Confronted by God

Confronted by God

The Essential Verna Dozier

Cynthia L. Shattuck and
Fredrica Harris Thompsett
editors

SEABURY BOOKS
an imprint of Church Publishing, Inc., New York

Library of Congress Cataloging-in-Publication Data

Confronted by God : the essential Verna Dozier / Cynthia L.
Shattuck and Fredrica Harris Thompsett, editors.
    p.   cm.
Includes bibliographical references.
ISBN-13: 978-1-59627-023-7
ISBN-10: 1-59627-023-3
1. Dozier, Verna J.—Religion. 2. African American
Episcopalians—Biography. I. Shattuck, Cynthia L., 1947– .
II. Thompsett, Fredrica Harris, 1942– .
BX5979.C66 2006
283.092—dc22
  [b]

                    2006014378

Church Publishing Incorporated
445 Fifth Avenue
New York, New York 10016
www.churchpublishing.org

Table of Contents

Editors' Preface

THIS INTRODUCTION to the life and witness of Verna Dozier began with a thick stack of interviews and an unfinished manuscript on the Bible and ambiguity. The interviews gave us her voice and the manuscript gave us the topic that seems to have been most on her mind in the past decade or so. Together they inspired us to attempt to capture the "essential Verna Dozier" on paper, and we have done our best to interweave her personal voice with her writings in order to show as much as we could of her life and the essence of her thought over the years. So we have drawn on interviews, sermons, articles, the ambiguity manuscript, and her book on the ministry of all Christians, *The Authority of the Laity,* to present a woman who has become for countless people a voice of extraordinary prophetic authority.

We are particularly grateful to Dee Hahn-Rollins, Verna Dozier's literary executor and close friend of many years. She and her family—Al Rollins, Stacey Hann Ruff, and Joseph Ruff—have provided invaluable help, encouragement, and support in putting this book together.

To the best of our knowledge, nothing remains of Verna Dozier's personal correspondence and family papers; she and her younger sister, Lois Dozier, together decided to destroy these materials sometime before Lois's death in 1998. In the absence of these writings, we would like to thank Carol Blakeslee-Collin for the transcripts of extensive interviews she conducted with Verna in 1999. We have drawn on these interviews extensively in chapter one and throughout the book, and Carol's work helped to recapture Verna's personal voice.

Mary Donovan's *Oral History of Verna J. Dozier*, an earlier interview compiled in 1990–91 for the Episcopal Women's History Project, was invaluable in obtaining a clearer picture of Verna's family life and early teaching career in Washington, D. C. James Adams, former rector of St. Mark's Church, Capitol Hill, has given us insight into Verna's years at that church. Janis Hoffman has also been generous in supplying written materials and personal recollections of her more than fifty years of friendship with Verna.

We also wish to thank the Christian Educators of the Twentieth Century Project, sponsored by the Talbot School of Theology, which provided the impetus to create a web-based biography and bibliography on Verna Dozier that helped in the earliest research on Verna's life.

Researching and compiling this small book would have been a far more daunting task without the help of two trustworthy editors. Vicki Black read through all the material we amassed and came up with a viable working outline for the book that succeeded in bringing these disparate materials together. She also designed the finished text. Charlene Higbe was not only responsible for putting into electronic form the chapters and articles from which we chose the final texts, but read patiently through a number of drafts, suggested some rearranging of the material, and brought previously overlooked "snippets" to our attention.

Most importantly, we wish to express our thanks and gratitude to Verna Dozier herself, who has graced both of us with her friendship and humor over the years.

CYNTHIA L. SHATTUCK
FREDRICA HARRIS THOMPSETT
April 2006

Introduction

by Fredrica Harris Thompsett

LIKE A BIBLICAL PROPHET she is focused and single-minded. Like a prophet she urgently witnesses to God's reign on earth, speaking the truth as she sees it, and commands your attention with a message that is uncomfortable at best. From first meeting her, you know that this woman—small in frame, dressed in blue, and feisty in spirit—is not to be trifled with. Verna Dozier is unforgettable.

Those who met her or ever heard her speak will particularly remember Verna's voice, rich and mellifluous; vibrant in tone, depth, and substance. Her voice is a modern symphony, full of complexity, paradox, and disturbing harmonies. When Verna quoted hymns and poetry, or confronted an audience with speeches from *Hamlet* or the prophecies of Amos, even familiar texts took on new life. Early on Verna felt an immediate attraction to the prophet Amos, whom she described as "the first voice of social justice in the Bible." She could read a favored hymn text out loud more musically than many could sing it, whether that text was "Love divine, all loves excelling" or the poetic crescendos of James Weldon Johnson's "Lift every voice and sing." As a child, Verna tells us, she loved to "orate" with "dramatic flair." With her deep appreciation for the English language, she had an ability to make students of all ages listen carefully.

This collection of her writings presents Verna as an impassioned and provocative teacher of the Bible and as a demanding prophet who speaks directly about our daily lives and the mission of the church. What vocational streams run through her life? What were early influences in her prophetic formation? What theological convictions and passions stirred early and later in her vocation? The brief biography which follows is not limited to being a "spiritual biography" for, as Verna would say, all of life is holy; indeed, as she repeatedly noted, "the ground on which we stand is holy." Verna knew we do not have to enter a church to find God. Throughout her life, in every dimension of her life, Verna Dozier has lived as one confronted by God, challenged by the quest for God's vision, or "dream" as she would later call it, for herself and for all humanity.

One of the first things Verna would want us to know about her life was the enormous influence of her agnostic father and her devout Baptist mother, and of the family patterns established in childhood. Another was that she has been a lifelong "Washingtonian," dedicated to and shaped by its public schools as well as by Howard University. A third factor, underscored in her autobiography, is the ever-present crucible of race in America as she has experienced it. The story of the journey from her Baptist upbringing to the Episcopal Church needs attention since it affected her emerging theological voice. These matters are addressed, in her own words, in the first chapter of this book.

Verna Josephine Dozier was born in 1917 in the Foggy Bottom section of Washington, D. C. As an adult, she proudly notes, she lived in only three different houses in the District. She and her sister Lois Gertrude Dozier (1919–1998), whom Verna called her "ministering angel," moved to an adult care facility in Maryland toward the end of Lois's life. At the time of this writing Verna resides there still, an impatient patient beset by advanced Parkinson's disease.

The two sisters, the family's only children, were lifelong companions, attending school and college together, and later in life sharing residences. In their childhood they took turns reading out loud from the Bible and from Shakespeare's plays. Anytime there was a reference to the Bible in school, their hands would shoot up. Laughing, Verna once observed, "We were the most annoying children!" Verna often speaks in generous terms about her younger sister and in comparatively derogatory terms about herself. Lois was musical, active, slim, and socially outgoing; she was a lifelong Baptist, raised in and buried from the same congregation. By contrast, Verna describes herself as shy, plump, and bookish, and remembers being a pesky, inquisitive child who repeatedly challenged her mother's religion.

Verna was a precocious student. Skipping two grades at Dunbar High School, the District of Columbia's premier high school for colored students, she entered college at age fifteen on an academic scholarship. The two sisters shared a love for learning and each went on to earn collegiate and master's degrees and become educators. Verna majored in English literature and wrote a master's thesis on African American hymns. Lois studied library science and had a full career as a university librarian, first at the University of Notre Dame and then at Howard University.

While both women lived busy professional lives and each had a lively sense of humor, their household patterns diverged during the years they lived together. Verna loved her creature comforts and enjoyed being cared for. Lois did the shopping, cooking, cleaning, bought Verna's clothes, entertained their guests, and attended her in other ways. Verna read voraciously; she lived in her mind. She could at times be impatient, arrogant, and less than sensitive to the feelings of others. It should not surprise us that one of

Verna's favorite biblical stories was of Mary and Martha: Lois was a homemaking "Martha" and Verna an inquisitive young "Mary." According to Verna, each brought a "different focus" to daily living.

By the time Verna entered college she was already, like her father, "skeptical of religion and those who practiced it." At Howard University's Rankin Chapel, she was inspired—"just carried away"—by the sermons of its dean, the brilliant theologian, poet, and preacher Howard Thurman. "I looked up to him as if he was the voice of God." Throughout her life she was fond of quoting Thurman's vision of God's desire for creation: "A friendly world of friendly folk, beneath a friendly sky." Inspired by Thurman and other "great minds" encountered at Howard, Verna started a lifelong habit of extensive reading in theology, although she majored in English literature. In addition to Thurman, Paul Laurence Dunbar, Countee Cullen, and Langston Hughes were among her favorite poets. Later in life she loved to quote Maya Angelou.

Early in her high school teaching days, Verna started the morning by reading *The Manhood of the Master* by the outspoken liberal Baptist theologian Harry Emerson Fosdick. She "just drank in" ideas that challenged fundamentalist scriptural interpretation and pointed toward social justice. "The first time that I heard someone question the divinity of Jesus, I was just so excited I didn't know what to do."

Her pursuit of God's dream propelled Verna to look for questioning, committed Christian communities and companions. Through a young adult study group convened by the Washington Federation of Churches, she first encountered Gordon Cosby, a young Baptist clergyman "from the South" who believed the core biblical story and who "led his life differently" because of it. Cosby founded the Church of the Saviour, a highly disciplined multidenominational community whose members committed themselves weekly to educational cell groups, meditation and prayer, tithing, and practical responses to his sermons on social action. Verna immersed herself in the Church of the Saviour's religious formation and made several lifelong friendships there. After a five-year commitment, its members were expected to move to a denominational church, and it was then that Verna entered the Episcopal Church. Verna had worked with Episcopalians in youth conferences and other educational events and admired the way Episcopal authors wrote. Then, through teaching Bible for the Diocese of Washington's School of Christian Living, she met Bill Baxter, a brash and energetic social activist whose justice-based parish preaching concentrated on the poor and oppressed. Baxter, who was serving St. Mark's Episcopal Church on Capitol Hill, invited Verna to join his small, declining, inner-city parish, noting that St. Mark's was "ready for a black."[1] Her entry into this parish in 1955 was at first controversial, and members of the parish "interviewed" Verna before they would accept her; eventually many of its members "fell in love" with the way Verna led Bible classes. Verna was drawn to the denomination's "beautiful liturgical language" and what she experienced as its intellectual freedom and appreciation for the mind.

Verna has remained at St. Mark's ever since: leading classes, serving as the parish's first woman senior warden, presiding over the parish during the sabbatical of a rector, and holding for life an honorary appointment as warden emerita. "When I discovered the Episcopal Church, it was as if I had been waiting for that all my life." Verna was gradually accepted at St. Mark's as a local prophet. One parishioner observed that, like the prophets, Verna's "powerful gyroscope" balances core biblical tradition with promoting justice in contemporary society. St. Mark's still describes itself as a place where "both skeptics and believers find a home."

A wise biographer once asked: what do we really know of someone whom we first meet in their middle age? This is an especially apt question when considering Verna's life, since many people interested in studying the Bible and learning more about their faith first met Verna when she was over fifty. Many of us knew that Verna had a "dual career"—she taught high school students for thirty-four years, first in segregated public schools in the District of Columbia. Not as many of us knew how distinguished she was both as a teacher of English literature and an administrator in the District's high schools. Nor have we fully appreciated the ways that a common set of values and interrelated pedagogical themes shaped her lifelong passion for teaching, which she called her "continuing ministry."

Verna was a demanding and caring teacher. She was also talented. When the District moved from segregated to integrated schools, she was shocked to realize how much her black students had been "short-changed." She vowed to help them realize their self-worth and authority, modeling and teaching lessons about respect and dignity that she hoped they would retain for life. Verna may have been the first African American to head a department—English—in the newly integrated school system. Later on she became a curriculum specialist in English and then a leading participant in the Urban Teacher Corps, helping a team of students and teachers to develop innovative curricula in which students' voices and authority were central. In 1972 she cooperated with the Folger Shakespeare Library on an award-winning project to enable tenth-graders to learn about Shakespeare. Then in 1975, after thirty-four years of teaching, she took early retirement from the D. C. schools to concentrate her energies on a full-time ministry as a Christian educator and theologian. Years later she was still in touch with former students and colleagues whose lives she had influenced.

Verna translated her skills, values, and pedagogy from teaching high school English to studying the Bible. She always emphasized the importance of historical context, both in English literature and in biblical texts. She insisted on beginning with questions and not answers, teaching by posing evocative questions and reminding other teachers never to ask a question to which they already knew the answer. She always invited different voices to be heard; just as students played different parts in Shakespeare's plays, she advised students of the Bible to read different biblical translations out loud. All of her study guides and curricula encouraged students to overcome any sense of powerlessness. Whatever their age, authority belonged to learners; it was not to be imposed on them from the "outside" by a "real" expert. Ideas, books, learning in community, and leadership mattered. As a teacher Verna defined a real education not as "what you believed," but rather by "how you lived" in the world. It was difficult work, going against the grain of common assumptions. She would later recall, "Sometimes when I was teaching, I was praying."

Verna's reputation as a public speaker and religious educator began to extend beyond the mid-Atlantic region when she started working with women's groups. In 1969 Dee Hahn (later Dee Hahn-Rollins), a volunteer working with women in the Diocese of Indianapolis, invited Verna to do a Bible study for women there. Verna became Hahn's mentor, teacher, and lifelong friend; eventually Hahn became Verna's literary executor. In her role as Coordinator of Women's Activities in the diocese, Dee Hahn helped Verna gain wider recognition as an Episcopal conference leader, first at diocesan gatherings and then at provincial and national meetings. Verna recalls that a career "highlight" was serving as one of three speakers and leaders for the 1976 Triennial Meeting of the Episcopal Church Women. Marion Kelleran and Carman Hunter, well-known Episcopal educators, were her colleagues. Over the next two decades Verna would be an invited speaker, retreat convener, or workshop leader in all of the provinces, most of the dioceses, and many parishes in the Episcopal Church.

Other denominations and ecumenical groups sought her skills as well. As recently as 2004, Michael Curry, the Episcopal Bishop of North Carolina, ordered hundreds of copies of Dozier's book *The Dream of God* (1991; republished in 2006 by Church Publishing), as a prophetic study text for shaping diocesan conversation about mission. Curry called Verna Dozier "his Moses."

Verna never formally studied theology in a seminary setting, yet she was widely respected by many in seminaries of the Episcopal Church and received two honorary degrees. As an adjunct instructor in the late 1980s she co-taught two courses with New Testament professor Barbara Hall at Virginia Theological Seminary. Both courses immersed students in the complexity of the Bible in addressing social issues and in preaching. Verna taught that responsible preaching was a "risky business" because it called upon clergy to admit to their congregations that "they did not have all the answers." Throughout this time, she kept up her reading and correspondence with contemporary theologians and Christian leaders. Marcus Borg and Walter Brueggemann were added to her list of favored scholars, as were two of today's powerful black preachers, James Forbes and Paul Abernathy.

Verna also worked as a consultant, focusing on leadership education and organizational development for groups and individuals. From the mid-1950s she was associated first as a volunteer and later as a staff trainer with the ecumenical group Mid-Atlantic Training and Consulting, Inc. (MATC). She served as a trainer of consultants for the Episcopal Diocese of Washington and the national Episcopal Church. She kept up this work although she was never fond of travel, highly valuing her creature comforts at home. Yet in the 1980s she twice went to St. Paul's Theological College in Limuru, Kenya, teaching biblical studies as part of the Women's Leadership Project organized by Jane Watkins, Jane Trent Surles, and Dee Hahn-

Rollins for the National Episcopal Church and the Church of the Province of Kenya.

Additional consulting opportunities, mostly in the mid-Atlantic region, came through Verna's association with the Washington-based Alban Institute, founded in 1974 to focus on strengthening congregations. An advocate of adult education in parishes, Verna began by drafting guidelines for studying the Bible. She also prepared, in 1978–79, audio recordings about her approach. This was the subject of her first published book, *Equipping the Saints: A Method of Self-Directed Bible Study for Lay Groups* (1981). Throughout her publishing career Verna prepared pamphlets and videos emphasizing that laity, not only clergy, need to use scholarly resources. Dictionaries, commentaries, and multiple translations would allow for the hearing of different voices, rather than settling for one biblical translation or interpretation. *How I Read the Bible* (1986) and contributions to *In Dialogue with Scripture: An Episcopal Guide to Studying the Bible* (1993) are other published resources where she emphasized that Christians must "study" and not just "read" the Bible to live faithfully in the world. Her basic method for studying the biblical record is presented and illustrated in chapter three of this volume.

Through Alban Institute engagements as a workshop leader, Verna increasingly expressed her conviction that laity need to claim their authority in the world. When Alban Institute staff members Loren Mead and Celia Hahn assisted Verna by taping her conversations about authority, the resulting text was *The Authority of the Laity* (1982). In this brief yet critical assessment of the institutional church, Verna is adamant that there are no "second-class citizens in the household of God."

Other publications, interviews, and articles followed. The most successful of these, and Verna's favorite, is a book called *The Dream of God: A Call to Return* (1991). In it she cautions that we are too often falling away from the dream

God has for us "to follow Jesus and not merely to worship him," and urges readers to live into their "high calling as coworkers with their Creator." This modern classic encompasses a summative, challenging exploration of the whole biblical story, emphasizing God's hopes for the people of God. It has been called a "small masterpiece" by Marcus Borg, one of today's foremost New Testament scholars. Borg recommends Dozier in his books, and even borrowed her title "The Dream of God" to head a chapter he wrote on God's passion for justice, in *The God We Never Knew* (1997).

The theme of equality as God's dream for humanity was often in Verna's work. She was a consistent advocate for gays and lesbians, for decrying tensions between Jews and blacks, and against the notion that men and women had to play different roles. In 1993 with James R. Adams, a long-standing friend and rector of St. Mark's, Verna co-authored *Sisters and Brothers: Reclaiming a Biblical Idea of Community.* The book was written at a time when women's place in the church and the world was for many an uphill road.

From the late 1990s, the topic of ambiguity has increasingly preoccupied her thoughts. Her final writing project was on the subject of ambiguity, a concept she found central to embracing religion and living in a multi-religious world. Significant selections from this unfinished manuscript are included in this book. They represent a theme which evolved throughout Verna's life and recalled the influence of her father's "searching mind."

Whatever the text, Verna's written voice is unmistakable in its quality. Because she thinks out loud, her writing can seem repetitive. Her words are blunt, often ironic, full of humor, and usually provocative. Verna wants us to *respond,* whether we agree with her or not. It is important to her that we are questioning, thinking through our beliefs. "I think the foundations of a simple faith should be shaken," she once asserted, so that "something new" may come into our lives.

This book honors and extends Verna's voice through her written work. Much of the material in this volume is being published for the first time, and is drawn from interviews, oral histories, and other occasional sources. An assortment of passages from previously published material, including *The Authority of the Laity*, is also included. Short selections, aphorisms, sayings, and stories from all her available work deepen our knowledge of her theological perspectives, particularly her concern that ambiguity is an essential component in understanding God.

It is difficult to find just one dimension that encompasses the complexity of Verna's life. Clearly she has been widely known, sought after as a speaker, and respected throughout the Episcopal Church and other denominations for her Bible teaching, conference leadership, preaching, and consulting work with laity to claim and live out their baptismal promises.[2] Verna has always styled herself a "radical" theologian, although she believes that sexism, racism, and her status as a layperson muted her prophetic voice. Some who are familiar with her work consider her a living saint, and others admire her as a visionary prophet. It is true that many knew her simply as their favorite teacher, whether in high school settings, church conferences, or delivering a sermon for the consecration of a bishop from the pulpit of the National Cathedral. For some she is the "ultimate" teacher, an energetic educator who is unforgettable, both encouraging and challenging. This is also the story of Verna Dozier, a black woman and layperson, who spread God's word in the nation's capital, across the country, and beyond its borders. While her high school students called her "Miss Dozier," Verna always insisted that her adult friends call her by her baptismal name. This book continues this practice because of our friendship with her, but mostly out of respect.

Short letters, notes, and cards from Verna were always closed with two words: "Truly, Verna." In this volume, we hope a fuller and "truer" picture of her teaching life and theological legacy emerges for generations to come. If you have met Verna already, add your own memories, filling out this portrait as you read from her writings. If you are new to her life and work, be prepared to learn from a committed and opinionated contemporary prophet.

1. For Baxter's version of Verna's integration of St. Mark's, see William and Jean Baxter, *Building Church: Memories and Myths,* ed. Jo Ellen Hayden (Washington, D. C.: St. Mark's Episcopal Church, 2003).
2. If you wish to learn more about Verna Dozier's life and impact as a Christian educator, I have written a fuller online biography at http://www.talbot.edu/ce20/educators.

One

My Father Had a Searching Mind

IF WE WERE TO SPEAK *with Verna Dozier about her life, one of the first things she would emphasize would be the influence of her father. Fortunately, in the chapter that follows we are able to hear this testimony in Verna's own words. Her early childhood, her religious wrestling, and her educational journey are chronicled here. The significance of her father's hunger for learning, his mistrust of institutional religion, and his "skepticism about religion" were all, as Verna says, "passed on to me." Steeped in discussions with him, Verna learned at a young age "the idea that nobody's work is to be taken as absolute." The concept of ambiguity, which foundationally informs her work, took root in these early encounters with her beloved father's "searching mind."*

Her experience of growing up in segregated Washington, D. C., deepened her pointed analysis of religious life. Recalling her childhood, she reflected, "Everything about me was part of being black." The care, cautions, and challenges of daily living led her to question pious, "pie-in-the-sky" religious declarations that did not address social justice in the here-and-now. She searched for religious communities where people worked on "living a Christian life day by day."

The material in this chapter is largely drawn from unpublished interviews conducted in the 1990s, oral histories, and short articles about Verna. Although Verna and her sister Lois burned their personal papers, Verna's voice remains in candid interviews with friends and associates about her life, work, and the manuscript she was writing on ambiguity. Some of her references have a dated quality, referring to past controversies. Other allusions are more recent, and most of her stories are timeless. We have edited these resources to give us a portrait of Verna's early life in her own words.

GROWING UP in the Baptist Church, I was a smart-alecky little kid in Sunday school. They asked all the children to define sin, and when it came to me, I said, "It's whatever the other fellow is doing." My heritage in the Baptist Church is a very rich one because my mother, Lucie E. Carter Dozier, was very devout, and she taught me the faith once delivered. My father, Lonna Dozier, taught me to be skeptical of the delivery. So I grew up with those two pulls on me.

In the tradition in which I grew up, being good was very important. This may not be doing justice to my childhood experiences, but in the Baptist Church the story always seemed to end on something you had to do. I never got the feeling as a child that it's already done, and there isn't anything you have to do. In fact, I now know there isn't anything you can do. It's all been done for you.

MY MOTHER was our educational foundation. There's a wonderful poem by Alice Walker that talks about mothers who never went to school but "they knew what we had to learn without knowing a word of it themselves." It's a marvelous tribute to black mothers of that time, and my mother was of that generation.

My father was a country boy in rural Georgia—black, poor. At a very young age he took off for Birmingham, Alabama, and worked in the mines. Then he thought, "There must be more to life than this," and came to Washington, D. C. That's where he met my mother, I think at some church gathering. She had a high school education, and he thought she was just a goddess. She was a graduate of Armstrong High School and then worked in the Bureau of Engraving and Printing, in those days a very good job for a black woman. To my father, she was someone who had *arrived.* He had bad teeth—his teeth stuck out—and my mother's first requirement was that he had to have his teeth fixed before she would marry him.

The reason I've never had any truck with men who thought men and women had certain roles is that I saw my father do everything to make life easier for my mother. When she married him she gave up her job to stay at home and rear her children. My father did not make enough money to support a family so we had hard days, very hard days. He would clean, he would wash clothes and cook—his first job in Washington was as a short-order cook—so he cooked better than my mother. I saw my father do everything my mother did, and there was never any question in our family that he was a man.

I guess you could say that my father was an agnostic. We didn't say that back then, and my father would never have thought of using that term. But that's what he was, and to have an agnostic father and a very traditional, devout mother gave Lois and me a shaky kind of childhood. We loved both our parents, so there was no problem of choosing between the two of them, but there *was* the problem of having two different ways to look at reality.

That's always disturbing. If you just have one and you know that's the straight line, then that is the straight line. Either one of those directions gives you a firm foundation. It's when you are tossed between the two that you have to think. Since we loved both our parents, we never thought that one was better than the other, or one was right and the other was wrong. There were two rights and two directions in which you could go. And we were just kids.

At a very early age we became very serious figures. I'm smiling because I'm thinking of the picture of those two little girls sitting there at the kitchen table, carrying on these very profound conversations. Race was a very serious topic for us. We talked about school, our lessons, and books that we had read. There's a quotation that comes to my mind. Aristotle said—I'm not going to quote it exactly—the curse is the unexamined life. Well, we didn't ever suffer from that curse. We were always examining our life and the life in which we were placed.

There was never any competition between my sister Lois and me, and our parents did not pit us against one another. They thought both of their daughters were wonderful, and we had different specialties. Lois played the piano, and I used to orate! I loved to read aloud—poems, stories, and essays, with great dramatic flair. Lois was also the popular one, and she loved clothes. I was fat, so nothing looked good on me. And Mother did what so many mothers do. Even when they've got daughters with different builds, they insist upon dressing them alike. So mother used to love these little dresses that had little ruffles and all that sort of thing, and they looked wonderful on Lois, who was very slim. Well, I looked like a balloon. But nobody ever mentioned that to me, so it was many years before I realized that I looked like a balloon.

I was two years older and would get to every grade in school first, so the teachers would always have an image of the Dozier children as very quiet. Then Lois came along with a mouth running like a bell clapper, and people were always saying to her, "You're not a thing like your sister!" And Lois would say, "No, I'm not!" She talked all the time, and I was very quiet and never said a word. Very shy, with a great inferiority complex. But I was the smart one, see. Lois didn't care much about school. She had all the gifts of a good body and personality and I had none—but I had a brain, which I used.

My wanting to question *everything* started very early. When Lois and I were younger, a friend of Mother's who had the usual critical attitude of the maiden lady toward the married woman rearing her children gave each one of us a Bible for Christmas. She didn't think we were getting enough religious faith. When I was in junior high I would read a chapter of that Bible every day before I went to school. I read it all the way through, marked it up, questioning it at every point. When I got to the end of it I thought, "That didn't make any sense at all! I must have missed something in that great book!" Then I went back and read it again. So now when people tell me, "I've read the Bible from cover to cover," I always say, "Hmmm. That's not the way to read the Bible!"

My mother was one of the innocent ones. She took her religion straightforwardly and as far as I know, she never questioned at all. The most disturbing moments in her life were times when I was ranting and raving in the kitchen about what I didn't believe. Or when we argued. There was a little hussy on our block, a wonderful-looking woman, and my mother held her in great contempt. I said, "You know, Mother, the first person you're going to meet when you get to heaven will be that young woman." And Mother said, "Oh, no! Not that girl." And I replied, "Well, I want to tell you, that's the first person you're going to meet!" Mother asked, "Then what would be the point in my having lived such a good life?" and I said, "Your response to that, Mother, proves that you haven't led such a good life."

My father had a very searching mind, and it helped me with my search because I could talk to Dad about these things. He was also interested in astronomy, and the psalm that says, "When I consider thy heavens, the work of thy fingers, the moon and the stars, which thou hast ordained; What is man, that thou art mindful of him? and the son of man, that thou visitest him?" (Psalm 8:3–4). It was one of my father's favorite psalms. I always said that if I were going to hate white people, it would be because of what happened to my father, who had a great mind but never had an opportunity to exercise it. He was born in the Deep South, in Cataula, Georgia, and when my father first went to the Washington post office to send a letter home to his mother, the man in the post office said, "There is no such place." My father said, "There is such a place, I just came from there!" It was really quite a little country town. In that town, there was a young man who was very interested in my father and wanted to send him to school, but my grandfather said that Dad was his oldest son and he needed him on the farm. He just couldn't give him up. And so my father never had the chance to go to school, and that great mind was just wasted.

I don't think my dad actually went to high school. I think he stopped with the eighth grade, but he read voraciously. He read all the books Lois and I brought home, all those novels I never read, and then he'd go to the library. He was a reading powerhouse. But my father was very antagonistic toward religion. That skepticism about religion he passed on to me. So he agreed with his daughter, who adored him and told him that religion was ridiculous. We used to have long discussions. I remember my father saying one day, "When I look around and I see how great this world is and how insignificant human beings are in all of that, I cannot believe in anything that says they are the crown of creation." The idea that nobody's word is to be taken as absolute—I got that from my father.

MY MOTHER was very proud, strong-willed, ambitious. Although I feel closer to my father, without my mother, I would never have gotten as far as I have. My mother and I have very little in common. My mother was a socialite, and I was never interested in that sort of thing. I was always into books, and my mother was very little interested in books. Mother read newsmagazines, but she was a great lady. She had so much strength. My father could never dream of a poor black man whose children would go to college. My mother said, "They have got the brains, there isn't any reason why they shouldn't go to college." And so we did.

My mother gave up her job at the Bureau of Engraving and Printing because she did not want to work while her children were going to school. My father was forever grateful for that, so he was always trying to make up to Mother for what she had given up for him. My father was always so proud that he had married an educated woman. He was proud of the fact that when he went off to work at night as a poor laboring man, Mother was home with his little daughters reading Shakespeare. We read the plays aloud so we could act all the characters in all the plays, and we had a wonderful time.

My father worked two jobs. He would have dinner by himself and then go to work at six o'clock in the evening and work at the Government Printing Office until eight o'clock the next morning. When he left the Government Office he went off to the hotel at Union Station, worked there a half-day, and came home about noon The Government Printing Office was really what killed him. He was a printer's assistant, which meant that he lifted the heavy plates, and that gave him his heart trouble. It enlarged his heart, and that's what killed him.

It was my mother, not my father, who impressed on Lois and me that we were as good as anybody else. It didn't make any difference that we were black and poor, we were just as good as anybody else. That was mother's religion. My father, born and reared in the South, had it instilled in him from early childhood that he was a nigger and could only go so far, or he would be smacked down. So he was pretty cautious in his relationships with the white people, and taught my sister and me the need to be cautious. My mother was a feisty lady, and she instilled in us that there was a battle to be fought, and that we had the weapons to fight it. It never occurred to my father that as a poor black man he would have two daughters who would go on to college and graduate school; it never occurred to my mother that it would be any other way.

Once when my mother was cleaning the office of a congressman—quite a comedown for my mother—she told him about her very intelligent daughter who didn't have any way of going to college. The congressman told her about the National Youth Administration and the scholarships that I could get, and that's how I went to college. My father would never have thought of doing that. He would never have had the courage. But mother had no fear—it just seemed a natural thing. Over here you have a brilliant young woman with no way of getting an education; over there, a congressman who has the access to that education. It never occurred to Mother not to put the two things together.

I MAJORED in English literature in college, and so I read the great ideas of the English writers about the dignity of human beings. Even as I read them, I knew they were not talking about me. I had some wonderful professors at Howard University. There were some great minds there: Howard Berman, Benjamin Brolley, John Knox. I never had Knox as a teacher, but his ideas about liberty and justice influenced our very being. So I lived in a world of ambiguity: I knew what the human race was supposed to be, but nowhere did I see it manifested.

One of the tragedies of being an oppressed people is that you take on, almost without intending to do it, the evaluation of the controlling community—which meant that black people had as little sense of their own worth as the whites around them did. Even as we fought against that belittling of ourselves, the fight itself in some way confirmed that they were right. The very fact that you are engaged in proving your worth means that your enemy is winning. Even the fight against it proves its power. I dealt with it the way my fellow black students did, by insisting we were just as good as anybody else. But the only people who have to insist are the people who sense that either they are not so good, or the culture has told them they are not so good, and they have bought into it.

Everything about me was part of being black. If you're black in America, there's no way to avoid it. If you were going downtown, you had to be very careful which store you went into because there were some stores that wouldn't serve you. So it was an ever-present factor in your life, yet you learned to live as if that factor didn't exist. I remember the first time that I mentioned to a high school friend that a new store had opened downtown and I hadn't "tested it" yet to know whether it was open to me. This friend said, "Do you realize that that is an issue that only black people have?" I had never put it into words before.

That's an awful burden to live under, and after awhile this way of living became natural. I remember a young black who was one of the new blacks—very good-looking, very smart, very dressed up. He couldn't understand why we lived like that, which was very stupid of him, of course. We lived like that because that was the price of living. I suppose you work your way out of it by finding out that there is more to life than black against white. But there was very little around us to support that. In fact, our very existence depended upon holding ourselves together with a bitter web of hatred. So we lost whatever creative possibilities we might have had, or at least they were diminished.

The question of race also affected me in my career as a teacher. I was committed to having my students know that they were worthy, and the world might not recognize it but I did. So I tried to make a haven in that classroom. I suppose the image I would use is that I was arming them for the world they were going to meet. This sense of struggle left me with an overwhelming earnestness not to demean those students. It was a religious commitment: I was not going to be a part of that world by how I treated them or by how I treated myself. There is no freedom in that life. We were focused on one goal and one goal only: presenting to the world an image of a successful, fulfilled, creative person, against all odds. There was no time for anything else. Even in a life-and-death struggle for existence, we couldn't run the risk of not doing that all the time. So when we saw the black children exhausted, there was a reason for their exhaustion.

Sometimes when I was teaching, I was praying, and I offered that to God as my effort to participate in God's will for those kids. I've had the experience of being in some situations in which something was happening that was very meaningful to me, and I almost held my breath while it was going on, and then I realized when I let my breath out that I had been praying.

I was not going to shortchange those black students in any way. I was going to give them the very best that I had, and I was going to demand of them the very best that they had. Because they *were* shortchanged in all kinds of ways. In the first place, they didn't have the textbooks that the white kids had. When they integrated the schools and black teachers and black students for the first time went into the white schools, we were appalled at the differences in equipment, and the buildings.

WHEN I WAS growing up, I could not conceive how a black man could forgive a white man—it seemed to me a weakness. Now I know it is not a weakness, and I can't conceive of any instance in which we should not forgive. But it can be a way of refusing to confront a problem, if by forgiving someone you let injustice roll on. So even forgiveness is ambiguous. I think I need to understand that where I stand is not necessarily the totality of where God stands.

In strange ways that only the faithful know, faith is not only the decision to risk but also the courage to be, to affirm yourself in the face of all that denies you. To be able to say *yes* to yourself when all the environment is shouting *no,* to be able to listen to that *no* and hear what message it is sending from which you can profit. In my experience, that is certainly beyond the possibility of fragile human beings. That takes a leap of faith.

I went on a tour of Ethiopian museums a few years ago given by a bitter, hostile youth. He said to me as he proudly showed off the figures of Ethiopian kings in all their splendid regalia, "I do not see why they always picture us as naked savages. We have always worn clothes." I wondered why wearing clothes was to him such a sign of worth. In the Genesis story nakedness was a sign of innocence. Human beings only felt the need for clothing when they felt the need to hide. But obviously my young guide was taking his signals from another drummer, and not necessarily the drummer of his fathers.

With sublime arrogance, the Englishman Sir Kenneth Clark wrote a book about a small part of the world and called it *Civilization*. Even those proud blacks who would protest it most were unwitting prey to that stance. Out of scores of definitions for "black" in the *Oxford English Dictionary*, only a few are not pejorative. Black hearse, black days, black moods. Black is bad. White is good. Howard Thurman noted that *Moby Dick* is the only instance in American literature where white is a sign of evil.

So blacks follow that example. If blacks have been condemned by whites, blacks will condemn whites. You hate me, I will hate you more. If you are a black child stepping on a streetcar filled with white children, if they are your enemies then you are theirs. There is a wonderful little poem by Contee Cullen:

> Once riding in old Baltimore,
> Hate-filled, heart filled with greed,
> I saw a Baltimorean looking straight at me.
> Now, I was eight and very small....
> And so I smiled, but he poked out his tongue,
> And called me nigger.
> I saw the whole of Baltimore
> From May until December
> Of all the things that happened there,
> That's all that I remember.

Now, I don't look at every white person expecting him to poke out his tongue and call me nigger, but I know there's always that possibility. The response is inevitable, since we all, I believe, participate in fallenness, but there is no redemption in the response. If I have to say a death-dealing *no* to you in order to say *yes* to myself, you still have power over me. I am still bound by the example you set. There is no freedom for me in that. I cannot point the way to a new reign of God that way.

WHEN I WENT to college, Howard University, I stopped going to our local church. The dean of the chapel at Howard was Howard Thurman, the first really exciting person I met in the area of theology. I always characterized him as a mystic, the only black mystic I know. He was a very early student of Mahatma Gandhi and in touch with religious traditions beyond Christianity; he saw truth and wonder in all of it. So that was the opening of my mind, way back then, to the possibility that Christianity was not the only way to respond religiously. Thurman was probably the greatest influence on my life next to my father, as far as religion was concerned—he was a poet and used language beautifully. He was also the first person I met who did not accept the traditional interpretation of Jesus as a savior. For Thurman, Jesus was a model, not a savior.

My father was a very questioning person, and he never particularly found himself comfortable in the Baptist Church, but we didn't know anywhere else to go. Then he found Howard University, and he went to chapel with me every Sunday to hear all these very gifted preachers. When I started at Howard I was fifteen years old. My father was a good-looking man, and when he came with me to church, the next Monday the kids all said to me, "Who is that handsome boyfriend you have?" And I said, "What boyfriend? That's my father!" and they said, "Oh, tell us another." So my father and I would trot along up the hill to Howard and listen to the great thinkers and leaders that Howard Thurman brought to that chapel. I was spellbound. It was the first time I had heard anyone question the divinity of Jesus, and the chapel did not fall down!

It was a breath of fresh air and an escape from traditional religion. Some people think questions like that can shake a person's faith. It can shake a *simple* faith—and I think a simple faith should be shaken! Sitting in the pew at Howard and listening to new approaches to biblical criticism and new ideas of social justice deepened my faith. Only when the foundations are shaken can something new come into your life. At that time most intelligent black people—and I suppose intelligent whites, too—questioned everything about traditional religion. I mean, it was a whole new world to them and to us because it did away with all of the traditional business about Christmas. Little baby born in a manger and all that sort of stuff, you know. You could appreciate the poetry of it, but you didn't have to make it history, because it was poetry. The church was singing its faith.

At that time I was beginning to have questions that planted the seeds of doubt with the Baptist tradition. The minister of our church, a very distinguished Baptist preacher, would say, "There is no other name given among men whereby we must be saved," and all those other exclusive kinds of things that Christianity dwells on. So when the *Revised Standard Version* of the Bible came out, our Baptist church was outraged, just outraged! "Isn't the King James Bible what Jesus used? Good enough for St. Paul, good enough for me!" I became very annoyed, very restless, after that. At that time the Washington Federation of Churches was very active here, and I started going to their events. It was still very traditional but much more liberal than anything I had ever experienced. Then someone gave me *The Manhood of the Master* by Harry Emerson Fosdick, and I used to read that every morning before I went off to teach school.

At the time I belonged to a young adult group, and we used to have retreats. On one of those retreats I spent the whole weekend by myself trying to wrestle through what it was I believed, and why I believed it. It was a very traumatic experience for me, but I think I came out of it encouraged, sure that even though I don't accept every single thing that the church says and does, at its best the church expresses what I believe is God's message to us, and I want to be a part of that. When I reached the point at which there was enough ambiguity so that I could doubt but still say that wonderful line, "I believe, Lord, help my unbelief," that was it for me.

I went from being a skeptic to being a believer—a believer in the action of God. There's a wonderful story by James Weldon Johnson which uses the language and the feeling of the old black preacher to recount the biblical story, and that was very important to me. He said that the Bible begins in God stepping down from space, and God looks around and he says, "I'm lonely. I'll make me a world." As far as the eye of God could see, darkness covered everything, blacker than a hundred midnights down in a cypress swamp. And God said, "Let there be light." And the light broke and curled around God's shoulder, and God said, "That's good."

IN WASHINGTON I belonged to a young adult group, the Washington Federation of Churches. Our young adult group was always looking for some new ways to express our religious faith. We were trying to introduce people to ministers who came to Washington, particularly the young ministers with new ideas, and Gordon Cosby was one of those ministers. So we decided to go explore this young man who came from the South to the city of Washington and who was going to have a church which would take Jesus seriously. We all trotted over to Gordon's Church of the Saviour to be completely and utterly flabbergasted by this man. I was just captivated by him, because I had been to churches all my life, but that was the first time I ever met anybody who really took it seriously. One of the things that propelled me to the Church of the Saviour was disgust with my mother's church, the church that I was born into—I found that such a stifling environment.

In the first place here was someone who believed completely in the traditional story and *acted upon it*. It wasn't just a matter of Sunday morning coming to church and mouthing these things, as if Christianity were just a matter of criticizing your morality. Instead, it had some kind of impact on the social situation. The Church of the Saviour was a very exciting, experimental community that has probably done more to improve life in the city of Washington than any other group. When I joined it was still a very small group with strict requirements—daily meditation, educational programs, tithing, social action, weekly study with a disciplined cell group. They wanted very much to keep it small: part of our commitment to the church was the idea that after a certain period of time, we would return to the denominational churches we came from.

Gordon Cosby always preached sermons that had to do with how you lived your life from day to day. If you were supposed to be a Christian and if you believed what Jesus was talking about, how would you live your life differently? Those were questions nobody had ever asked us. We had weekly sessions in which we talked about living a Christian life day by day, and Gordon told us the first thing you dedicated to God was your money. You didn't just put a quarter in the collection plate—you *tithed*. When we left that session, a friend of mine with a very wonderful sense of humor looked at me and said, "Do you think that man is crazy?" That was the first time I even considered taking tithing seriously, and I'm sure most of the people there had never thought of taking it seriously before either. We thought there were a few religious crackpots there who did that, but not us intelligent folks. But at the Church of the Saviour we all tithed.

I really think that the Church of the Saviour needed a Gordon Cosby, which was its flaw. That's the flaw in the dream—it needed somebody who was a little crazy. I always think of the little band who gathered around Jesus, who were as radical in their day as the Church of the Saviour was in its day. But, you see, every little band has a possibility of doing that. Every church community, strange though it may seem, has the possibility of being in its own way Jesus of Nazareth and the little band he ran with.

Of course, if we were to meet people who took that radical way of living seriously, we would think they were crazy, and I am sure there are people who thought Gordon was crazy. It was exciting. So you wonder how I happened to leave? Because Gordon had this powerful system whereby we were expected to move on; we were going to take what we learned back to the traditional church. Finally, though, they had to give that discipline up because no one ever wanted to leave!

At the time I was thinking about the Episcopal Church and reading books by Episcopalians, and I would say to my friends, "You Episcopalians write so well and live so poorly!" So after five years at the Church of the Saviour, I was going to go to the Episcopal Church. I know there are a lot of snooty people in the Episcopal Church, but maybe I've come up in society and so I don't feel so inferior. At the time there was a class barrier that corresponded to the religious and racial barrier: my classmates, for example, who were Episcopalians were always the fairest-skinned. They were always the ones whose parents had gone to college, and whose parents didn't have laboring jobs. Episcopalians were always a more privileged group, and they just seemed a world apart from me—I never dreamed of associating with those people.

But I entered the Episcopal Church through *liberty*. I was drawn to the liberty of the Episcopal Church because they seemed to me to gather up all that I thought

Christianity and the biblical story were all about. I found that exciting. I had never experienced that before. It was the language of the liturgy, and the fact that the worship service took us Sunday after Sunday to what I thought, and I still think, was the great Christian story. For me, the great Christian story is about a God who cared enough about God's creation to struggle for it, and that is made so clear in the liturgy. It strikes me now that I don't think I've ever seen this before. It is the Christian story stripped of morality. Isn't that interesting?

Bill Baxter was the rector of St. Mark's, and St. Mark's was a dying church. In fact that was the reason he was sent there—the bishop said Bill couldn't do any harm because the church was already collapsing. When I joined I was already becoming well known in the educational structure through what the diocese called The School for Christian Living. The night we were going to teach a course on the New Testament, we were lined up outside the door at All Saints', Chevy Chase. I was the only woman, the only layperson, and the only black. I said to the clergy waiting with me, "These dear little old ladies are going to be very disappointed that the one class they really want to take is not taught by a priest and or even a white person. But if they have the courage to come the first time, I guarantee they will come back." And that is what happened: you could almost see their little faces fall, but they went in there and came back the next week.

So that is how I met Bill Baxter. He said to me, "Verna, I'm making some great changes at St. Mark's. I think we are now ready for a black person, and I would like you to come." Well, it didn't make any difference to me, but Bill, with his creative response to reality, had not presented the situation accurately. St. Mark's was *not* ready for a black! And that is a story in itself.

When I first came, they really thought that I was a spy for the NAACP because those people at St. Mark's had such a terrific fear of black people. They also had the very exalted idea that blacks would be trying to infiltrate any white church. They imagined that when I got into St. Mark's there would be a flood of blacks coming right after me. And for the whole time I was at St. Mark's, not one black person came! I said to those fellows when I was talking to them, "Black people aren't standing outside the door waiting to bombard your church. They have their own churches and they have no desire whatsoever to come into this little church!"

LOOKING BACK on my life in the church, I don't like to use the word "victim" because I think that is a very bad stance to take, but in my life I have experienced racism in a very interesting way. I say often to people that I am a woman of few ideas and many repetitions! I am probably one of the most radical people in this church today, but people respond to me with great affection and love because I look like Aunt Jemima. I may sound like Sojourner Truth, but they don't pay any attention. I think that is a manifestation of racism. They cannot believe that this fat little old lady is a radical. I have the maternal look: people are always telling me, "Oh, you look like my grandmother!" I have that look because I am fat. That is a function of racism and sexism, too, because I think a lot of men do not hear what women have to say. I don't think there is a woman operating in any of our church systems who hasn't experienced that special kind of condescension.

Now the biblical story is unimaginable without the prophets. My favorite, Amos, saw an injustice at the very heart of human relationships and he railed against it, the first brave voice for social justice. Amos was a rough Judean shepherd who lived in the hills a few miles from Bethlehem.

He was impelled by a call from God to go and preach to the idolatrous and very prosperous northern kingdom of Israel. Amos was not a professional prophet like Elijah or Samuel, who belonged to a priestly brotherhood. He was rough and prickly and saw himself as merely "a herdsman, and a dresser of sycamore trees." No, he didn't let up, and I'm sure they caught him in an alley some night and shook the life out of him. That's the only way they silenced him. But when you look for ambiguity, or tolerance, or compassion even, I don't think you look to the prophets, then *or* now. The Old Testament prophets came at an evil time, and they were inveighing against those evil times. They had no room for charity, or compassion, or mercy.

In the conservative movement to convert homosexuals to heterosexuality, they think of themselves as modern-day prophets. We often see them as modern-day Jonahs or worse when, full of consternation, they wonder why God doesn't smite those "horrible people" who refuse to see the evil of their ways. From where I stand, I don't think they are speaking the truth. I think the prophets had a much firmer grasp of reality, and I think the prophets were under the judgment of God, whereas too many in the antihomosexual movement set themselves up as God.

For me the modern-day intolerance for homosexuality is another example of "We have to be right." The way we want to do it is the way that we think it should be done, and so we immediately equate our response with God's response. We think that homosexuals are sinful; they are wicked and they are dirty. Because *we* have made that response, we think *God* makes that response. But God is quite a different matter—you can't gamble on what he will do. I think we experience a God who changes his mind.

There is nothing in the Bible that talks about homosexuality as being against God's law. The people in the Bible who objected to homosexuality objected to it on very practical grounds. As a people, they needed to grow and expand.

Homosexuals do not reproduce, so it was very important that they not have homosexual practices among them. There is no moral reason why people shouldn't have homosexual relationships, so we try to drag in all these other reasons that don't really have anything to do with it at all. And once again, it's "You have to do it the way I do it, because the way I do it is right, and God forbid that anything would happen that isn't right."

What happens to all of us is we decide on our position and then we go out looking for justification. We seek an answer as to whether homosexuality is intrinsically good or evil. We go to the Bible to see if it is acceptable and even find strong hints now and then one way or the other. The same was true for the role of Gentiles in the early Christian church or the role of women in the clergy today. The cultic practices of circumcision in Judaism and open communion in today's Episcopal Church provoke similar searches for justification. Sin is never what we're doing; it is always whatever the other guy is doing. Sin is in the eye of the beholder. Too often our response is, "We just can't have that," and we proceed to do what Christians have always done, which is to bend the Bible this way and that and find some moral reason.

I grew up with the understanding that homosexuals were not only different, they were also dirty. How blacks could fall into that trap, since whites thought all blacks were dirty, is beyond me! To this day I'm sure that my frantic necessity to bathe every single day, to put on clean clothes every single day, comes from my childhood. Blacks were said to be dirty, and by God, I'm not going to be dirty, so I'm washing, washing, scrubbing, scrubbing. It's real easy to pass that kind of judgment on to other people, and it annoys me that homosexuality is always put within the same category: "It's dirty." When I was an adolescent, all sexual activity was dirty to me. There are all kinds of sexual relationships that are perverted, but we lay on the homosexual the burden of sexual sin. We are simply trying to find reasons to dislike people who are different from us. It is another instance of our making one point of view absolute and not facing up to the possibility of ambiguity. All of life is ambiguous. There is no position which we can point to and claim, "Thus says the Lord."

I am depressed by the resolution by the [1998] conference of Anglican bishops declaring homosexual activity to be "incompatible with scripture" and advising against the ordination of homosexuals. I have always believed the Episcopal Church represented the breath of reason in our religious fervor. It was personally embarrassing to me because I realized that I had put so much faith in a denomination that I saw as enlightened. I saw it as nearer to the heart of God in its humility; the Episcopal Church didn't claim to have all the answers, and other people with different answers could exist. But at Lambeth we Anglicans came down as rigid and intolerant as any other part of the Christian family. That was part of the reason I left the Baptist Church! For me, the Episcopal Church held out a promise that religion could be different. It didn't have to be dogmatic, it didn't have to have rights and wrongs, and it could be open to other possibilities. But at this meeting the loudest voice was the voice of intolerance, and I found that a betrayal of my commitment to the Episcopal Church. I realized I had put too much faith, too much dependence on the human structure of this particular institution. However gracious it may have seemed, however intelligent, the Episcopal Church is not God.

I can remember when I was younger, there was nothing more comforting to me than to come into my house at night and shut the doors. I felt safe and secure, and that's still a part of me. If anything goes, then nothing goes and nothing works. There have to be some boundaries or rules, but what God is really calling us to is the kind of freedom that accepts all possibilities. These things do not last, but we have to live with the shadow. How do we live within that shadow? Do we just say there was a lapse on the part of the cooler heads within the church? I can see some hard days ahead, but the fight is already on. And I'm going to align myself with the side that's fighting it.

DYLAN THOMAS has a wonderful poem, written to his father who is dying.

> Do not go gentle into that good night,
> Rage, rage against the dying of the light.

That is one of my favorite poems, and I was saying to someone recently, "I wish I would do that. I would like to think that I would do that." And they said, "Well, you do it all the time. Talking about death is a way of raging." Well, isn't that an interesting idea! So that's the way you rage. So I thought that was pretty good insight.

I've been quoting just recently from *Julius Caesar,* "Oh, Caesar, dost thou lie so low? Have all thy glorious triumphs sunk to this low measure? Fare-thee-well." I think about that about myself. I had an exciting life. I don't have one now. So I very often quote Mark Anthony's farewell to Caesar, because I'm not lying dead, but practically.

"What's new?" is the classic American greeting, and growing old is a fate worse than death. Our folk heroes are those who lived hard and fast and died young. The specter of turning forty traumatizes the nation. Midlife is a crisis. Robert Butler aptly titles his book about growing old in America, *Why Survive?* And the question is not lightly asked. Our culture writes the aging off. We can look forward to victimization by young hoodlums in the decaying neighborhoods to which our lowered earning power condemns us, and victimization by our government because we are increasingly powerless and dependent. Our wrinkled skin and slowed movements are all-too-vivid reminders to the young of the fate that awaits us all, and they would just as soon forget it.

The good news for me in growing old is that the old have the possibility of breaking that vicious human history of living by the death of the other. Older people have an invaluable gift to bring to the world—the gift of reconciliation.

Now I'm telling the Spirit, "No more!" I wanted to die at seventy, and my friends say I'm always sending God mixed messages—I say I want to die and then I'm starting new projects every day. One thing I do have in mind, which I am not going to do, is a book on the theology of ambiguity. The first chapter is going to be called, "You Are Not Wrong." And the second chapter, "You Are Not Right."

The appeal of religion, I think, is the promise of something beyond this world, and I think that that is quite an appeal. Like those wonderful spirituals, "All God's children are going to have a place"—that is quite a promise to people who have no place: joy, fellowship, blessings for everybody. It's unbelievable. You can only believe on faith, because we don't know anything about that in this world. But we have it on faith, "In my Father's house are many mansions: if it were not so, I would have told you. I go to prepare a place for you." That's a pretty good promise.

Faith risks that there is something beyond this world, and it's better than this world. And if you find out it's not so, it won't matter anyway. You have nothing to lose, and a whole possibility of joy to meditate on and to write wonderful poetry about, and of dreaming great dreams. So if it turns out that it's not true, you still have those poems and those dreams.

Two

The Sleeping Giant

EVEN BEFORE VERNA DOZIER *formally became an Episcopalian in 1955, she was called upon to teach the Bible at youth and adult education conferences. Here she found two enormous challenges. First, many Christians were unfamiliar with the biblical record, particularly its larger story, so she prepared guidelines and lesson plans for Bible study. However, she also discovered that many more newcomers to biblical study had "abdicated" their responsibility as learners, choosing to believe that only experts and "authorities" could answer their questions. Here Verna describes the church, which she called the People of God, as a "sleeping giant." She believed church members were hiding from their responsibilities as Christians in the world and depending on others (mostly clergy) to give them answers rather than wrestling with their own faith. The institutional church was asleep.*

This reluctance to take up the hard work of wrestling with what the Bible has to say to our lives led Verna to write what for many years was her signature book, The Authority of the Laity *(1982). At the heart of this powerful text, the accumulation of years of thinking and teaching, is a dilemma about authority that Verna had previously encountered in her thirty-year "ministry" (as she called it) as an English teacher of "downtrodden" students in the District's inner-city schools.*

To address this tough learning environment, Verna began her classes with challenging questions, the "A-1 principle in teaching." She emphasized again and again that "the authority lies with the students," rather than looking to teachers for the answers. She vowed that "her students were to be respected" as she urged them to embrace and exercise their own authority in conversation with others.

In The Authority of the Laity, *which is the central text in this chapter, Verna similarly encourages us to believe that we too are accepted, upheld by "God's boundless assurance of love." She prods us to study with others the stories of "God acting in history," stories that help us struggle with and shape responsible journeys in faith. Such stories, she assures us, do not offer us a clear and unambiguous "book of rules" but models for living with faith.*

A FUNNY THING happened on the way to the kingdom. The church, the people of God, became the church, the institution.

Even in the gospels you can see the beginnings of the process of institutionalization, the story of how "the people of God" became "the institution." The concern about the institution that marks the later epistles is not yet there, but it is clear that it is the church that produced the gospels. We cannot ever get back to the Jesus of history. The flaw in the "Jesus of history" versus the "Christ of the church" controversy was pointed out by Albert Schweitzer. We can know Jesus only by responding to the risen Christ in an act of faith. There is no way we can ever go beyond that act. The gospels themselves were the response of the people of faith to this new experience, the risen Christ. So, as I see it, the church's fingerprints were on the record from the beginning, in the choice of what fragments were saved. What is saved is always a response. What do we believe about this? There is very little in the Bible about what we are to *do*, very little about actions apart from what we call "spiritual." Paul does say something about the marriage relationship. And there is some effort to deal with the work relationship, at least with that then-powerful institution, the relationship between slaves and masters. But the Bible describes the results of the organized community's decisions about what was right and wrong, not the individual wrestlings that took place.

There is a shift in focus in the New Testament. The shift occurs somewhere between the letter of Paul and the later epistles, when the church becomes the focus instead of the life of faith. This shift is a movement from an unorganized response to the risen Christ to an organized response. The shape of the community was a little freer during the earliest periods of the church. In the earlier writings we hear the community around Matthew saying, "This is how we saw Jesus," and the community around John saying, "This is how we saw Jesus," and Paul saying, "This is how I saw Jesus." In the later writings we hear, "This is how Jesus must be seen." In Acts one can begin to see the process of doctrines being formulated and decisions being made about who is in and who is out. That is the kind of shift we have, and it was a necessary shift. That was the process by which the Christian community moved into institutionalization. If we are going to perpetuate the faith we have, we have to get it organized and catalogued so that people can know who is "in" and who is "out." It became very important to detect heresy.

The early church was very much threatened by other religions. A great diversity of religions proliferated in the ancient world as they do in our modern age. So the early Christians *had* to have some way of saying, "Who belongs here? Who is with us?" That kind of activity is both very necessary and very dangerous, because the minute the question "Who is with us?" is asked, tests for membership begin. Tests for membership are always based on beliefs and creeds rather than on loving relationships with one another. We have a hard time creating clear criteria for membership on the basis of loving relationships. It is not surprising that people would pick up the Bible and decide that correct belief is the purpose of its use; not surprising, but tragic. The way we have often used the Bible is one more manifestation of human sin.

I HAD THE unhappy experience recently of hearing a capable, intelligent woman executive say how insignificant she felt in a meeting with some distinguished clergy. She said, "I felt I had no ground on which to stand that was important enough to claim their attention." Tragic. Her very *being* was ground for claim to their attention! She was the reason for their existence. How topsy-turvy it has all become!

Unfortunately, I often feel more alone and isolated when I am with institutional church groups than as a black person with all-white groups or as a woman with all-male groups. Consciousness-raising has worked well enough with whites and with men that they at least understand, even if they do not heed, the protest I bring from my sex and my race. The cry that I raise from my lay consciousness is not even *understood* by many in the institutional church—either clergy or laity!

People are more likely to talk about "lay ministry" than about the ministry of the laity, and I think appropriately so because it is something very different! In the clerical mind, "lay ministry" ranges all the way from "finding something for the laypeople to do" to "getting some help with the work because I can't do it all." In the minds of most laity, "lay ministry" means being let in on the institution's work—or being trapped into it. But to me the ministry of the laity is not parish renewal nor liturgical reform nor sharing the ministry. All of these may be a part of it, but all of these are shifting the cargo in the ship. For me, the ministry of the laity means changing the port toward which the ship is headed.

This is not the first time the ship has been diverted from its course. Long ago Israel, the chosen people, became Israel, the nation. Amos and a long line of prophets following him cried out, "We've missed the mark! This is not what it is all about."

What are we about? What are we called to? And what does that say about our basic understanding of ourselves?

For me the problem is that church has come to mean institution and not people—not the people of God. I do not think that most people, in response to the question "What is the church?" would answer "the people of God." They (accurately) view the church as an institution with a professional hierarchy, concerned about maintaining itself. That is what institutions are always all about. They could not possibly be about anything else. And their contact with the world outside of them is designed to maintain themselves. That is one reason why evangelism has gone astray, as I see it. Evangelism has become putting people in the pews; it has become equated with church growth because numbers are necessary to maintain the institution.

Laypeople err in the direction of idolizing institutions by the deference they pay to clergy. Laypeople see clergy as somehow being privy to esoteric knowledge that is very important for life after death or very important for comfort in this world. Laypeople believe that the clergy have the inside track to that kind of knowledge and that laypeople must be enough in touch with the clergy to assure themselves of safety after death and comfort in this world. Most people seem to think the Bible is some kind of magic book containing the secret of how to live my life. When I am in trouble, if I can decipher that secret everything will be all right. When I fall sick or somebody in my family falls sick, that secret is the magic by which I can make them get well. It is wisely accepted that the church holds that kind of secret because there was a time in the history of the church when church people had the power to make sick people get well. We have now for the most part lost that secret, though clergy, it is believed, have a better chance to break the code than laity.

That approach of reading the Bible to recapture the magic started very early in the church; it is not just a twentieth-century American invention, as we sometimes suppose. We now inherit a malaise of the church that began a long time ago. Periodically the church has fought battles to break out of that bondage to "magical" thinking, with its implicit dependence on clergy. But each time, when the victory was won, almost as soon as the battle was over the victory was institutionalized. I always think with great sorrow of how people lost their lives so that the Bible could be translated into the language of the people. That battle was fought and those people were willing to die because they understood that the Bible contained no magic remedy, but a life-giving message that people needed to have in their own language. The tragedy was that the message was never released. People were too firmly in the habit of letting somebody else do the deciphering of the mysteries for them. Although the Bible was put into the language of the laity, the laity still would not accept the responsibility for learning how to use it.

Another battle was fought to open the Lord's table so that everybody could partake of the bread and the wine. That very important battle was won. But the end result was institutional: now you have a church that gives communion in both kinds and a church that doesn't, and that's all the victory has now amounted to. It is an old, old struggle that we are talking about, and a struggle that threatens to continue, because we are trying to change a centuries-old way of responding.

Interestingly enough, those battles were fought by the very people who were the leaders of the institution, by enlightened clergy who saw that something was seriously wrong in the church. Laypeople never really participated in those reforms because they had long since given up believing that the church was anything in which they really had any ownership. Laity were always the *recipients* of the church's bounty. They were the *objects*. The institution's history has been dominated by that kind of theology.

To turn all that history around is very difficult. Both laypeople and clergy have a hard time understanding what I am talking about. It sounds heretical. I believe that in the Bible we have only one part of the story, though I know that is not an idea that people are going to warm to. The church has always acted as if one needs to know nothing outside of the biblical record. The theory about the inerrancy of the Bible got its strength from people's fear that if part of the structure was attacked the whole thing would come tumbling down. As if that structure was something that could be destroyed! The Bible was rarely understood as the response of people who saw God acting in history. We could tear apart all those records that are left to us and not destroy that witness. We can sweep the house clean of all the ideas that we have had about the Bible and the church and fill it with a new content. Most people do not see that. We cannot bear the void. We think that if we sweep the house clean, the devils are going to rush in immediately, but the story is that the devils rush in only if the house is left empty.

ARE WE SERVANTS of God, or are we servants of the status quo?

We can come to the Bible with a new understanding of what it says that will itself be a new response to that revelation: that God came into history to create a people who would change the world, who would make the world a place where every person knew that he or she was loved, was valued, had a contribution to make, and had just as much right to the riches of the world as every other person. That is what the church is all about, to bring into being that vision, that ideal community of love in which we all are equally valuable and in which we equally share. Every structure of life comes under the judgment of that vision: our politics, our economics, our education, our social structures. Even the church! Nothing is exempt from that challenge. Every member of the church who lives and works in any of those structures or any combination of those structures is called to carry the message that this structure will be redeemed to the glory of God.

But laypeople have very little idea of that high calling. True religion binds together and undergirds all the structures of society as the redeemed people of God infiltrate those structures, changing the world. We act as if religion were a compartment separate from those structures. I think the first Christians were all excited about the promise of making a difference, of changing the world. The ecclesiastical structures had not yet emerged, but they were not long in emerging. They were in place before the biblical record was all written down. The problem—now as then—is holding the structures under judgment. Not that ecclesiastical structures in themselves are evil, rather they are always under judgment. The structures are there, not for themselves, but in order that the people of God may be let loose into the world.

We have turned the whole thing upside down. Instead of the structures being tools to help the people, the people became subservient to the structures. Then the church as a structure among structures gave up its power. The church as one structure became subservient to another power: to kings. It became the handmaiden of the state. The church lost its vision of being a disturber of the status quo and became a supporter of the status quo. In the movie *Breaker Morant*, the priest blessed the troops that were going out to fight a "holy war." He said, "God can use to his purposes war as well as peace." The reason the church got into the business of supporting "holy wars" was that kings were determined to have wars and anybody who said war was wrong was going to be executed, exiled, or rendered irrelevant.

In those days kings held the power of the structures. In our day the industrialists, the financiers, and the great corporate managers hold the reins of power. And the church goes along with the structures of power. A comforting message is: "If you are really living a good Christian life you will be successful in business. You will be the chairman of the board or an executive." That is one way in which the church has gone along with the structures in our time, as in other times the church went along with other structures. The church, having become just one institution among many, had to bow down and support one of those structures in order even to maintain its life. Those kings and those financiers became most significant. The church became irrelevant. The church as a structure became subservient to the principalities and powers—then, and now.

The people of God have been diverted. If the true business of religion is to search for some truth about how the whole of life fits together and how we might live it, it simply cannot be just one department alongside others. Religion cannot be the glue if it is one of the pieces.

I can remember that when I used to go to youth camp, the leaders showed a little diagram of a triangle. One side of the triangle was personal life; one represented work; another, church. Church was always just one of the three sides. Some people divide life into religious, intellectual, and social aspects. Again religion is just one of the aspects. The whole idea that religion is the totality of life is completely lost.

Jack Spong's book *The Hebrew Lord* has a fascinating series of drawings that shows the movement from the Hebrew understanding of life to the Greek. To the Hebrew, the human situation was enveloped by God; the Greek saw the human situation as "down here" and God as "up there." Where the two touched was "religion." That is very different from the image of the whole of life as religious. If you tell most people that the whole of life is religious, they think of somebody who gets up in the morning and says prayers, stops in the afternoon and says prayers, says prayers again at night, wears a cross, and says the Jesus prayer. We seldom recall that being religious means that our whole life is so ordered that every moment we are aware that we are not the final explanation for ourselves. It means that the ethics that control our work are the ethics of a servant, because we are not our own masters. It means that our relationships to our fellow human beings are under the lordship of our Creator—whether we are married to those fellow humans or are their parents, whether we are their friends or coworkers. We do not have to stop and think about being religious because that is the way our lives are lived.

The covenant image of the Old Testament means all of this. Amos inveighed against every part of the Hebrew people's life because they had lost their awareness of being the people of God. Isaiah proclaimed the judgment of God: "Even though you make many prayers, I will not listen;

your hands are full of blood" (1:15). The prophets railed against religious activity as a substitute for a religiously aware life. Very early in the church's history people who wanted that totality of religious life were separated off into convents and monasteries. They were called the "religious." It was not expected that other people would participate in that total offering of life. The sense that all of life is played out before God was lost for ordinary people.

When chancel dramas in Washington churches first started, people wanted to put on "religious" dramas, so they chose plays like *Murder in the Cathedral* and *Everyman*. At St. Mark's Church we wanted to do plays by Arthur Miller and Ionesco. We put on a play by Miller in which the set showed dilapidated housing, a lavatory on stage, and inhumane working conditions. People were offended because they thought it was so inappropriate to show things like that in church. Very often churches allowed that sort of drama to be performed in the parish hall but not in the chancel, not in front of the altar. There was an idea that somehow you kept that kind of activity a secret from God. Nowadays that attitude is less common. We used to think we had to walk into the nave with hushed whispers and come before God with our Sunday best dress on. The fact that God was where we were in the world, in the office on Monday, at the party on Friday, in the cellar on Saturday, was somehow not recognized.

At a conference for women married to clergy, the conversation turned to their sexual life. They had difficulty talking about it. When the discussion did turn in that direction, one woman said her husband was pastor of a church that met in their own house for worship. She said living in the church really affected her married life because "after all, the Host was in the house and you couldn't have sex with the Host in the house." It was apparently not part of her awareness that anywhere she had sex, God would be there. That is the kind of separation we have created, a separation that is not only ridiculous but harmful because it legitimizes keeping important parts of our life away from God—as if we could! We murmur sweet prayers on Sunday morning that do not affect what we do when we go off into the voting booths on Tuesday. We vote our own self-interest and greed in that voting booth on Tuesday as if we had never prayed about being members of one another on Sunday.

I WAS AT A conference recently that concluded with a Eucharist. We had been working all day in one room, and the Eucharist began in that room with the liturgy of the Word. At the end of it, we were told that we would all participate in making the "sacred space"—because where we were was not a "sacred space." So we joined hands and danced our way from that room, through another room, to pick up the communion vessels, the bread and the wine, to a third room where the table was prepared, and we celebrated the Eucharist in a "sacred space."

There were good reasons to move to another room. There was a piano there, and singing was to be a joyful part of the Eucharist. It was also a room in which we had lived some life together. We had eaten our meals there. The troubling part to me was the suggestion, however subtle, that the "sacred space" was a place different from where life was lived, that the "sacred space" was where the institutionally ordained preside.

I believe the sacred space is where the institutionally ordained preside. I believe it is also where mothers tend their children, teachers guide their students, doctors care for their patients, police officers patrol the streets, executives make decisions, laborers ply their trades—laity everywhere doing the work they are called to do.

The ground on which we stand is holy ground. God is where we are. What space could be more sacred than where God is? As long as we, intentionally or unintentionally, believe and therefore act out that we have to go somewhere special to meet God or do something special to be close to God, laypeople will see themselves as second-class citizens in the household of faith and the work they do as second-class activity. They will not perceive their work as a calling; they will not perceive themselves as called.

The sacred space the clergy provide is to give laypeople the opportunity to celebrate together the God we have met in the sacred places of our homes and offices and communities, to confess our failures to identify what God has made sacred, to be renewed so that we know all our life is holy. No other understanding of sacred space, it seems to me, takes seriously the ministry of the laity.

WHY HAVE we strayed so far afield from where the church began? For me the answer lies in our great human need for definite answers. We resist living with the doubt, incompleteness, confusion, and ambiguity that are inescapable parts of the life we are called to live. Living by faith means living in unsureness. We cannot bear the uncertainties with which the gospel message calls us to live. We cannot bear having to take a *risk* that this is the way to go. We cannot bear our inability to *know* absolutely. So we hurry up and create some certainties that will relieve us of that anxiety. The temptation in the Garden of Eden is that "you will be as gods," knowing all things, and we succumb to that temptation all the time.

Clergy often fall prey to the illusion that they do have the answers. Sometimes the laity encourage that illusion. Often in a church conference when we divide into small groups, clergy refuse to participate in the small groups because they think that they have the answers and they will "overpower" the laity. Withdrawing from the groups, of course, suggests that they *are* different, that they *do* have the answers. I was working with a group once that I had worked with many times before. We had had wonderful times and lots of participation. A bishop came to visit and he just sat there, silent. The discussion was killed because the people felt there was one present who had the right answers. Afterwards the bishop and I talked about the event. He told me that if he kept silent, his power as an authority figure would be less oppressive. I felt that his silence made him more of an authority figure, and that he would have been part of the group if he had risked participation like everyone else.

What gives clergy the feeling that they ought to know everything? All too often laypeople give them that feeling, and clergy feel guilty if they don't meet those unreal expectations.

Another problem is that laypeople need to be experts both in their own vocational area and in theology. Laity really need to know what God has done in Christ, as profoundly as any ordained minister; and then they need to know their own discipline as well. Clergy need to know that there *are* other areas of expertise, but they do not need to be experts in those areas. So laypeople really have the harder job. No one wants a harder job, so it becomes easy to give up and say, "I'll just take care of my profession, and leave the profession of ministry to the ordained person." So the whole structure communicates to the layperson, "You do not know," and the layperson replies, "Yes, I do not know." Of course the layperson really does have to know. One has to "know whom you have believed," and that means knowing not only in the biblical sense of participating in a reality but also in the intellectual sense of being able to say to someone else what that gospel is. It is the task of the clergy to be sure that the people with whom they work *do* know what their faith is all about. Clergy are called to be rabbis. Rabbis do not profess to have any more spiritual genius than the congregation; they merely profess to have the learning. The learning that laypeople themselves need is really not academic learning. No layperson has to know Greek or the history of the church or all the arguments that the church fathers put forward. They *do* need to know the gospel story. The training of the clergy should give them a set of tools for helping laypeople know that story, the story of the people of God.

Periodically the Christian church produces prophets who say there is something fundamentally wrong with the direction we have taken. One of the most eloquent of these was Hendrik Kraemer. In 1958 he wrote a profound little book which he called *A Theology of the Laity*. In a very learned way Kraemer reviews the theological struggle with the issue of the laity. The general conclusion that can be drawn, he said, is that for the greater part of its history, church thinkers have provided little place for the laity in their understanding of salvation or of the church. At best the laity was the flock; always it was object, never subject with its own calling and responsibility.

In the Protestant Reformation, a strong vindication of the laity as *subject* and not merely *object* was made, but it broke down in concrete reality for two reasons. On the one hand, the laity were generally unable to function according to their biblical calling. On the other hand, the church was preoccupied with the nature and function of the ordained ministry. Though there was an attempt to reshape the theology of the ministry, the new ministers were, in sociological and psychological reality, a metamorphosis of the former clergy. Milton said, "New presbyter is but old priest writ large." The priestly, sacramental notions related to the clergy were of course largely eliminated and reinterpreted in religious-moral terms, but in actual fact the "standing" and "apartness" of the new "ministry" were in many respects similar to those of the former "priesthood."

That temptation to establish a "set apart" ministry of the ordained haunts the church. We have great difficulty grasping the idea that *all of us* are called, *all of us* are ministers. If a layperson evidences a particular interest in Bible study or theology, soon someone is bound to ask, "Have you ever thought about being ordained?"—as if only the clergy need to know their spiritual roots. Or we promote special orders and ranks of laity, a sort of religious version of "all are equal but some are more equal than others."

Kraemer goes on to his basic point: The church *is* ministry. He prefers to use the Greek word for ministry, *diakonia* ("serving"). Kraemer says the *diakonia* of the church is correlative to and rooted in the *diakonia* of Christ. The ministry of the ordained clergy and the ministry of the laity are both aspects of the same *diakonia,* each in their proper sphere and calling. He moves on to identify that "proper sphere and calling": "The main part of the ministry of the clergy should be to enable the laity to fulfill their peculiar, inalienable ministry." Kraemer spells out how the church carries out that enabling function: "Not as a haven of refuge, which is in most cases another form of escapism, of letting the world go to the devil. But as the nourishing and understanding mother, the community which by prayer, sacrament and ways of true fellowship sustains its members in the battle."[1]

The more recent thinking of the Grubb Institute in Great Britain speaks to this point. Grubb Institute theorist Bruce Reed describes the way we oscillate between "intradependence," the mode of being sure and competent and equal to what is required of us, to "extradependence," the mode of being needy and drained and not equal to any challenge. In that latter mode Christians turn to the church (remember Kraemer's image of the "nourishing and understanding mother"). When the church is healthy, and the clergy are in their proper calling and role, the needy are cared for, the drained are replenished, and the droopy are reminded who they are and to what they have been called. Back to the battle they can go, strengthened for *diakonia*. Reed describes this as "controlled regression." "Contained regression," the unhealthy manifestation, keeps one trapped in that warm cozy community, and both clergy and laity forget their high calling.

"Contained regression" is as if a shop in the business of repairing broken-down buggies became so fascinated with the apparatus of repairing the buggies and so proud of the rehabilitated buggies that it disdained returning them to the customers. The customers went on to motor cars and airplanes while the factory workers, happily unaware, spent their time perfecting their repairing technology and looking for more broken-down buggies to fix.

Kraemer has a stinging insight on this point. The institutional church, in an effort to fulfill her prophetic role in society, has issued many pronouncements on the great topics of the day. "But," he contends, "if the laity of the church, dispersed in and through the world, are really what they are called to be, the real uninterrupted dialogue between church and world happens through them. They form the daily repeated projection of the church into the world."[2]

Such a ringing call as Kraemer's should have made a difference, but the religious situation is not a lot different today than it was when he first wrote about it.

The situation has not changed because the institutional church has a vested interest in its *not* changing. Changes threaten the institution. In Martin Luther the Roman Catholic Church saw the threat of its own demise. Its leaders did not have enough vision to see that someone was bound to start a counter-reformation and keep the Roman Catholic Church in place. For every Pope John, you have a Pope Paul. But there is always a potential threat. Jesus was a threat to the synagogue in his day. Every institution strives to maintain itself, to ensure its own safety and stability and protect itself from threats. All organisms try to survive. No organism yearns to follow the example of the dinosaurs. Institutions *can* change, though very slowly. Of course, many people do not *want* institutions to change. They hope that the structures of society will give them some stability. One hears people wailing because society's institutions are breaking down. They find that fact very threatening. They have never heard, "Behold, I am doing a new thing." Christianity should be troubling: it should threaten every institution.

All structures, principalities, and powers stand under judgment—even when the structure is the church. There is a way to be a part of an institution under judgment. There is a way to belong to an institution and maintain some tension, so that we can measure it by its declared purposes and look at the possibility that the institution may be in error. When we can do those things, we are no longer captives of the institution. God always has thousands who "have not bowed the knee to Baal" and thousands who have not accepted institutions as the idol that the institutions would like to be. We do not know who all those people are. We do know they come from every Christian tradition, and that many of them are clergy or even bishops who have broken the mold in one way or another. There are models for living in tension. But I would not for one minute want to institutionalize the models. When we work frantically to institutionalize the way we live in tension, we fall into creating another institution, which is what Protestantism has done continually. Every time a Protestant body has broken out of the tradition to uphold some new insight, we have set up another denomination. Or "restructured" an old one. Over and over we show that we are not willing to live in the uncertainty. We grasp that new insight and hold on to it anxiously. We have to see ourselves reproduced in order to know that we are right. Then the vision is lost again.

Kraemer said that when church bodies deliberate, the world is out of sight. The only concern seems to be continuity with the past. The new challenges come from the present and the future, and the church's intensive concern about continuity with the past, always looking back to see how it was done at the beginning, is a force that presses in the direction of institutionalization rather than in the direction of living in the tension by faith. We are called to walk by faith. We cannot do that if we are unwilling to live in uncertainty; we willfully grasp "a piece of the rock."

So the Christian church continually denies its Lord.

AS THAT BEAUTIFUL line in *Romeo and Juliet* has it, "My love is boundless. The more I give to you, the more I have." That is the quality of love. The more you love, the more you are able to love. The more people you love, the more people you *can* love. If we find that to be true in our human experience, how much more would that be true for God?

We may object that children growing up do not experience love as inexhaustible. Siblings feel that there is only so much to go around, and if my brother gets a lot of attention, there will not be much left for me. But why reduce God to human terms and cast love in one form only, the form of attention? I do think that a person has only so much attention to pay at any given moment. If I am looking at you, I cannot be looking at John. But the fact that I am not looking at John does not mean I do not love John at that moment. The problem lies in our definition of love; the terms in which we define love limit it. We need always to hear the gospel telling us about a God who is very different from anything we can imagine.

It's so interesting the way we modern people talk in superior tones about how the ancient people thought of God in anthropomorphic terms. I think that today we try to reduce God to our understanding, to our experiences, and that is equally anthropomorphic. In the picture language of the Pentateuch (the first five books of the Bible) the images vary. If we are going to talk about God (and we must talk about God) then it seems to me we should be very careful constantly to use varying images, or else to be very clear that whatever image we are using is limited. We need to do that for ourselves when we are alone thinking, or aloud when we are talking to others. I was told once never to express an idea without prefacing it with "as I see it." I find the practice useful because it reminds me that there always have been and will be other views. Anthropomorphic though the Old Testament was, it gave us ever-varying images: a light behind the cloud, a man walking in his garden, a mother hen brooding. A lot of ways to say the unsayable—because when we talk about God, we say the unsayable.

You are accepted

HERE IS ANOTHER reality to remember: my belief that I am fully accepted, though I am unacceptable, is a faith statement. I can never prove it. It may not be true. The whole biblical myth could be just a delusion. A risk is involved. But what the Christian community at its best is doing is living as if that myth were true. We are not going to find any validation of that myth in the world around us because the world marches to another drummer. We cannot talk about God only in terms of our experiences, because we are marching to a drummer that says our experiences are only a part of reality, not the whole of it. And our interpretation of our experiences is always skewed and distorted by our self-hatred and pride.

I have two choices. Either I make reality small and concrete and unequivocal enough that I can grasp it and own it. Or I admit that the truth is so far beyond what I can grasp and comprehend and own and control that my relationship with that truth is very tenuous. I have to walk by faith. I believe that while the Christian witness calls us to walk by faith, most of what we do in the institution denies that. The institution always moves toward making reality certain, pinning it down in liturgies, in organizational structures, in educational systems, in any way we can pin it down. Because of that tendency, the institution has to be broken open again and again and again. That breaking-open process doesn't happen often enough, but it is the thread through the church's story. We need to go back and look at church history, because people are always tempted to cling to the idea of the church as a way to get to be all right. The clergy are trained in that approach, and the laypeople accept it because that is all they have ever known. Note that I am making a distinction between what many people honestly believe they believe in their hearts and what they *do* corporately in the institution. Few clergy or laypeople profess belief in a rule-making God. Indeed, most clergy would be denied ordination if their examiners even suspected such a belief on their parts. No. The leaders of the church do talk and try to believe the grace game. But they *play* the law game. There's the rub—the difference between religion of the lips and religion of action.

Being made right is not the church's work. That is God's work, and that work is done. The work of salvation is finished. The unfinished part, the part that is ours, is to work out our salvation with fear and trembling, in a world threatened by nuclear extinction, ravished by greed that secures the very rich at the expense of multitudes of the very poor, seething with age-old racial and religious hatreds.

This is the world *we* are called to turn upside down. In many ways it is very much like the world into which the incarnate Lord came, and in many ways it is very different. The major difference today is that "Christianity" is a powerful establishment. Religious establishments all act alike; they all arrogate to themselves the exclusive right to speak for God. Laypeople must take upon themselves the awful burden of yielding that right to no one.

If our salvation is already accomplished, we will want to act that out in our lives everywhere without compartmentalizing them. If we are already all right, we can probably tolerate more ambiguity, freedom, and chaos. For instance, we will not be so concerned about who is in and who is out. And if we are already all right, we need not grasp for the kinds of certainty we can possess, but will know ourselves to be held by a certainty that is ungraspable. We will not leave church knowing just what we ought to do. If we come away from hearing a sermon and know exactly what to do, then it is possible that the sermon missed the point, because that sermon would have structured our lives. The sermon in which the gospel is preached gives no rules and regulations about how to live our lives, but points to a great vision. I am always happiest when the preacher says, "This is how I see it; this is what I am called to do," and then I can decide that I want to march with that person, or I can decide that I am not called in that way. Even the person who knows "This is what I must do" knows it only for that moment. I may be called to do that on Monday, and I may *not* be called to do that on Tuesday. We are called to freedom, and the awfulness of decision. To know that we are accepted is to receive the gift of freedom. Love God and do as you please. Such freedom gets scary. We see too much space out there, so we tie things down very quickly. By the time we come to the written gospels, the figure of Jesus has already been tied down to a certain extent, but we can still see that free spirit moving through the New Testament. Christ's spirit cannot be tied down.

Now, I know we need some structure. There is something comforting in saying, "This is the way we usually do it." Those little rituals structure our lives so that we have some containers for all the chaotic experience that goes rushing through. I would hate to wake up every single day and say, "Well now, here is this marvelous day. What shall I do today? Shall I start by brushing my teeth?" In fact, I think people who live in a totally unstructured way have set themselves up another structure. They have made anarchy their God. But the love of structure can grow to the point where you have all banks and no river. The structure becomes the idol. The important thing, it seems to me, is to hold the structure loosely. As a servant. I think "servant" is a beautiful word, too, for institutions. Robert Greenleaf wrote a series of papers and books on the idea of servant, and one of them was on the institution as servant. The real definition of the church as institution is servant. "Servant" is like the word "symbol." It points beyond itself, it is limited, it is finite, it has a purpose, but it is not ultimate. Neither servant nor symbol is ultimate reality. The institution is not ultimate. It points to God, when it is doing its job. When it begins to *act* like God, it has capitulated to fear, making itself an idol.

If people really believe that the work of salvation has already been accomplished, how would it change the way they related to churches? I think they would participate fully in churches as institutions. They would serve on the boards. They would contribute their money. They would be faithful in attendance. But they would hold it all loosely. Just to give some concrete examples, they would not be devastated when the church changed the form of worship or the hymnal. They would not consider all lost if the church opened up the ordained ministry to women. It would not disturb them if some people found meaning in other denominations instead of the one they happen to belong to. There would be a kind of lightness in the way they encountered all those bits and pieces of ecclesiastical life.

The gift to them from the institution would be community. They would have a place where they were understood. No matter how peculiar and crazy they were, there would be somebody there who would understand them, somebody who would love them. And they would hear that message proclaimed, falteringly perhaps, but proclaimed on Sunday morning. The sacraments would give them the opportunity to participate in that continuing drama. And I think all those gifts from the church would be important to them, often vital. Even though people knew their salvation was accomplished, I do not think they would separate themselves from the institutional church. I think they would have a spirit and a lightness and a grace so that everyone would know they had a different quality of life. There would be no lightness about the way they encountered the essence of their call to be about the business of their Lord. With grace and humility, they would name the demons of oppression, care for the victims, march against the powers and principalities, and constantly challenge the church, the institution, to be the church, the people of God.

They would be leaven in the lump, not always recognized. While they would be very faithful in their participation, I think they would find it possible to bring judgment on the church. Because the prophets in our midst know that their salvation is accomplished, they are free to say of any structure: "That's not helpful." I do not think they would necessarily be serving on the highest boards, although they might be so called. They might be very annoying people, so they might not get elected to anything. People who hold the institution lightly are not always celebrated by those who do not hold it lightly.

I AM INCREASINGLY convinced that the biblical injunction to "go into all the world and preach the gospel to all nations" has been narrowed from our Lord's broad vision to just a churchy activity. In St. Mark's gospel, Jesus does not just come preaching the kingdom. He comes as the embodiment of the kingdom. Where he appears, life is different. I always think of this hymn stanza as a synopsis of the Jesus of Mark:

> Hear him, ye deaf; his praise, ye dumb,
> Your loosened tongues employ;
> Ye blind, behold your Saviour come,
> And leap, ye lame, for joy.

Where Jesus came, life was different. He proclaimed the gospel by being the gospel. "And greater things than I do shall you do," he said. It is not enough to heal the sick. Heal the systems that make them sick. It is not enough to visit the prisoners. Question the structures that imprison people. Some great churchmen have had this vision— Martin Luther King, Reinhold Niebuhr, Walter Rauschenbusch—but the implementation of the vision is the ministry of the laity.

Christian economists must be about the business of asking: *What are the systems and structures that will give dignity to all people? How can we bring those systems into being?* Christian political scientists must be about the business of asking: *How can life be so ordered that people will have increasing control over their own lives? What changes must be set in motion so that those dreams can become realities?* And so on, in every sphere of life. Christians must be about the business of making real for every man, woman, and child the kingdom that has come among us.

The ministry of the laity is being open and sensitive to every structure of society that puts a millstone around the neck of one of the least of these. As the poet William Blake put it:

> I shall not sleep
> Nor shall my sword rest in my hand
> Till I have built Jerusalem
> In England's green and pleasant land.

That's the ministry of the laity. Building Jerusalem where you are.

What would have to happen for some of these things to take place? What do laity have to do that might turn the situation around?

First, laypeople need to become informed about what the faith actually is. Laypeople have to be experts in the theological realm as well as in their own vocational realm. What kind of adult education do we laity need to be looking for that will help us build up that theological strength? I think laypeople need to study the Bible and be cognizant about church history. We do not have to become scholars, but we need to be well enough educated to know that whatever form of polity our particular denomination practices is not sacrosanct, that it developed in response to certain historical events and that it is under the judgment of the faith like everything else, including the Bible. Any educational venture that brings laypeople together to study seriously is a helpful intervention in the life of the church because out of serious study, questions arise.

Terms like "ministry," "church," "faith," and "baptism" need to be wrestled with, as if they have never been wrestled with before. The old containers will not do. New wine needs new wineskins. Small support groups need to be developed—groups where laypeople can have the freedom to doubt and challenge and wrestle. In Bible study groups, people can discover for themselves, for instance, that the nativity story is not at the heart of the gospel. Insights like that can encourage us to ask ourselves, "What else have we been paying attention to that's really peripheral?" And in answering that question we are going to fumble; we are going to make some mistakes.

I recently received a card from a woman in Virginia, where I had been delivering some of my biblical iconoclasm. She wrote, "I want you to tell me if I am off the track." She had gotten the idea that the resurrection was not essential to the Christian story. Well, she *was* off the track, of course, because what I had been saying was not that the resurrection was not essential. But I think getting off the track is not so terrible; at least she was thinking. She and I are now in conversation. Now she knows she need not be in a garden or an upper room or by the sea to meet the risen Christ. She is beginning to understand that Magdalene's experience was not like Peter's, and Peter's was not like that of the disciples on the Emmaus road. Paul's experience wasn't like any of theirs, and hers doesn't have to be, either.

Out of serious study, real questions arise. For example, the Church of the Saviour in Washington, D. C., has accomplished a revolution within the institution simply by having committed ongoing cells of people who study together. They focus on the world, not the church. They focus on important things: families who have nowhere to live, people who are hungry, countries that are going to war. They really deal with those issues, and they do not care too much about institutional church structures. So there is one model of what laypeople can do.

There is another in the Society of Friends, a lay movement. I find it fascinating that whenever laypeople are really empowered, the issues of the world become their agenda.

Now, I am sure that is a generalization. No doubt there are laypeople who are missing the point as the ordained have often done, but those are two instances of laypeople really getting at the heart of the matter. What is important in the gospel is a new world, not an institution. The institution should always be at the service of laypeople in the world. It is a servant institution.

Study groups are one way of raising these questions. Liturgy is another place at which the questions can be raised. A young woman I know who was on the worship committee in an Episcopal church tried very hard to have the congregation rise when the offering was brought forward. The custom was that the offering was brought forward and received by the priest, and then, when the priest lifted the bread, everyone stood up. My young friend said that the congregation's practice was the exact opposite of the witness that the movement in the liturgy was supposed to make: that when the offerings of the people were brought forth, the people stood up because that was *their* offering. Rising in response to the priest's action conveys the message that what the priest does at the altar is the important thing. We pay homage or respect to a holy thing rather than participating in the offering. When we participate in the offering, that means *we* are important, we give the offering of *our* lives. Asking questions like that about the liturgy could lead laypeople to understand that this is *our* service, the work of the people.

Another liturgical form about which laypeople ought to be raising questions is the way the gospel is read. In many churches, when a layperson reads the lesson, everybody stays seated. Then there is an impressive procession of the gospel into the pulpit, with the ordained person standing in front, the cross behind him or her, and candles on either side. It is the most impressive moment in the entire service, and only the clergy can read that gospel. The ceremony is supposed to be exalting the gospel. What it does is exalt the ordained person. What a different witness it makes when the gospel is processed *into* the congregation. You can look at the liturgy and ask, "What is being communicated here about the gospel? About the laity?"

We can come at those questions from hymnology. We can study the hymns and ask, "What is it that these hymns are saying?" I often have people pay attention to hymns when I lead retreats. Some people read the words of the hymns for the first time. Or we can always use ethics as a starting point. We can look at what is going on in the world today and ask, "What is to be my response as a Christian? How do I become informed?"

There are many ways in which the educational program, the worship, or issues in society or the church's life can provide laypeople with opportunities to deepen their faith. During that great battle about the ordination of women in the Episcopal Church, it interested me that people studied what the ordained ministry was all about more than they ever had before. There were some serious questions raised. Anything that will get people excited, stir them up, so that they can ask the question, "What is it that we are trying to bear witness to?" can be an occasion for laity to grasp their true calling. The questions are there, all around us, all the time. Will we take the responsibility and authority to pay attention to them?

The laity have abdicated their authority

WHEN WE REALLY study the Bible (and I make clear distinctions between *studying* the Bible and *reading* the Bible or using it devotionally), we will find out very soon that the Bible is the record, the witness, of the people of God about how God has acted in their lives. And that witness is borne by laypeople. Although the beginnings of institutional development are clearly in the Bible, it is not an institutional book. There was no well-organized hierarchy. The Old Testament story starts out with a little bumbling band in the wilderness with a very gifted leader. Those travelers looked around at what was happening and they said, "That was God acting." That was a faith statement. It would have been possible to look around and see all kinds of other things going on. But that community said, "This is God acting."

Now the community that wrote the story down was not the original community that traveled through the wilderness, but a later community that looked back on its life together and asked questions like "Who are we?" and "How did we come to be" and "What has shaped us?" The Old Testament people were a fairly fluid community of men and women, laypeople and some ecclesiastical people, who saw themselves as the people of God. That is the subject of the Old Testament: the life of the people of God. And the being of the people of God went furthest astray when they gave over their being as the people of God to the temple authority, to ecclesiastical authority. The temptation was there even in the beginning. When they got scared in the wilderness they asked their priestly leader for a golden calf, a beautiful idol to reassure them.

When the people of God let someone else tell them what to do, when they should offer sacrifices and wash their hands and all that sort of thing, they lost their vision. Then the prophets came on the scene and said, "God does not want all those noisy hymns and all your incense." But finally, when ecclesiastical structure seemed to encompass everything, then came the great light that Jesus brought. He made it very clear that those structures were not the point. The next scene showed again a little bunch of laypeople fumbling around, trying to figure out who Jesus was and how he could be the incarnation of God.

The story keeps repeating itself. Laypeople become weary of the struggle, and they give over the responsibility to some kind of ecclesiastical hierarchy. It happens in the Hebrew scriptures and it happens again in the New Testament. The last books of the New Testament show a fairly well-organized structure telling all the people what they must do at this time or that time—exactly as the Old Testament ended with Ezra telling all the people what they must do at this time or that time.

The tendency toward increasing rigidity happens not only in religion; we do the same thing in secular life. The medical profession finds a new way to deal with illness, and then the institution closes in and that becomes the only way. Perhaps the reason we have made so little headway so far against cancer is that the medical profession has concentrated on treating cancer rather than finding a cure for cancer. The institutional way is to preserve what we know; do not risk the unknown.

The economy is another area in which we give up the struggle. We laypeople do not know what to do. We let the experts tell us. It is a very natural tendency. We just happen here to be concerned with the nature of the church, but it is no different anywhere else.

Our tendency is to say, "Oh, I'm tired of struggling—let someone else do it." In my opinion, this is another manifestation of the tendency toward sin that is deep in all of us. The minute you let someone else do it, that "someone else" will work to remain in power. So, when laypeople say about their religion, "Well, the clergy know more about it, let them do it," then you tip the balance of power to the institutional church. Laypeople then say, "Well, who cares about the institutional church?" and they go off to their jobs in organizations where that same kind of institutionalization has taken place.

I think that if laypeople do not give up in the church, if they fight for the insight that God is concerned about us as

God's people, those same laypeople will be out there making a difference in the world. When we give up in the church, then we are saying that what is going on in the church is not really very relevant in the world. We are really saying that we do not believe that God can work God's mighty acts. And if we have no *faith* that God is still acting, we have no way of *seeing* God acting. So I think it is essential that laypeople do continue to own not only their own vocational expertise but also their expertise as theologians. Unless laypeople struggle to hold together all their worlds, religion cannot be what that word means: "That which ties it all together." When laypeople give religion over to the clergy, it becomes an irrelevant little side issue, which is exactly what it is today—a reservation, as Kraemer says, for those with specialized religious needs. We have our little ceremonies, we have some religious-type saying a prayer when our president is inaugurated, but the administration that goes into action the next Monday cares little about that prayer. And, worse, the fellow who intones the little prayer is selected because he is *not* going to say anything that is going to upset anybody. Well-known evangelists can be hand-in-glove with Democratic presidents and Republican presidents and never say anything that could offend the powerful. The clerics that shake the establishment get pulled out. The church was the handmaiden of the state way back in the Middle Ages, and before. That is what Amos was arguing about with Amaziah. But the Amaziahs of this world have always been rushing out to warn the kings, saying, "Watch out for those people; they might upset things." They do.

Indifference is the natural response to timid, irrelevant religion. We must not confuse weariness with indifference. Most laypeople are bored, rather than exhausted with the battle—or else they are wearied by activities irrelevant to the real struggle. Reinhold Niebuhr described accurately what most laypeople feel: "Religion is no longer radical;

religion is now irrelevant." People pop into church on Sunday morning to pay their dues. They have a good deal of religious superstition. But they are not weary. They are not struggling to bring their faith up against the issues of their lives.

Paul warned, "Let us not weary in well doing." It is so easy to get weary, because being a conscientious layperson is a struggle. It takes work. We have to keep fighting always against the institutional structure closing in. Of course there has to be some way for the real weariness of laypeople to be acknowledged and dealt with in ways that don't encourage them to abdicate their responsibility. When people grow really weary, that is what the church is for, that is what the sacraments are for, and that is what the gathered community is for. People who are weary from the battle need the Sabbath rest.

Scripture says that there were two women to whom Jesus was devoted. He went to their house often and sat and talked with them, and it must have been so exciting to have this guy come in from the city, with all the aura of the big city and all the excitement that he brought with him, and they both adored him. Mary was the one we generally think of as the spiritual type—she hung on to Jesus' every word, she didn't do any cooking, she didn't wash any dishes. She just sat there staring up in his face, whereas Martha was the responsible type. (It was Martha's house, incidentally, that's what the gospels said.) And so she was out there in the kitchen getting the dinner ready, but she kept looking back to see what Jesus was doing and what Mary was doing. Finally she appealed to Jesus and said, "Master, doesn't it trouble you that I'm doing all the work out here in the kitchen and my sister is just there, looking up in your face and doing nothing?" And the Bible says that Jesus said to her, "Martha, you are troubled about many things. Mary has chosen the better part."

That is one of the most misinterpreted verses in all of scripture, because everybody assumes that Mary was the spiritual one and Martha the busy one, and that Jesus was valuing the spiritual over the business and the organizational type. But I think what he was saying is, "Whatever your choice is, value that and concentrate on that." If your choice is cats and dogs, then choose cats and dogs, but don't run around and wonder what the rabbits are doing. Very few are able to have that kind of concentration, particularly if there is something exciting going on somewhere else, that undivided attention to one thing.

Jesus was also busy about many things. Jesus was into politics, he was into social action, he was into quiet. He was a man of many moods and many activities, and he was not looking to any one of those activities as a savior.

1. Hendrik Kraemer, *A Theology of the Laity* (Philadelphia: Westminster Press, 1958), 143, 167, 175.
2. Kraemer, *Theology*, 170.

Three

Yes and No

SHE STANDS IN THE *midst of a room crowded with people who are seated around tables piled high with Bibles in different translations, a few scholarly commentaries, plus scattered notes and cups of coffee. She begins by intoning a verse from a hymn and then quotes a short story from the Bible. At the front of the room on a chart pad, three blunt questions are clearly printed: "What do we hear the passage saying? Why do we believe this passage was preserved? What meanings does the passage hold for us today and what is it calling us to do?" Verna Dozier, a small woman with a booming voice, is at work "equipping the saints."*

Her method revolved around three foundational questions that regularly produced multiple responses and resulted in debate, disagreement, and dialogue. Verna was seldom "at the head of the class." Rather, she moved in and out of small groups, asking even more questions, each one seemingly more challenging than the last. As conversations deepened, she often quoted the words of the Old Testament prophet Amos, railing against the injustice of religious and other authorities. Amos was her favorite prophet.

Verna encouraged those studying the Bible to answer both "yes" and "no" as they wrestled with the Bible and with ethical living. She had learned from her father that every time we say, "as I see it," we need to make room for the opinions of others. Urging adults to become learners full of questions, responsive to the ambiguity and diversity of the biblical record, Verna asked questions that lingered deeply: "Does this passage make enough sense to me that I want to risk living by it?"

This chapter is a compilation of Verna's responses from interviews on her approach to the Bible and excerpts from her unfinished manuscript on ambiguity. The latter was a project she was especially intent on in her later years, although the idea of ambiguity has been central to her work all along.

WE COME TO the Bible looking for the wrong thing. Luther cautioned us that the Bible is only the cradle in which the Christ child is laid, pointing beyond itself to God. The reason we choose not to see it that way is that we are terrified of freedom. That is the great sin of human beings. We want to have our life structured so that we will know every minute that we are right. We do that, however, in only one area, the religious area. We want to make sure that we have the right religion; then that frees us to do whatever we please in all the other areas of our lives. People who say the Bible is inerrant are looking for one place where there is absolute certainty. But the Bible is not that place. It points beyond itself. It points to God. Even though every single moment we may have to make terrifying decisions, we are not alone.

WITH JESUS, goodness is ambiguous; Jesus did not make little golden rules. He took the world as he found it, and I think that many times he was not saying, "This is what you should do." Many times he was saying, "What can you learn from this?"

To me ambiguity embraces the totality of reality. There isn't any one position that can do this—it is only one part of the totality of reality. And that is the most difficult thing for us simplistic humans to accept. I remember I had a student once who was so annoyed with me because I was always pointing out another possibility. She would say, "Miss Dozier, just tell me what you want and I will do it."

The comic strip Kudzu poses the issue very succinctly. The preacher and a young friend are sitting on a mountaintop. The young man sighs, "Life is full of ambiguity." He turns to the preacher. "Right, preacher?" he asks, and the preacher answers, "Yes and no."

The Bible: a collection of rules or an assurance of love?

THE BIBLE is being used in ways that it was never intended to be used. The Bible is being used as if it were an answer book, a rule book, a guide for every hour and every day of our life. That is not what it was intended to be. The Bible was the worshiping community's book, written by a people who wanted to express their faith in how God acted in history. The unspoken preface for biblical books is always, "This is how *we* see it." That preface is explicit in the gospels. The gospels are always called "the gospel *according to*..." and what that means is, "This is how this faith community saw it." They do not say, "This is the absolute, not-to-be-challenged way it is." The wonderful thing is that as we read the gospels we see very different pictures of Jesus in each one. There is no way to put those pictures together, because they are faith statements: "This is how we saw it, and this is the way we responded to it."

Five

Called To Be Saints

THIS CONCLUDING CHAPTER *focuses on Verna Dozier's hopes and dreams for the faith community, the people of God—who, she insists, are "called to be saints." With the Bible in mind, her portrayal of "saints" is down-to-earth and realistic: saints are definitely part of fallen humanity. Like the Old Testament prophets and like Verna herself at times, saints could prove difficult, impatient, and demanding. They did their best to resist God's call. Yet through grace, all could be and were called by a God of love.*

Notice that Verna always addresses "saints" as plural members of the body of Christ and not as "scrupulous individuals." She dislikes religion that focuses on the self, and was once tempted to call her book The Dream of God *by the title "The Sorry Journey from We to Me." Here clergy and laity alike are called to live out their different callings. With carefully delineated responsibilities and a special plea that laypeople claim their power in the secular world, Verna issues a collective summons to ministry.*

The selections in this chapter sum up many of her thoughts on calling and also point toward the future. Selections from The Authority of the Laity, *portions of the unfinished manuscript on ambiguity, and other writings show the way. The chapter concludes with a sermon by Verna on the costs of ministry. With a clear voice this provocative and outspoken "saint" proclaims that ministry is at best uncomfortable, always disturbing, and always new.*

TO BE CALLED to be saints means we are called to be members of the household of God. That's what a saint is. A saint is a person who knows that God has acted for him or for her definitively in Christ, that God has acted for lots of other people, too, and that all those people make up the people of God.

When I, as a free-churchwoman, heard the Roman Catholic dictum "There is no salvation outside the church," I was just furious. I thought that was Roman Catholic arrogance, and I would have nothing to do with it. Since then I have learned the profound truth of that affirmation. The church is the people of God, and there is no such thing as a solitary Christian. A Christian is a member of that body. A saint is not necessarily a good person or a wise person, but a saved person. Sainthood has been very much distorted to mean I'm called to work on all my faults and be more spiritual and pure and "better and better." That's another distortion of the biblical message. Paul's instructions to the early Christians were instructions "downward." Because God has done this for you, giving you a new life, this is what that life is going to look like. Since God did this for you, therefore, here is how you act. Gradually, those descriptions became directives. "Saint" began to mean someone who successfully followed the directives and became an especially holy person—a scrupulous individual rather than a member of the body.

That was a denial of the meaning of sainthood as the New Testament people originally saw it. But laypeople believed it. It was a way to make some people better than others and to take the others off the hook. If I'm not specially called, I don't have any responsibility. The church had begun to consider the institutionally ordained as the only people who had *callings*. The rest of us had *jobs*.

During the time of the black revolution, when blacks were marching on Selma and holding sit-ins in restaurants, the white people who joined them were generally ordained ministers. Some of their parishioners were furious. Many others sat back in the pews and thought they had taken a stand because their minister was down there marching, and they had given him leave to do that and paid his way. Actually *going down there* was his responsibility; that was what he was called to do, to make that kind of witness for the church (a witness that, for some, meant imprisonment or loss of life). And decades later, laypeople in the governing bodies of the land are overturning the victories won.

It has all gone so far astray! We have denominations making pronouncements, while all the church people sit back and congratulate themselves: "My, we've been noble! We've made a resolution." But if we take our sainthood seriously, we know that we have missed the point, that sainthood means putting our own lives on the line.

I don't know how we have slipped so easily into thinking that sainthood means being a very good person, that only a few people ever make it, and they only become saints after death. All of that is contrary to the New Testament, where sainthood happened in life, right then. If we believe the whole point of the church is to show us the way to get to be all right, that distorted idea of sainthood is understandable. It would make sense to believe that the institutional church has the right to say who is and who isn't a saint, that the church, rather than the cross of Christ, determines who is a saint. Jesus' sacrifice was not enough, according to that view. We are always trying to add to Jesus' sacrifice. Laypeople need to claim the grace of his all-sufficient sacrifice, accept their acceptance, and, as the people of God, turn the church, the institution, around.

THE BIBLE is about very real and human people who resist God's call. When we try to give meaning to or find a message in many of the stories, the result is often ambiguous at best. Isaac's blessing of Jacob is such a troubling story because it's very difficult to understand why God loves Jacob after he impersonated his brother Esau.

> Isaac said to Jacob, "Come near, that I may feel you, my son, to know whether you are really my son Esau or not." So Jacob went up to his father Isaac, who felt him and said, "The voice is Jacob's voice, but the hands are the hands of Esau." He did not recognize him, because his hands were hairy like his brother Esau's hands; so he blessed him. He said, "Are you really my son Esau?" He answered, "I am." (Genesis 27:21–24)

From the very beginning the Bible is not about setting up role models: Jacob is a rat who stole his brother Esau's birthright and walks away with the prize. These are real human beings interacting with one another. But the interesting thing is that they are the chosen people. God is not choosing people because they are good, or holy. He is choosing people because they are real people and he loves them.

Later in the story Jacob wrestles with an angel. He refuses to let go of the angel until he is blessed. The angel tells Jacob, "You shall no longer be called Jacob, but Israel, for you have striven with God and with humans, and have prevailed" (Genesis 32:28). It's a story that for me is surrounded in mystery. In antiquity, selfhood was expressed in the name given a person. Jacob's new name signifies a new self. The name Israel is interpreted here to mean "the one who strives with God." It's obviously the story of a man coming of age, finding out who he is, being tested, and being prepared for what's ahead of him as one of the leaders of the chosen people. It's a story of a rather imperfect young man being pulled into the future.

We insist on heroes who are completely heroes. They have got to be strong, beautiful, and brave. But those are not the biblical heroes. God didn't go around choosing the most perfect people. Sometimes they have more strength, sometimes more wisdom, sometimes more sensitivity, but they don't have all those virtues. The biblical heroes are fallible human beings.

The story of young Joseph is the story of another nasty little brat (Genesis 37). Joseph parades himself in front of his brothers with all of the things his father has given him, spinning dreamy tales of his own future greatness. I can just see the brothers saying, "We're going to get him"—which, of course, they did. They left him to die in a pit in the wilderness. I have always said the greatest change that ever came over any human being happened to Joseph between the time he was thrown into that pit and the time he was dragged out. The humor is more understandable and even poignant when we realize this is how the faith community that produced the record saw it. It should never be absolutized as "this is the way it was." The story always points to an understanding of God that is greater than the facts themselves.

I think any understanding of the biblical story that fails to see it as a human response to God is itself an idolatry. Look, for example, at the irony of the people of Israel's call to leave slavery in Egypt and live in their own promised land. That call was to witness to a new possibility for humankind, to be something new in the world. But it is a sorry story, as the people of God long for "the fleshpots of

Egypt," the lures of a consumer society with all of its glitter and gloss. Over and over the people of God succumb to the temptation to be just like the people around them.

In the book of Jonah, the prophet is called to preach to the people of Nineveh, the capital of the Assyrians, to get them to repent. Jonah expects the judgment of God on the Assyrians but, much to his surprise, the people of Nineveh do repent. So God, once very threatened and angry, stops in his tracks and changes his mind. He gets angry, but when the people respond and do his bidding, he repents of his anger and gives it up. He just melts like the wind. Jonah can't bear that and is incensed. Once angry, he's always angry. Repentance doesn't affect Jonah at all. And repentance always affects God. Jonah goes and sulks outside the city in the shade of a vine. God makes the vine wither, and Jonah is saddened by its death. God then chides him for having greater concern for the vine than for the people of Nineveh, who are also loved by God.

God's love is less important to Jonah than God's consistency, and that begins to explain what ambiguity is all about. Ambiguity is not consistent, but we are rigid little creatures who prize ourselves for being consistent. We value consistency. We want our God to be steadfast and dependable, and we ignore the evidence when God is not like that. The biblical God responds to our responses, and we just can't understand that. The biblical God is very personal, ambiguous, and unpredictable. I think that was how the people of the Bible experienced God.

I think the Hebrew experience of God was very different from the Greek experience, which was much more abstract and impersonal. The parable of the father and the prodigal son was the Hebrew experience of God. There's no story in Greek mythology like that. And like Jonah, we get annoyed with our God. He says, "I'm going to zap those people!" and the people say, "Oh, no, God! Don't zap us, don't zap us!" And God says, "I won't." Well, that's pretty annoying to the people who are depending on God to zap their enemies. The only dependable quality about the Hebrew God is that God will love.

Chosenness

I REALLY LIKE the idea of chosenness because it is sort of one degree beyond acceptance. We're all accepted, but more than that, we are *chosen,* and that gives us a role we have to discover and carry out—a responsibility. It also gives us, if we can experience being chosen, the sense that we were wanted. Our lives are not accidental.

We can disappoint God. God can weep over us, you know.

The wonderful parable of the prodigal son is a great image of God. With all that the father did, he could not stop the son from saying, "To hell with you, Dad. I'm leaving!" But whatever the son did, he could not destroy the love of the father. And that's a remarkable image of God. I always like to remember that it was Jesus who told that parable— Jesus who knew more than anybody else what God was like.

THE HEBREW people, even with their powerful conviction that God had chosen them, needed their prophets to set them straight. Over and over again, they asked, "What's with God? We have a better deal." They constantly defied God, exchanging his call and his commandments for their own sense of what was right.

The ones who have the power to say how things should be and what they mean are not necessarily the ones who are right. The people most threatened by ambiguity are those whose way of life is most threatened by the possibility that it is not the right way. War is a good example. Human beings have always gone to war; they've always decided things by sending out armies and killing people off. But what is decided in war is not necessarily right; the proof is that we go to war over and over again about the same thing. And people justify war by saying, "It's in the Bible!" The Bible is only the record of a people's experience, but so many Christians need to believe that it is what God actually told us to do.

Our longing for authority is another instance of our making one point of view the *only* point of view instead of facing up to the possibility that all of life is ambiguous. There are no absolutes—there is no position of which we can say, "Thus says the Lord." But we humans insist on this business of being right. A law, whether passed by Congress or by a conference of Anglican bishops, is a good example of ambiguity. It can be used for good purposes, to protect the weak and provide safety for a society, but the same law can also be used for destructive purposes—to control, to put one group of people ahead of another group. The law is a necessity, since without it the strong would overpower the weak. But then some laws are even worse for the weak if the strong take hold—the law can act to protect the weaker members, but it can also crush them.

In the Bible, law is always softened by grief and forgiveness. We see the power of mercy in Shakespeare's *The Merchant of Venice* as well, when Portia says, "We do pray for mercy," and in that same prayer she teaches all to enter the gates of mercy: "The quality of mercy is not strained; it droppeth as gentle rain from the heavens...." If each one of us was judged solely by the demands of justice, none of us would be saved.

REBELLION IS another alternative to the status quo. In the Declaration of Independence the right to rebel is written into the law, because that gives the individual citizen some way to respond to the law. King David is a wonderful example in the Bible of a rebellious response to the tyranny of law. He was also another example of God not choosing the perfect in order to carry out God's will, because although David was a very exciting and strong-willed person, he was also a greatly flawed one. That kind of ambiguity makes us doubt ourselves. If we can't name the hero and the villain, the person who is right and the person who is wrong, then our perception of reality starts to get shaky. As my father used to say, "Always leave room for another opinion."

When people make the Bible a rule book, a how-to and how-not-to, they misunderstand the Bible. How much more exciting it is to see the Bible as the story of human beings responding to whatever life brings them. As their lives change, their responses change, too. But that is too troubling. In its place, we see churches with big signs in front: "We believe the Bible" or "God said it, the Bible records it, and I believe it." Don't you dare question! No ambiguity allowed! And yet we've seen how full the Bible is of ambiguity. People like to invoke "what Jesus would do" or "what God would have us do" because it is impossible to argue against or disagree with God or Jesus. There is a certain irresistible persuasiveness to appealing to the ultimate authority. It is another way of getting control and avoiding ambiguity; it is also a way of protecting our privileges.

It is even more frightening to people, in matters of faith, to admit there may be more than one possibility. People work very hard to get every little detail of their belief system worked out, so they can cast it in concrete and let it work for them, and so they do not have to think about it anymore. Any serious questioning scares people to death, and then they don't know if they can believe anything. But the lack of questioning creates the worst kind of hypocrisy when our belief system sits on the mantle next to a picture of Jesus in the garden and has no bearing on the decisions we make from day to day. It also makes people tight, mean, and fearful. Any suggestion that things are not the way they want it to be threatens the whole little theological house of cards that they have built. In a way, it is a sad and fearful response, when it could be so freeing to say, "Well, it could be this way or it could be that way. I don't have to decide—I can think of it as enriching or interesting or complex."

As human beings, we long for an infallible source of authority. Our particular Christian tradition of Anglicanism has resisted this over the centuries, but often at the cost of what seems like impending chaos. We look to God as our source of authority but this God is, to use a wonderful phrase from Kathleen Norris's *The Cloister Walk*, "alarmingly alive." Faith is ambiguous by its very nature because there is no certainty. It is as if we were way out on a trapeze and we can't really be sure anyone is going to catch us at the other end. And every now and then somebody lets us fall. There's no certainty. We just have to trust that God is going to be at the other end to take care of us.

Faith is not the assurance that what we're working for is going to happen. Faith is only possible when the answer is not clear; otherwise it isn't faith. Instead, it is being pulled unknowing and sometimes kicking and screaming into the future. It isn't faith if it's dependable, if we know in advance what's going to happen. That's not faith; that's a calculation, and very often we confuse the two.

Think how much courage it takes for the little fetus in the womb to go toward the light, because it's all very comfortable in the womb, you know—plenty of food, no disruptive noises. It takes a lot of courage for the little fetus to get himself together and risk that strange unknown. It is very cold out there, so unfamiliar. I really think that if the fetus had to make a rational decision, it would say, "Hell, no. Nothing out there is worth leaving this!" It takes a lot of courage. But it's a journey each one of us makes to be born—and one thing about that journey, you can't go back. Once you've stuck yourself out of the womb, there's no going back. So it's a once-for-all decision, a one-way street. When you stop to think about it, this is a tremendous decision.

The healing ability to change, to reflect, to start again comes from God. Certainly that's what the Genesis story tells us, that God made adjustments in God's plan. There is no final answer: it is always out beyond us, or maybe sometimes it's behind us, but we can never pin it down. And the best insight today will change tomorrow, if we're still living, because we'll have another insight. So we never pin it down, though that's what we are always trying to do. We write books to pin it down, or we tell stories to get it pinned down, but we can never pin it down.

Christians incognito

WHEN LAYPEOPLE actively try to bring their faith into some relationship with the world about them, the church often describes them as religious specialists. I think about a man like Bill Stringfellow, who really worked very hard to make his legal profession an expression of his faith, and who became one of the great radical theologians of the church. We are likely to think of Stringfellow as a theologian, not a lawyer. But from my point of view it was as a lawyer that his struggle was most meaningful. I think of a person like Bill Diehl, who consults with the Lutheran Church in America and makes important contributions to "Laos in Ministry." Bill Diehl was a Bethlehem Steel executive who took the relationship between his faith and his work very seriously. We are likely to think of Diehl as a churchman rather than as a businessman today. There's something insidious about the pull of the institution. It is unfortunate that we value these men more as church leaders than as searching laypeople.

I think that Bruce Reed had a telling insight when he said that Christians need to go out on Monday morning into the kingdom of God as doctors or salesclerks, not under the Christian label. When I taught school, I never once talked about being a Christian. I hope I was *operating* as a Christian, with my commitment to the fact that my students were valuable and my belief that there should be a certain integrity in the way we worked, and that how we worked made a difference in the world. But the *content* of my teaching was never about being a Christian. In fact, there were three instances in which I disappointed my fellow teachers for that very reason.

In the first instance, they wanted to have a Bible club in the school and they asked me to be a co-sponsor. I struggled with the issue but decided not to do it. In the first place, I felt the school was not the appropriate place for Bible clubs. I believe the religious community is the place to study the religious faith.

In the second instance, the teachers were going to form a little cell group early in the morning to meet regularly as Christian teachers and strengthen one another for the day. I thought that was a wonderful idea, so I agreed to join the group. When I got there, however, I found what they really wanted to do was to convert the students. They were going to hand out little tracts during the school day. They were going to proselytize the Jewish students. Well, I didn't think that was what Christian teachers ought to do. I thought we ought to work on being good teachers, not "missionaries in the school."

The third event had to do with prayer in the public schools. I was with a group who thought all the Christian teachers ought to go out and lobby for prayer in the public schools. I had to conclude that precisely because I was a Christian I could *not* battle for prayer in the public schools. I know that a lot of people start talking about public prayer the minute they think about being Christian. Many Christian members of Congress get together and have a prayer breakfast. For me, that is not the point. I do not think parading piety is what makes a Christian congressman. Whether they are Christian or not, their job is to be out there campaigning against the arms race, against putting burdens on the backs of those least able to bear them, against the exploitation of resources. No matter what their label is—Christian or Jewish or agnostic—their integrity as members of Congress has to do with the stands they take. From my viewpoint, we should not go out in the world waving our Christian credentials. Unfortunately, evangelism has too often been reduced to parading labels rather than proclaiming with our lives the Life that led to a cross.

We often tend to think that New Testament people always identified themselves publicly as Christians. In fact, I think they were careful about when they let their faith be known, witnessing only when there was a point to be made. The fish symbol was a secret way to reveal their allegiance to one another. So I am sure they did not go out saying everywhere and at all times, "I am a Christian." But even if the early Christians had habitually proclaimed their allegiance openly, that would not tell us what *we* are supposed to be doing. We forget that we live in a very different world from the world they lived in. They lived in a world that was *not* Christian, so for them to proclaim their faith would have been a courageous stand. They might have ended up being eaten by a few lions the next afternoon. We, in contrast, live in a world in which Christianity is the norm. If I say I am a Christian, that isn't a startling statement; it says I go along with the status quo. So the last thing on earth I want to do is go out and announce randomly that I am a Christian, because I think that is easily misinterpreted. I need to ask myself very carefully what I will gain by the announcement. A cross or an accolade? (And please don't confuse unpopularity with the cross!)

The true calling of the laity

IF LAYPEOPLE are the subjects and not the objects of Christian ministry, to use Kraemer's distinction, how do all the pieces fit together—the role of the laity, the role of the clergy, and the purpose of the church?

When we come to the church building, the ordained leader has a very special role there. The pastor holds that church together. He or she has the primary responsibility for overseeing the work of that institution. Laypeople can bear the chalice, serve on committees, even preach, but the ultimate responsibility for the institution belongs to that ordained person, who has chosen that responsibility and has been chosen for it. I do not and should not have final responsibility for administering that institution. My primary responsibility is my job.

Laypeople gather in the church to worship but also to learn. One of the more important activities that takes place in a church community is Christian education, for which clergy have the ultimate responsibility. As a layperson, I can teach classes and I can chair the Christian education program, but the ultimate responsibility for the educational direction of that community, as I see it, belongs to the ordained leader. I think it actually *works* that way. If the pastor is charismatic, the church is charismatic; if the pastor is existential, the church is existential. I think the clergy ought to be open enough, though, to have their vision under judgment. There is always more than one possible right answer. We only know in part.

The sacramental office belongs to the ordained person. I participate in that, but I do not see laypeople as called to celebrate the mysteries. I know there are places where they do, and it's always interested me how those communities distinguish between ordained and non-ordained people, but I do not have to wrestle with that problem because I do not belong to that kind of religious community. But the idea that when the priest is at the altar he or she is no longer a "person" is not my theology. I like priests to look me in the eye when they give me the bread. I don't want them to stick it in my hand and move on like some disembodied floating spirit. But I do believe that for that moment the priest is in a peculiar way the bearer of the holy for me. I can be that for someone else in another time and in another way, but for that moment I think that is the ordained person's role.

And I believe it is also the calling of the ordained to know the story: to hold that story in our remembrance, to recall it in the educational program, to act out that drama in the sacrament, to hold that community together so that the word can always be preached and the sacraments offered. Within that setting the layperson operates always in conjunction with the pastor—teaching, counseling, administering.

Laypeople do carry out those functions in church, but to me they are always *secondary* functions for laity. The layperson's primary function is out there in the world, and it is a problem when the church becomes the primary focus of their lives. I can remember that when I was most unhappy on my job, I was most active in the church. When

I was escaping from my primary function, I was in the church day and night. When we see laypeople doing that, we ought to ask the question, "Why is that person here every time the doors of the church are open?" Something's wrong, either in the family or somewhere else in that person's world. Somewhere the person is in trouble. I think such devotion to the institution on the part of a layperson is a danger signal. I suppose as long as this time of retreat to the church has as its purpose getting ready to go back out again, it may be useful. But that purpose can easily get lost, because the church needs workers to do jobs and the minister is relieved and helped to have them there.

Of course, there are laypeople who work professionally for the church, and they therefore have in a different way the same kind of function as the ordained person. But for the majority of laypeople the institutional church is secondary. I think laypeople working for the church are, to a certain extent, an anomaly. I am one of them now. It is always something of a painful experience for me when laypeople are attracted to do what I do. Ironically, the gift I would find most affirming is a layperson inspired to do what I say, not what I do.

Unfortunately, our churches have become so elaborate that they do need a great deal of work from laypeople. The kingdom of God is never going to march triumphantly forward as long as so much activity is concentrated in churches! Those "greater things than I do" need to be done by laypeople in the world. Governments are never going to learn a way to live together that is better than blowing each other up every twenty-five years or so until laypeople who have a vision that human beings can live together another way are in positions of power, in the halls of government, in the structures of society. If wars are ever going to stop, they are going to have to be stopped by laypeople with a vision of the battle flags furled, people who have a vision and who work hard to learn the skills to bring that vision into being.

And that would be a greater thing than Jesus was ever able to do, because the Roman Empire was slashing right and left during his lifetime. Wars did not stop for Jesus.

Nations will never produce food wisely and distribute it fairly to the poor until laypeople are in power who have a vision of new economic possibilities that embody the compassion of the Creator. It was Karl Marx's understanding of the Bible that contributed to his scathing criticism of capitalism as a system that keeps many people in poverty while a few are wealthy. Heeding the biblical message leads to questions about our economic system. Many important changes in our society have come about because someone asked, "What does it mean that I believe in the biblical message?" When someone takes that message very seriously, it is likely to turn the known world upside down. And, in my opinion, anyone who remains comfortable in the known world cannot be paying attention to the biblical message.

We have lost the capacity to dream great dreams. We reduce God to the personal, private, "spiritual" sphere of our lives so that ministry becomes only personal, private, "spiritual" acts—a good deed here, a good deed there, a cup of cold water here, a loaf of freshly baked bread there, a prison visit here, a hospital call there, a night in a shelter here, a time with a troubled friend there. We see no need to challenge the systems that make these "ministries" necessary. The people of God are called to a possibility other than the kingdoms of this world. They must be ambassadors in every part of life.

Bread for the World is a group of Christians concerned about feeding people. They are not romantics—they do not collect little baskets for the poor and send missionaries out to deliver them. They go to Congress and carry out a legislative program skillfully and consistently. There is a wonderful story about Jesus feeding the five thousand, but five thousand are a drop in the bucket compared to all the hungry people in the world. Bread for the World, actually a very small operation, is an example of the "greater things than I do" that only Christians can do. (And a lot of people who do Christian things are not Christian.) That is the kind of evangelism that excites me, and that is the ministry of the laity.

Laypeople have power in the secular world, but they lose it when they feel they need to be ordained in order to have a significant ministry. The church has not understood the power of the laity. The church has felt it had to make an impact on the world through what the clergy said or through institutional pronouncements. The black church bears witness to another possibility. The black community was not fed as much on "pie-in-the-sky" religion as the white community liked to think they were. They were talking about a very real world. They heard the message: "You are worthwhile. You are just as good as a white person, and you don't have to sit in the back of the bus." It was that kind of message, fed into blacks week after week by black preachers, that really communicated the gospel and inaugurated the revolution. And that is what the gospel really says, that regardless of who you are, you are worthy of the world's respect. In the face of the worst kind of deprivation, black people held their communities together because they heard that message. Spirituals were a safe medium in which to put the message, but blacks heard those spirituals very differently from the way whites heard them. Black people knew they were singing revolutionary songs. The black experience is a good example of what the gospel message really does mean and can mean to laypeople. That is the message we need to hear when we go to church. I know too many people who think they are not worthy, they are not accepted, and I think, "They've been going to church Sunday after Sunday, and they've never heard the message that they are worthy?"

We *are* worthy, we are the people of God, and we are called to change the world! Let's accept the authority that has been given to us.

From Sunday Christians to Monday Christians

THE BOOKS IN the New Testament were written primarily for and about the gathered church. But if we read between the lines we can find hints about how the New Testament people made sense out of all that on Monday morning, when they went out to do all those other things that the Bible is almost silent about. For instance, we get some clues about how two social institutions, slavery and marriage, were understood in new ways.

People eventually overthrew slavery because they saw that if they really took the Bible seriously and saw themselves as brothers and sisters in Christ to every other person, then slavery made no sense. Some were fond of quoting Paul's words in Colossians that slaves should be subject to their masters, but the word that shook slavery was Paul's word to Philemon to receive his slave Onesimus "as a beloved brother." Paul had a radically new understanding of the master-slave relationship after both had accepted Christ. So there is a new word about slavery in the New Testament.

In the same way, Paul's new word about marriage is not the oft-quoted, "Wives, be subject to your husbands," but his message to husbands and wives that each has an equal demand on the other, which neither has the right to deny. There we really hear Paul working out his understanding of what it means to be equal in Christ. The other quotations became more familiar to our ears because it was very convenient for slaveholders to quote Paul saying, "Slaves, obey your masters." Men have loved to repeat the line "Wives, be subject to your husbands," but seldom recall Paul's words about equality in relationships. We remember the rules, but we avoid the difficult wrestling.

We do not possess the stories of what those early Christians were doing when they were dispersed, but we do have some clues about the issues they confronted in their daily lives. Obviously the people in the early church were concerned about what it meant to pay taxes. That story in the gospels has been left in the New Testament record because that was a troubling question: What was their responsibility as citizens? It is very interesting that Jesus did not answer questions like that. The answer to that question was thrown back on the person who asked it: "Render therefore to Caesar the things that are Caesar's, and to God the things that are God's" (Matthew 22:21). Now we have taken Jesus' response and made it into a doctrine about the separation of church and state, but he was not talking about that. He was talking about the fact that we have to make decisions about what the ultimate authority in our lives is going to be, and how we will live with lesser authorities. And our decisions have ambiguity, risk, and difficult questions as inescapable attendants. Jesus' response was relevant for those people, and it is relevant for us. That part of scripture is no pat answer; it stands as a challenge to exercise freedom. That conversation about paying taxes is a magnificent example of an issue that those New Testament Christians had to face.

We catch a glimpse of another everyday problem when Paul talks about eating food presented to idols. Those Christians had to buy their food in the market, and some of it had been offered to idols. Their problem was, "How do I know what to buy?" In his letters Paul tried to help them to wrestle with that question from their daily life, how they should operate in the marketplace. So we do catch glimpses of how those early Christians dealt with Monday morning issues. But what has happened to those wonderful passages that give us glimpses into those flesh-and-blood issues they were struggling with? We have transformed them into pious, churchy moralisms.

Those New Testament people did not face the same issues that we face. They lived in a different world. To suppose that every issue they had would be an issue for us is to deny the historicity, the particularity of our faith. Bible people lived in a world without telephones and televisions and computers. The Bible will not give us "how-to's" because that is not its purpose. What the Bible does is to lift up the God who was shown forth bodily in Jesus of Nazareth. We look to that God, and then we make our own decisions, under judgment and under grace.

WHAT IS THE cost of ministry? I am not going to pretend that we can identify the true disciples by those who are in prison for their beliefs and actions, by those who will not eat more than they need while others hunger, by those who put their bodies on the line with the victims of brutal systems. Surely the disciples, the ministers are there; and they pose a silent judgment on those of us who are not—but I will not settle for any absolute answer. T. S. Eliot, the Christian poet, reminded us we can do the right thing for the wrong reason; and George Bernard Shaw, who was not a Christian, gave us a memorable image of the foolish era in Christian history when Christians rushed to martyrdom as a way of ensuring entrance into heaven.

The fact is, however, we do not know where our commitment to Jesus will lead us, any more than Peter and John knew. St. Paul said he died daily.

I know not where the road will lead
I follow day by day,
Or where it ends: I only know
I walk the King's highway.

I want to suggest some of the daily deaths the ministers of God are heir to—the cost of ministry.

First, we must die to conventional standards. That is one of the strong messages of Jesus' parables. Jesus did not tell his parables to give us models for behavior. He told them to give us graphic pictures of what life in the kingdom is like and to offer us a choice. Do you want to be a part of this way of life? The parables disturb us greatly. They were intended to disturb. We say they are not fair. The Pharisee was a good man. At least he tried. And the publican went down justified. He didn't even repent! Probably went right back to his tax collecting. What kind of a God is this?

And those laborers in the vineyard! Some people bear the burden and heat of the day, and the Johnny-come-lately, who had spent the day lounging around the market-place, gets the same wage. We can identify with that indignant spokesman: "You have made them equal to us!" And if we can give up our sentimental identification with the prodigal son, we will realize that the crux of the story is the elder brother's response, as he details all the really good reasons why he is indignant.

What kind of a God is this, anyway? A God of grace. Grace turns the whole fabric of our way of life upside down, but grace is the mark of God's rule among human beings. That rule we name the kingdom of God, that rule we are called to show forth in our lives.

Matthew Fox thinks the spirituality we need to develop is a spirituality of compassion; and he agrees that a more accurate translation of that verse "Be ye therefore perfect as your Father in heaven is perfect" is "Be ye therefore compassionate as your Father in heaven is compassionate." The "perfection" translation sets us on a private journey for our own salvation. That is not what ministry is about. Compassion opens us up to caring for the world. That is what ministry is about.

> It is the way the Master went,
> Shall not the servant tread it still?

A second cost of ministry is that we can no longer settle for our own security. "Do not think that I have come to bring peace to the earth; I have not come to bring peace, but a sword," Matthew quotes Jesus as saying. And lest anyone think that is an anti-pacifist argument, hear what the sword is. Matthew continues in the section of teaching for the disciples:

> For I have come to set a man against his father, and a daughter against her mother, and a daughter-in-law against her mother-in-law; and one's foes will be members of one's own household. Whoever loves father or mother more than me is not worthy of me; and whoever loves son or daughter more than me is not worthy of me; and whoever does not take the cross and follow me is not worthy of me. (Matthew 10:35–38)

Oh, those hard sayings of Jesus that we don't pay much attention to! In this age of sweetness and light, the exaltation of the nuclear family, and gene-altruism, doesn't he sound like a fanatic?

Has anyone called you a fanatic lately? And if they did, was it because you were so set on establishing a morality for someone else, or because you were intent on a private piety, or because you were willing to risk every known security that someone else might have a richer life?

So how should we live? Jesus' answer: "Do not store up for yourselves treasures on earth, where moth and rust consume and where thieves break in and steal; but store up for yourselves treasures in heaven" (Matthew 6:19). And again, "Love your enemies and pray for those who persecute you" (Matthew 5:44). This is all getting very impractical.

Suppose we say Christ is the answer? That's theological enough to distance us from troubling reality. Ah, but to say Christ is the answer is to plunge us into the very heart of the issue of ambiguity, for no one can say who is the Christ except by the power of the Holy Spirit. Flesh and blood will not reveal it to us. We cannot think our way to the knowledge of the Christ. We cannot will our way to it. We cannot even worship our way to it. Only by faith can we look at a Palestinian rabbi and say, "Thou are the Christ."

Let's try the church as the answer. The institutional church from the days of Rome has fostered that image of itself. We've even used the term Mother Church to underscore the parental image of a source of all wisdom and authority for the little children. Some of the little children couldn't stomach that authoritarianism, so they broke away and set up the Bible as the answer. So we turned from the infallibility of the Pope to the inerrancy of the Bible.

But the Bible inveighs against idolatry and resists all efforts to be made into an idol. It will not take any faithful student of that record long to realize the Bible raises more questions than it answers. It is the story of the people of God wrestling with the questions of their lives and finding their own answers and, if faithfully attended to, it will challenge you to do the same.

So is there no word from the Lord?

I always say Jesus did not get crucified for singing and praying—or even for doing good works. Jesus was crucified for challenging the powers that be, for offering human beings a new possibility for life. He didn't get into trouble for healing the sick, but for healing the sick on the Sabbath. He didn't get into trouble for being pious, but for challenging piety.

Christian ministry is response ministry, not an in-order-to ministry. The kingdoms of the world—and the devil who boasts that they are his—would like us to spend all our time earning our passage to heaven because then they would never be disturbed. As Paul Laurence Dunbar, an American black poet of the nineteenth century, wrote:

I am no priest of crooks and creeds,
For human wants and human needs
Are more to me than prophets' deeds....

Take up your arms, come out with me,
Let heaven alone; humanity
Needs more and Heaven less from thee.
With pity for mankind look 'round;
Help them to rise—and Heaven is found.

What does your theology of ministry say about your understanding of God?

The promise of institutions is that they will preserve for the future all the glory of the past. The cost is that the gifts of the present get short shrift. The promise is a steady witness. The cost is the silencing of those who deviate.

The Christian church emerged victorious in its struggle with the synagogue and with the Roman Empire and with the so-called barbarian hordes that swept down from the north and with the Muslim forces that threatened the east. Mistaking, as we are wont to do, that God is on the side of the winners, the church as institution established itself as the mediator between God and human beings, a position it has maintained in one form or another for over ten centuries. There have been many internecine struggles in the institution, but generally the faithful have found their place within some form of the institution and have not seriously questioned it as the medium through which their commitment to God would best be expressed. If they didn't like the way one church did it, they went to another.

To give up on the institution of the church altogether was to give up on the biblical revelation of God in Christ. And that is the way the church wanted it. After all, there were budgets to be met, buildings to be maintained, and services of every kind to be offered.

Somehow the absolute primacy of the baptismal rite as qualifying one for citizenship in the kingdom was lost, and instead membership in the church became the important criterion. Good deeds—good church deeds—became ministry: how many hours you taught Sunday school, how many terms you served on the vestry, how many years on the altar guild, how much time you gave to maintaining the institution. All of this, of course, qualified as lay ministry. The institution defined a distinction between the callings of Christians and rank ordered them.

Ministry was no longer one. As in *Animal Farm,* all were equal, but some were more equal than others. Of course, everybody profited by this arrangement. The clergy got easy status, and the laity got off the hook of living up to the high calling of the baptism charge.

Why haven't our lives as the people of God lived up to our glorious baptismal beginning—sealed by the Holy Spirit and marked as Christ's own forever? I'd like to suggest three reasons why I think we haven't, and they are so tied up with one another, it will be very difficult to separate them. I shall seem to be saying the same thing in different ways.

The stumbling blocks to our claiming the gift of our baptism, as I see them, are these:

One, we have been concerned with earning our salvation rather than living it out. *Two,* we have mistaken membership in the church for citizenship in the kingdom. And *three,* we have read the Bible in bits and pieces rather than as a total story, so we don't know who Jesus was or what he was about.

I think number three is the clue to all the others. I like to compare our study of the Bible to the way in which we look at paintings. We do not first view a painting by going up close and examining a detail. We first stand back and get a grasp of the entire painting, and then we study the details. In that way we know what each detail is about. We don't begin our viewing of the Sistine Madonna by looking at the cherubs, for example, yet that is how we approach the most important record for our history. And this in a country where television evangelists shout the name of Jesus every day. Their followers fill up the pews in churches across the nation, and their success is the secret envy of those churches whose enrollments are down.

Not everyone who cries "Lord, Lord" will enter the kingdom of heaven. Ministers of God, I think we have missed the mark of what Jesus was all about, and I believe that any thinking about Christian ministry has to begin with Jesus. Christianity is forever bound by that revelation of God which began among the Hebrew people and culminated in the life and ministry of the man of Nazareth and flows on in the life of God's chosen people, the church, you and me, sealed by the Holy Spirit in baptism and called to be the continuing witness in the world that the kingdom has come.

Ministry is always disturbing because ministry is always new. God will always raise up prophets from among us, prophets who will speak the new message from the Lord. Great as Moses was, Jesus was greater. The synagogue didn't like to hear that. It had become comfortable with Moses. But God is a living God, always going ahead of God's people, always raising up new prophets to speak with authority God's new word.

And so we are called to be prophetic and pastoral—called to feed the sheep and tend the lambs, called to confront the systems and care for the victims. It is an awesome call.

The peace of God, it is no peace,
but strife closed in the sod.
Yet let us pray for but one thing—
the marvelous peace of God.

How I wish we paid attention to the words of the hymns. Yes, some songs we'd never sing again if we paid attention to the words—and some we'd sing only in fear and trembling! The gospel according to John remembers that on Jesus' last night on earth, he said to his disciples, "Peace I leave with you; my peace I give to you. I do not give to you as the world gives" (14:27). He was talking about something other than what the world calls peace. Not quietness. Not serenity. Not a calm floating above the troubles of the world. Not an escape. "Do not let your hearts be troubled, and do not let them be afraid." That was not gratuitous advice. They were going to encounter that which would trouble their hearts and make them afraid. They could not so easily avoid the issue of the cost of the choice they had made.

One form of the closing prayer at the Eucharist in the Episcopal *Book of Common Prayer* says,

And now, Father, send us out
to do the work you have given us to do,
to love and serve you
as faithful witnesses of Christ our Lord. (BCP 366)

I would like to submit to you that this is the definition of ministry, the work God has given us to do: to love and serve God as faithful witnesses.

Ministry is not a discreet act, not a series of discreet acts. Ministry is discipleship, the giving of the total self over to being God's agent for making God's new creation known to God's world. And this is dangerous work because the fallen creation still powerfully holds sway. Ministry had its cost. It had it then. It has it now.

Sources Used

Books and Manuscripts

Dozier, Verna. "A Sacred Space" and "Toward a Theology of the Laity" in *The Calling of the Laity: Verna Dozier's Anthology.* Washington, D. C.: The Alban Institute, 1988.

Dozier, Verna. *The Authority of the Laity.* Washington, D. C.: The Alban Institute, 1982.

Dozier, Verna. Unpublished manuscript on ambiguity, 1999.

Interviews

Arbogast, Marianne. "Stumbling in the Dark," in *The Witness,* 80: 46–47.

Blakeslee-Collin, Carol. Unpublished interviews with Verna J. Dozier, 1998–1999.

Donovan, Mary S. *Oral History of Verna J. Dozier.* Episcopal Women's History Project, 1990–1991.

"Passion for Teaching and for the Bible Come Together in Verna Dozier," in *Senior Link.* Episcopal Senior Ministries for the Diocese of Washington (December 1997), 4–5.

"Verna Dozier: Helping People Find Meaning," in *Caring People* (Spring 1997), 28–31.

1. Genesis

My journey to Iraq started at a pub in Hackney. It was a Saturday night in 2004 and the place was heaving. The barmaids were struggling to keep up with the crush at the bar and some revellers were already drunk enough to start dancing to the jukebox. I was playing pool. Playing well for a change. I was two games in and looking secure in the third. There were a satisfying number of coins lined up on the edge of the table indicating those who would take me on next if my game did not go to pieces. It was near midnight, I had friends around me, and there were enough girls around to hint at possibility. It was a good Saturday night.

I sank a yellow, looked up, saw the people shouting at each other over the cacophony of music and voices, and realised that being there was not going to be enough. I had hoped it would be, had tried to break the habit that for the previous decade sent me back and forth across the world, but I knew at that moment that it was not yet going to happen. All I could think about was not what my next shot would be, who was getting the next round, or even the girl in the corner in her tight black top. It was a conversation that I'd had with my boss the previous day.

He had e-mailed me to come over to his desk and then

1

asked if I had any concrete plans for the future. I didn't. I had spent the previous two and a half years working in the United States and I had only arrived back in Britain three weeks earlier. I was still trying to find somewhere to live and was dealing with the customs documents that would allow me to retrieve all my belongings from storage. My boss had then asked me whether I fancied going to Baghdad.

I had been there before. I was a journalist and worked as a foreign correspondent for a British newspaper, the *Daily Telegraph*. It was the *Telegraph* that sent me to live in the States. I had arrived in September 2001 a week after the World Trade Center came down. The following months were spent covering the impact of 9/11, criss-crossing the country to ask Americans how their world had changed and their reaction to it. Then, as the drums of war began to beat and Washington marshalled its legions to fight in Iraq, I was assigned to cover a US army company in the 1st Battalion of the 15th US Infantry Regiment, 3rd Infantry Division, which was to be at the forefront of the upcoming invasion force. In March 2003 I crossed the Kuwait border, travelling in the back of one of the unit's armoured vehicles. Seventeen days later I reached Baghdad. It was a bloody and brutal journey. The invasion may have been completed quicker than anyone in the Pentagon or Whitehall dared hope but it was still a merciless experience for those like me who had witnessed the fighting. There were long days advancing under gunfire, mortar attacks, the spectacle of burned cars with corpses hanging out, and then the final push to Baghdad when it seemed that civilians were as likely to be killed as any of Saddam's soldiers.

I was now being asked if I wanted to go back. It was while I was playing pool in Hackney that I realised with utter certainty that I did. I did not actually have much choice. I had to go for the same reason that I had left the States and tried to start afresh in Britain. Even surrounded by people enjoying their Saturday night out, I could not forget the bodies I had witnessed.

I had never seen a corpse before I joined the US troops for their invasion of Iraq. I can remember the first time. It is as clear as if it had just happened. I was in the back of an M88, the armoured pick-up truck that accompanied tanks into combat. We were driving down a road outside Nasariyah, an Iraqi city just north of Kuwait, as the Americans fought to seize a nearby military airstrip in one of the first battles of the war. I was looking out of the back hatch when we rounded a corner and there, by the roadside, were two Iraqis crumpled in a hole in the dirt, their skin crisp and black. A helmet had been fused to the top of one of the dead soldiers' skulls. Lips and eyes could still be made out on what remained of a face, but the eyelids had been burnt clean off, the cornea turned grey by the heat of the explosion that had killed him.

Before we crossed the Kuwait border the American soldiers had been excited at the prospect of putting into effect the skills that they had trained long and hard to master. Tank crews talked about the tickertape parades they expected when they returned to the States, and laughed about which Hollywood actors should play them if a film was made of their coming heroics. By the time we reached Baghdad, no one was joking around. The unit's commanding general had told his men to expect welcome parades from the Iraqis and not to anticipate significant resistance before they reached Saddam's elite units entrenched around Baghdad. What they had received was a very different kind of welcome. From the moment they entered Iraq, US forces were hounded by mortar and sniper fire. Iraqi soldiers cast off their uniforms to attack from the anonymity of crowds of civilians, while members of the Saddam Fedayeen, a paramilitary organisation established to hound the invaders, emerged from sandstorms to fire their rocket-propelled grenades. Those bodies near Nasariyah may have been the first I saw but they certainly were not the last. In Baghdad, at night I heard the screams of the American soldiers as they suffered their nightmares and during the day watched as with ruthless efficiency they hunted down those seeking to kill them.

The Iraqi Ba'ath Party that Saddam led had first emerged in the 1940s as an idealistic organisation committed to working for pan-Arab unity. Its name means renaissance and its founders had hoped that it would bring about a Middle Eastern revival by ending foreign control of its lands, introducing economic modernisation and easing the worst suffering of the poor through a mass of socialist initiatives. After Saddam seized control of Iraq in July 1979 it had not experienced a renaissance. The Ba'ath Party became a body that did not look after Iraq's citizens but oppressed them. Its leadership was purged of any who would not bend to Saddam's will and the security apparatus he created snuffed out opposition with a mixture of intimidation and torture. Saddam dominated the party and through it he dominated the Iraqi people, leading them into a catastrophic war against Iran in the 1980s and then into the

1991 invasion of Kuwait that united almost the whole world against him. Now he had led them to his downfall.

On the 9th April 2003 Saddam fled Baghdad and went into hiding while his state buildings were occupied by US troops and his statues were pulled down across the city. America had invaded with two official aims: to remove the Ba'athist regime and to uncover the weapons of mass destruction that Washington and London believed Saddam was stockpiling. The first of these had been achieved: Iraq's leaders were now either dead or scattered. Few of the American soldiers I was with expected it to be long before the first chemical or biological weapons were uncovered. It was difficult to doubt their existence if you had been wearing chemical weapon protection suits since first crossing the Kuwait border and had spent weeks before the invasion drilling how to don a gas mask in the shortest time possible. The soldiers in my unit had been promised that the weapons of mass destruction were there, believed they had fought to ensure that they were never used, and now presumed that all there was left to do was locate and secure them. This was not expected to take more than a couple of months and so they were talking as if the war was won. In late April 2003, I said my goodbyes and was flown out of Baghdad airport in the hold of a C-130 military transport plane.

Life in the States had been less enjoyable after I returned from Iraq. I found myself feeling lonely. I had friends but it was not home and that was where I felt I needed to be in order to put all I had seen behind me. So I asked to be reassigned to London – moved back to the *Telegraph*'s newsroom in Canary Wharf – where my plan was to start afresh and enjoy the delights of normality.

Back in Britain, however, I still could not forget those bodies. It was not only the sight of them, the ease with which a person's life could be snuffed out, but also the way they reproached me for what I had been thinking in the days before the war started while I was in the Kuwaiti desert waiting for the order to invade. My primary concern had not been whether the war was right or wrong but merely whether it would happen. I was excited and naive and had not considered whether those in positions of power might either have deceived me or could be able to misinterpret the situation in Iraq so badly. What I knew was that I was going to be covering a massive story, be a reporter in the right place at the right time, and that was what I had wanted more than anything else.

The war did not end when those statues of Saddam came down. The weapons of mass destruction were never found and pockets of stubborn resistance emerged as the invading armies became forces of occupation. Rebellion was met by military suppression. Barely a day seemed to pass without reports of the latest victims of the violence. The difficulty in using Western armies to force an Arab country to run on Western precepts was becoming clear. Since I had left Baghdad there had been thousands more bodies; thousands more corpses that would not have looked dissimilar to the ones I had seen lying on the roadside by that army base outside Nasariyah. This was why I wanted to go back. I needed to know if anything worthwhile could result from the deaths I had witnessed; if those lives had been lost for a reason that could ever be justified. Knowing the answer to that would hopefully let me move on in my life and start to forget.

I arrived in Baghdad a month later, a year almost to

the day since I had last been there. I was not due to start my new post until the beginning of the following year but it was considered sensible for me to see the situation on the ground before I started. I flew to Jordan on 25 April 2004, and the next day caught the plane that took me back to Iraq.

The best way into Baghdad was on board Royal Jordanian Airlines. No one I knew in the UK could quite believe that I could simply fly into Baghdad on a commercial jet. However, Jordan's ruling monarch, keen for his country to establish itself as the preferred entry point for the international companies selected to spend the billions of US dollars earmarked by Washington for the reconstruction of Iraq, had instructed its national airline to start running two flights a day.

Some Westerners were still risking the land route, the road from Amman that passed through the Sunni city of Ramadi and on into the Iraqi capital. Even at that relatively early stage of the conflict it was a foolhardy thing to do. Only a fortnight before I arrived in Baghdad a British reporter from *The Times* and his American colleague had had the tyres of their car shot out and been bundled into a waiting car. I was later told that it was the internet that helped secure their freedom. Their abductors googled their names and learned that they really were bona fide reporters rather than spies. They were fortunate to have been captured by Iraqis who were still willing to accept there was a difference.

They were the last reporters I know of who took that road. Within weeks, whatever Washington or London may have claimed, the Sunni heartland was unambiguously in open revolt as people's anger erupted at the affront to their dignity of their loss of sovereignty. The only non-uniformed Westerners still driving the road were the security contractors who ran the convoys that ferried supplies to the American bases spread across the desert of Western Iraq. These were employees of private firms, mostly American and British, hired by the US government to supplement the work being done by its military. Though civilians, most of them were ex-forces and their convoys resembled something out of a *Mad Max* film. The lorries were stripped down for speed, festooned with strapped-on armour, had machine guns pinned to the top, front and back, and had armed men in every cab. They went fast and did all they could to avoid stopping. The primary principle for survival most adopted was to treat anything suspicious as hostile, and if in doubt deploy maximum force. According to the Iraqis, cars that got in their way were fortunate if they received a couple of rounds in the engine chassis rather than through the windscreen.

Travelling into Iraq by plane was a very different experience. The destination may have been Baghdad, but the crew's studious commitment to normal airline custom made me feel I could have been on my way to Brussels rather than to the most dangerous city on earth. Two perfectly made-up South African stewardesses, resplendent in their Royal Jordanian uniforms, used their most dazzling smiles to greet the procession of hacks and security contractors climbing on board. The Fokker F28 we were flying in had blue leather seats and a free magazine to read. Once we were up in the air, a trolley appeared and was wheeled down the aisle to provide drinks. A meal was served.

It was an hour and twenty minutes into the flight when the descent began. Suddenly things were not so routine. The Americans could only guarantee that roughly a square mile around the airport was cleared of those who might want to shoot down an approaching aircraft. It was a tight space to keep a plane in as it dropped towards landing, especially one that wanted to get down fast. Sitting in the window seat, I was pushed against the fuselage as the plane banked steeply and the nose dropped into its sharply turning dive. It was then, as we fell into our corkscrew descent, that the streets of Baghdad emerged in front of me.

It is a view stuck indelibly in my brain. This was the city that, a century after the time of the Prophet Mohammad, had become the centre of the Islamic world, the capital of its governing Caliphate and the setting for Scheherazade and her tales of Ali Baba. It had survived being ransacked by the Mongols in the 13th century, absorbed the Ottomans when they came two hundred years later, and been host to the British when they marched in during the First World War. It was at least 1,200 years old and was lived in by seven million people. It was now to become my home.

No people were visible from that height, only ordered lines of streets and the loop of the Tigris river throwing off reflections in the sunlight as it casually meandered its way south. Rows of buildings disappeared into the shrub desert that marked the city's outer edges. There were the minarets of the mosques, the remnants of Baghdad's ancient defensive wall, the lines of bushes just visible along the largest avenues and the flash of green that marked the city's park with its lake and clusters of eucalyptus trees. Looking down, I could imagine Baghdad the way elderly Iraqis described it as being before Saddam Hussein's grip got too tight; still that sedate place where couples courted in the shade of palm fronds on the banks of the Tigris and friends wiled away afternoons playing backgammon in a tea house off a side road in Karrada. Baghdad looked serene. The shock of that, I think, is what helped make the sight of it so memorable.

As we flew lower the outlines of Saddam's palaces emerged with their ornate domes and ceremonial battlements. I could make out Ba'athist statues: the Monument to the Unknown Soldier, with its raised copper sphere symbolising a shield dropped from the dying grasp of an Iraqi warrior, and the Martyr's Monument, its split blue dome sheltering an eternal flame. The airport appeared in my line of sight, the US transport planes lined up on its runways like a row of grey metallic cigar cases. Around the terminal spread thousands of military tents and barrack blocks, the size of the camp filling the view through my window and providing the first tangible clue as to the scale of the operation being played out there.

The ground was close now, close enough that I could make out the soldiers unlucky enough to have been assigned to the top hatches of the military Humvees on the surrounding roads, yet the plane still seemed to be standing on its wing tip. At the last moment it shuddered as the flaps were lowered to force the final, acutest turn. We levelled out and the wheels touched tarmac.

As we taxied to the terminal I saw a DHL transport plane with scorch marks down one wing, the result of a missile attack that had hit it shortly after take-off five months earlier. We passed the main airport building, its façade still showing the battle damage from the fight to secure it the previous year.

'We've now landed at Baghdad International Airport,' the stewardess said over the Tannoy system. 'I hope you enjoy your stay and will choose to fly with Royal Jordanian again soon.'

Unexpectedly, I did enjoy my stay. Baghdad was on the turn and Western civilians were getting killed (four, in fact, while I was there) but it was still recognisable as a functioning city. I went out to restaurants at night, stayed late at parties, visited shops, drove outside Baghdad and even walked down streets after dark – the simple pleasures of life that within a year were too dangerous to risk. There was still hope, not only among the American and British soldiers and officials, the vast majority of whom seemed to have no doubt they were going to win, but even among many Iraqis, who remained pleased Saddam had gone and were excited about the possibilities the future held.

The intended focus of my visit was a British security firm, Arawn Security Management. This firm and the other civilian military outfits operating in Iraq were controversial because they were the hired guns who had been brought in to do the jobs too menial or too messy for the soldiers stationed in the American-led coalition to take on. Their supporters maintained that their presence was essential because, it was said, there were not enough troops to stabilise Iraq without them. Their critics called them 'mercenaries' and highlighted that they were not directly under the power of a sovereign government and were less tightly controlled by the rules and customs that guided soldiers at war. It was a debate made urgent by the scale of these organisations' contribution to the Americans' reconstruction project. Thirty security companies were in Iraq with twenty thousand people on their books, which made them the second largest force after the Americans, twice as big a presence as the British.

Arawn's personnel met me at the airport. This was fortunate because they knew their business as far as personal protection was concerned and at that point I had no idea what I ought to be doing to try to keep myself alive. They gave me a bullet-proof vest and helmet, sat me in the back of a car with windows made of reinforced glass, and made sure I was flanked by two enormous Fijians, both armed with folding stock AK-47s. The car itself was a navy blue Nissan that had a dent down the side and was in urgent need of a wash. It looked in the same condition as almost every other vehicle in Iraq, which was entirely the point.

As we pulled onto the airport road I learned my first lessons about how to travel around Baghdad, all of which remained as pertinent during my final days in that country almost three years later as they were then on what was almost my first.

The most inescapable of these lessons was that in Iraq no one cared about official traffic rules. This was not a new development. Pile-ups had been a routine occurrence during Saddam's time. The Iraqis' imperative was to try to keep moving forward whatever might be in front. This was done by driving down the wrong side of the street, ignoring traffic signals, going the wrong way around roundabouts and accelerating as fast as possible whenever they found a clear stretch of road. Iraqis were particularly proud of their road anarchy. One later told me that he considered his countrymen the best drivers in the world because no one from anywhere else would be able to navigate Baghdad's streets successfully. He was almost as proud of the fact that he had never bothered to take a driving test but instead bribed the official responsible to obtain the necessary documentation.

The second lesson was that any opportunity to go fast for any distance, which in Baghdad was anything more than 20 mph, happened very rarely. The city was almost always on the verge of total gridlock. This was partly because no one obeyed the rules of the road, making every junction a battle of wills, but it was also because the war was resulting in lanes shut off, bridges bombed and army checkpoints set up where guards would insist on searching passing vehicles for illegal weaponry. More and more streets were closed as the war went on. Within a year I risked spending hours each day stuck in traffic, not going anywhere and with only the hope that my dark hair and the Iraqi clothing I wore to obscure my identity would be enough to stop someone looking through the window and recognising a foreigner.

The third lesson was the most important. This was the never-to-be-broken rule that if an American military patrol drove past, you pulled into the side of the road and stopped. These patrols had signs in English and Arabic strapped to the front of the leading vehicle telling Iraqis they risked experiencing 'lethal force' if they either failed to keep a distance of one hundred yards or did not park and turn their cars away from the passing convoy. As these signs were normally too small for anyone to read at a distance of a hundred yards, and as the people of Iraq had had no prior experience of being in the midst of an occupying force, it was the litany of deaths that the first few months of the war brought which had primarily made sure people understood the urgency of keeping out of the Americans' way.

Steve Myers, a journalist I knew at the *New York Times*, told of a car caught up in the violence of Baghdad during that time. The car had been in the middle of a highway when a truck had driven at an American column, a gun mounted on its back. The US soldiers had directed a hail of bullets at it, sending the truck careering across the central crash barriers and into the stranded car, causing it to burst into flames. A mother and her three children, the youngest an infant, were badly burned. Her husband, their father, was seen lying by the roadside, barely moving.

By 2004, there was usually no mistaking that a patrol approached. The Americans would sound their horns and a GI would be placed half out of the hatch of the front vehicle to blow a whistle and wave everyone out of the way. If a car did not move fast enough then a rifle might jump to his shoulder, the power of that message being the knowledge that he might just use it. When everything was gridlocked, and no vehicle could possibly be a hundred yards from another, the soldiers would dismount and start shouting in English at people to move. The Iraqis, trapped in their cars, would try to look as meek as possible while not understanding a word of what was being said to them. The thrust of the message, however, was clear and, despite it seeming hopeless, space would still be found, even if cars had to drive almost into the front of shops to let it happen.

Everyone did all they could to get the Americans moving again as it was terrifying when a US patrol was anywhere nearby. It was not only that you never knew if they were going to panic and start shooting. Far more worrying was that you did not know if the patrol you were trapped beside was going to be one of those attacked that day. If it was, then you were going to be the one in the wrong place at the wrong time when that roadside bomb went off. I knew an American aid worker who died like that. She drove down a slip road and found herself beside a line of Humvees at the exact moment when the explosion happened. She was so badly burned the authorities had trouble identifying her body.

The drive from the airport with the team from Arawn was the first time I had properly seen Baghdad. When I was last there, during April 2003 when American tanks started to roll through the city, its streets were empty as people stayed inside to avoid the fighting. Occasionally you would see a car making its way slowly down a highway but it was a rarity. The people in those vehicles would be acutely aware of how exposed this made them and the danger which came with it. White handkerchiefs would be held out of windows to signal that they were not out to cause trouble.

Now, a year later, Baghdad was alive once more. The occupation was ongoing but people still needed to work and shop so the streets were bustling. Taxis with their dirty orange-painted bonnets and boots touted for passengers. Youths dragged wonky carts piled high with sacks of grain. A boy led a donkey laden with baskets of wood. At one point we followed a flock of sheep around a roundabout. Restaurants had posters outside showing luridly coloured kebabs. Photograph shops displayed portraits of chubby babies. Cigarettes, fizzy drinks, fruit, rolls of cloth, electrical appliances and cans of petrol were stacked in shop fronts. Shelves were filled with gold-plated bracelets and earrings. There were towers of water bottles, racks overflowed with newspapers and magazines, kitchen equipment spilled out onto pavements.

Baghdad is primarily a concrete city, the box-like buildings resembling above all the Soviet style commonly found in parts of Eastern Europe, though with walls stained a dirty yellow by sand and dust. Saddam's close ties with the Soviet Union had led to thousands of East Germans and Poles coming to Baghdad in the 1970s to build a modern city paid for by Iraq's oil money. A few apartment blocks boast touches reflecting the country's heritage, the occasional Assyrian-style bas-relief incongruously etched onto a wall, but most ornamentation is determinedly twentieth century: typically modernist in style with concrete triangles or zigzag motifs. Balconies consist of intricate designs of connecting rhomboids and doors are inlaid with friezes of ever-diminishing circles.

It was not the buildings, however, which most demanded my attention on that journey, but the people. They were everywhere, filling the pavements and spreading out onto the roads. Most of the women had covered their heads with an Islamic headscarf, called the hijab, but not all of these were coloured black. There were yellow ones, blue ones, cream ones and patterned ones consisting of a mix of purples and reds. Some did not even wear a hijab at all but instead boasted the pleated power jackets and bouffant hairstyles not seen in the West since the 1980s. Most men were dressed in ankle-length robes but jazzier types sported Turkish shirts with long pointed collars and garish stripes. Clusters of children in their school uniforms took over sections of the pavement, the boys in blue shorts and clean white shirts and the girls in long skirts and pleated blouses. Exercise books were clutched to their chests or satchels dragged behind them.

I had read about the money pouring in to finance reconstruction and had expected forests of cranes working to build a new city. Instead there was no sign of any building at all and the poverty of the place was inescapable. It was partly the age of everything: the battered cars, the fading paint on shop signs and the rusting air-conditioning units sticking out of buildings. However, it was also the rubbish that abounded. The streets were thick with it. Even in the car I could smell the filth as it rotted in the heat. Sometimes there would be a break in the lines of houses where a wasteland was piled high with rubbish bags. Almost every ditch was littered with packing cases and plastic bottles. Sewage ran along the edge of pavements where street children hawked confectionery or domestic bric-a-brac.

Not even the damage caused by the war had been repaired. Street lights bent double by tanks lay untouched. There were bullet holes in the walls of buildings. At a street corner, one of the Fijians sitting beside me indicated where the pavement had been destroyed by a bomb that had recently killed a Western businessman. A crater and shattered bricks competed with potholes to mark the spot. We passed the sites targeted by the air bombardment that the US had intended would both shock and awe. The attacks were so precise that the buildings next to them appeared completely undamaged, whilst the targets themselves lay crumpled like a collapsed house of cards, the shattered layers of each floor lying one on top of the other amid the skeleton of a few obstinately unbowed supports.

We drove through a wealthy residential area. It was quieter there, the energy gone and the houses hidden behind high walls. Many boasted intricate hedges with bushes cut into the shape of animals or geometrical designs. We then turned onto an avenue that followed the banks of the Tigris. It was late in the afternoon so the sun had softened and the river was at its most beautiful. A woman was doing her washing. The Fijian on my left pointed her out to me, and then gave a grunt to make clear how filthy he considered the water.

Our objective was a side entrance into the Green Zone, the great fortress in the centre of Baghdad that housed the administrators sent from Washington with instructions to turn Iraq into a Western-style democratic state. They had taken over the buildings that had formed the administrative heart of Ba'athist rule, set up their offices and ringed the site with blast walls and concertina wire to keep out those who wanted to stop them. The checkpoint at the entrance that we approached was manned by half a dozen American soldiers. A tank, its gun barrel pointing down the road towards us, was stationed behind them. As we drew close a soldier raised his palm to tell us to stop and then came over, his hands gripping his rifle, to demand identification. A plastic ID card was shown to him and we were waved through into a parallel world.

At the checkpoint there had been cars queuing as

Iraqis with grievances tried to persuade the troops to let them pass in the hope that they might be able to address their cases personally to one of Iraq's American rulers. Many had files of paper they waved in front of the soldiers' faces. Others were trying to explain in halting English exactly why they deserved compensation for some loss. None of them were getting anywhere. The soldiers, nervous of possible suicide bombers and not enjoying a shift exposed in the centre of Baghdad, kept back the cars with hand signals and the pedestrians with an occasional shove. Inside the Green Zone, however, it was calm and for the first time since I had left the airport I felt safe. The Fijians flicked the safety catches on their Kalashnikovs and the man sitting in the front passenger seat, a Zimbabwean who had not spoken since we started our journey as he scanned the road ahead for dangers, turned around and asked me if I was a fan of cricket.

In the rest of Baghdad cars had looked like they were held together by love and a few pieces of string but in the Green Zone we passed lines of brand new Chevrolet Suburbans, every single one of them presumably brought in specially from the States. I saw a jogger running in a grey army T-shirt and a group of American soldiers wandering to one of the mess halls who were not even wearing helmets. In the shade of a tree a man in slacks was sitting reading a book, seemingly without a care in the world.

The Green Zone's name was a designation set by the military. It means a secured area. A zone that has not been secured, which in Baghdad meant almost every other part of the city, is called the Red Zone. Some reporters did not like the artificial atmosphere of

Baghdad's Green Zone but there was no denying its classification was deserved. Mortar rounds were thrown into it and suicide bombs detonated at its entrances but at no point while I was in Iraq was there a significant breach of its perimeter. Compared to what was happening in the rest of Baghdad, it was secure. Inside the Green Zone I felt protected and it never ceased to amaze me how a semblance of order was maintained however bad things became outside. There were speed bumps and traffic signs. Military police would come up and berate those driving too fast. Lawns were mowed. The lighting worked.

The Green Zone was also big. I quite routinely became lost. You could drive around it for almost an hour and still not see everything. A dozen blocks of central Baghdad had been sealed off to house administrators, diplomats, military commanders, Western security companies and US troops. It had its own helicopter landing pad, a shopping complex, military messes, a hotel, private restaurants, a State Department bar, gyms and even a radio station. The British Army had its own base within it, located in the complex of buildings where Saddam was said to have previously housed his mistresses. They were pleased with that. It was why, the British maintained, they had secured some of the most comfortable accommodation on the entire site.

At the heart of the Green Zone was Saddam's Republican Palace. This was where Iraq's most senior US administrators had set up their headquarters. It also housed Arawn's office and it was therefore to the Republican Palace that we now drove. By its main entrance was a car park in which more than two hundred vehicles must have been stationed. We stopped, climbed out of the car and walked towards what had been the heart of the Ba'athist regime. Stretching up six floors and arched in a quarter-circle, the palace's roof was capped by two forty-foot-high bronze busts of Saddam dressed in a traditional Islamic helmet. The building had been spared during the American bombing campaign as it was thought to hold important documentation. It had not, however, escaped the looting which followed Saddam's defeat. That was so thorough that even some of the palace's heavy gilded doors disappeared.

We walked through the main entrance and into bedlam. There were people everywhere. Some were in full combat gear, others in the bureaucrats' fatigues of blue shirt and tan chinos. American soldiers and marines, Brits, even an Italian soldier, rushed past me. There were Romanian and Polish troops; Australians in their uniform with its incongruous bubbly-shaped camouflage design. Gurkha guards were dressed in tan jackets and floppy-rimmed hats. They had been hired by the private security firm that protected the palace and were desperately trying to maintain a semblance of order.

I was led through the throng and along a particularly ornate passage, up some stairs, across a room where figures stared at laptops and a Coldplay song played through a computer, then into a vast chamber that must have once acted as a reception room. A chandelier hung from the ceiling and a mural covered one wall. It was presumably of Saddam but its subject's face was hidden by rough brush marks of black paint. In one corner a dozen sleeping GIs lay on the floor. I passed a shiny black door behind which, I was told, were the offices of the

Green Zone's most senior official, Ambassador Paul L. Bremer III, and was then led down a stairway. There was a memorial to the victims of 11 September 2001, a sign of how, in people's perception, Iraq had become linked to the events of that day despite the absence of evidence that Saddam was in any way involved. The two towers of the World Trade Center were depicted and above them the words: 'Thank God for the Coalition Forces and Freedom Fighters at Home and Abroad.'

We passed a mess hall in which scores of soldiers with rifles slung over their shoulders lined up to eat. In the larger rooms wooden partitions had been erected to provide temporary offices. Military canvas cots were placed beside desks. People were sleeping while others worked only yards away.

Another door was opened and we stepped outside into the sunlight. We rounded a corner and in front of me was a vast kidney-shaped swimming pool with a multi-level diving platform and a stone cabin that acted as a pool house. The water was perfectly blue. Soldiers in swimming trunks were doing back flips off the high board. Women lazed on recliners in bikinis. It was like walking into a holiday brochure. I was told it was time for a swim. There was clearly to be no work that day.

'You should've been here last Thursday,' one of the Arawn guys, an Australian called Mike, said to me. 'At ten at night there must've been four hundred people here, dancing and swimming, when two mortars came over. Everyone stopped, and then someone shouted, "It didn't hit me. Party on!"'

2. The Hands of Victory

The next day I received the Green Zone tourist treatment. Two of Arawn's employees were assigned to show me around, the Australian Mike and a Glaswegian former marine called Danny who had a handlebar moustache and a delight in finding fault with the English. They revelled in the opportunity to take time from their daily routine to see what entertainment was on offer.

We started with breakfast at the site's Burger King, a restaurant which operated out of a converted lorry and had been sent to Iraq to supply soldiers who were hungry for home. We then visited the 130-foot Hands of Victory triumphal arches dedicated by Saddam in 1990 to mark his 'victory' over Iran. Shaped like two pairs of crossed swords, they were surrounded by five thousand Iranian helmets taken from the battlefields of the Iran–Iraq war, most set into the ground for Iraqi troops to walk over as a symbol of their foes' humiliation. Many still showed the hole made by the bullet that had killed their original owners. A group of Iraqi guards let us climb inside the arches after we gave them $10 to bend the no trespassing rules. They then charged another $5 to take a photograph of us looking out from the top.

In the afternoon we visited the palace where Saddam's

son Uday had lived, a building which had three lions housed in the back garden in an iron cage covered by wire mesh. Uday – reputed to have turned into a full-blown psychopath after a failed assassination attempt left him impotent – was widely believed to have enjoyed throwing his enemies into the cage to see them torn apart. Some Iraqis claimed that the largest lion used to have a gold chain around its neck and prisoners were told that if they could remove it, and get out alive, they would be set free.

The lions did not look particularly forbidding when I saw them. In fact they looked more tragic than terrifying. I could see shoulder bones through their emaciated flesh as they sat looking dispirited in the shade of an over-hanging tree. A South African vet turned up with a dead donkey for their dinner and he threw it into the cage. That succeeded in rousing them and they went at the carcass with notable fervour.

The vet told us it was his job to look after the animals left at Baghdad zoo and, as no one else knew how to care for them, Uday's pets had fallen under his remit. The lions had apparently suffered terribly in the first weeks of the war when, with Baghdad in chaos, they had not been fed and had almost died from malnutrition. Plans were being drawn up to have them released into the wild in Africa. In the meantime the vet provided their daily meal and tran-quillised them when the cage needed to be cleaned. No human bones had yet been found, he assured us.

The vet's time in Iraq had not left him impressed with the average American soldier. He recounted how he had lost one of the lions housed at the zoo after a pair of bullish GIs decided to pay a visit. One stuck his hand through the railings and a lion had fastened its jaws around it. He only got free after his buddy shot the animal through the skull with his pistol. US High Command had apparently declared the zoo out of bounds when another group of soldiers threw a dog over the fence to watch the lions hunt down and eat it.

That evening we visited Mike and Danny's favourite restaurant in the Green Zone. It was a Chinese place, established amid the shell of a looted Ba'athist villa, some of its windows still broken and most of its rooms empty or covered in dirt and litter. There was a courtyard in front on which stood groups of plastic chairs and a few tables. To try to brighten up the place a line of red paper lanterns had been hung off a piece of rope to one side, but their colour had faded almost to white from the daytime sun and as a result they looked more forlorn than cheerful.

A solitary waitress took orders dressed in jeans and a Disney T-shirt. I could not see why Mike and Danny were so keen on it, although there was an intriguing smell of exotic spices and sizzling meat coming from the kitchen. The food was tasty enough, particularly the beef in oyster sauce, but it was when they began talking about a Chinese masseuse plying her trade in one of the restaurant's back rooms that I thought I might finally have cracked the secret of its appeal. Neither would go into details about what sort of service she offered so I could not determine if she was simply a masseuse or if this was a money-making venture selling extras to the Green Zone's sex-starved security industry. Either way she was clearly one of the main attractions and all those I met that night were insistent about what a kind person she was, which only deepened the mystery as to her true profession.

From their time in the forces, Mike and Danny knew half a dozen of the other contractors eating there and they introduced me to them. They were a motley bunch with their tattoos, penchant for shaved heads and the obligatory pistols strapped around their waists. It took them time to stop viewing me with a mixture of distaste and mistrust, but when they did they delighted in recounting horror stories involving some of the smaller security companies working in Iraq. I learnt that many contractors were required by their employers to drive around in bullet-proof 4x4s. Instead of being made safer by these vehicles' armour, their size and modernity made them stand out amid the rusting saloons that filled Baghdad's streets, a conspicuousness which invited the attention of every jihadist in the area. As a result, those riding in them often concluded that it was prudent to take shots at any car that got too close just in case those in it might be out to kill them.

Although all Mike and Danny's friends had a military pedigree, I learnt that this was not obligatory for those undertaking their line of work in Baghdad. There were firms that they respected, and consequently worked for, but the more amateurish outfits would apparently take on almost anyone willing to brave Iraq's dangers. It was because they could pay these employees less, I was told, making their bids more competitive when contracts were put out for tender. This was deflating wages in the industry, which might partly have explained their rancour. Mike and Danny knew of contractors whose only previous experience in security work was as night watchmen at office blocks in the States. An Italian security contractor who had been kidnapped and then murdered earlier that month had as his qualifications merely that he was a military reservist who liked doing martial arts in his spare time.

These were the kind of people, I was told, operating in Baghdad with their guns and nervous trigger fingers. They were working on site security, guarding convoys, delivering supplies or protecting visiting businessmen. As employees of military security firms, none were under Central Military Command therefore and neither could be court-martialled nor bound by the Geneva Convention. Under a law issued by Iraq's American administrators those working on government contracts could not be tried for murder if they killed someone. It sounded as if a new Wild West was being created.

Although Arawn operated in the same questionable legal sphere, it was one of the more reputable organisations. It was a security firm that sought to mirror the practices of the British military with comparable methods and required standards of conduct. There were rules of engagement and an emphasis on discipline. Its employees had served in the Army, many in elite regiments or the special forces, so such behaviour came naturally to them, indeed made them feel at home. No one was hired unless someone in the company could provide a personal recommendation as to their suitability, which helped promote a camaraderie of purpose. Most were now in their late thirties or forties, experienced heads back for one last big payday, only too aware that they were as reliant on the professionalism of others in the organisation as on their own if they were to stay alive.

That was probably why the company had invited me to spend time with them. The owners knew its employees were not trigger-happy cowboys and wanted to get that message across, presumably in the hope that if there was a backlash against the private military companies working in Baghdad they might avoid being discredited by the behaviour of others. Graham, the cricket-loving Zimbabwean who had driven with me from the airport, even argued that they were better suited for the job to be done in Iraq than the young men in the military. 'We're better trained,' he told me. 'We're older and we've got families at home we want to get back to.' Or, as one of his colleagues bluntly put it, they would not panic when things turned nasty. 'Old warriors like us already know that war doesn't bring flowers but death and bullets, and that you'll lose good friends.'

Despite the repeated reminders from those I met at Arawn about how controlled and professional they were, it was nevertheless clear they were enjoying themselves in Iraq. While primarily attracted by the £650-a-day pay-cheques, most of them could not believe their luck that the war had come along to save them from lives that had seemed humdrum compared to their time in the military. Mike had been stuck organising security at the Athens Olympics when the call came from a former colleague suggesting he join the company. Danny had been unable to reintegrate into civilian life and had left Scotland to live barefoot in an Aboriginal village in northern Australia. Others had been glorified drivers for rich businessmen in the UK or reduced to being hired hands to keep the paparazzi away from pop stars.

They were now allowed to be soldiers once more and had new war stories to prove it. Mike and Danny described with joy how over Christmas they were guarding government offices in Hilla, a city south of Baghdad located near the ruins of ancient Babylon. They were attacked along one side of the complex's perimeter. Mortars had come in and the night had been illuminated by muzzle flashes as they fought for forty minutes to hold the ground while waiting for the nearest foreign troops, a Polish contingent, to arrive and drive their attackers away.

One of their favourite stories was about an incident shortly after that firefight. A taxi had drawn up outside their base in Hilla and a 23-year-old Swedish backpacker dressed in a T-shirt and sunglasses stepped out, asking if anyone knew where the ruins of Babylon were. She had apparently crossed the Turkish border into Kurdistan and come down to see the sights. They stuck her on the next military plane out of the country. 'Silly cow,' was Mike's view. 'Good tits though,' was Danny's.

Spring 2004 was the era of the Coalition Provisional Authority (or the CPA as everyone called it), the governing body designated by the United Nations, but established by the Americans, which from April 2003 to June 2004 ran Iraq like a colonial administration. It was staffed primarily by foreigners, controlled all aspects of the state and had been given the responsibility of building a new Iraq. This would be a country, the White House said, that would be secular and modern, a beacon of democracy in the Middle East.

Later it became clear that the likelihood of the CPA having ever been able to turn this aspiration into reality had been greatly reduced by the fact it had largely been made up of the wrong people doing the wrong things at the wrong time. Point-scoring between the US Defence and State Departments meant that the Pentagon, which

President Bush made responsible for the CPA, chose to exclude the experienced Iraqi hands in the State Department from the reconstruction process. Donald Rumsfeld, the Secretary of Defence, thought Colin Powell, the Secretary of State, too liberal so sought to limit his influence over Iraq by preventing his people from having involvement in it. Political ideology was as important as practical experience in determining who the Pentagon sent to Baghdad. Republican Party-supporting youths fresh out of Harvard Business School were hired to help establish a new country. A 25-year-old was overseeing the creation of a stock market and another the same age was helping write the interim constitution while filling out his law school application.

At the CPA's head was Paul Bremer, a man who had never been to Iraq prior to his appointment and gave every indication of wanting to have as little meaningful contact as possible with Iraqis while there. Looking like an American celebrity divorce lawyer with his white teeth, tailored suits and carefully combed hair, he would be helicoptered around the country for photo opportunities at a newly built school or hospital before returning as quickly as he could to the security of the Green Zone. His intent seemed to be to change as much as possible in a short period of time in order to shock Iraq into becoming the modern, Western-leaning state the White House demanded. Iraq was being taken apart so it could be rebuilt to American specifications. Laws were changed and legal procedure overhauled. State-owned businesses were privatised, Ba'athist institutions closed down and tariffs slashed.

Two decisions Bremer made in the first few weeks after his appointment in May 2003 proved to be the most momentous in determining Iraq's future because they contributed in particular to creating the Sunni insurgency that emerged to resist the American occupation. It was Bremer who issued the proclamation that disbanded the Iraqi army, thereby sending thousands of trained troops to their homes with guns but no pensions, and who initiated the de-Ba'athification process that removed hundreds of senior and middle-level Ba'ath party members from government jobs, many of them civil servants and school teachers, even though a significant number had been party members solely for career advancement rather than ideological conviction.

Sunnis were the Iraqis most affected by these decisions because of the nature of Saddam's state. Saddam did not trust the Shia, particular after the Shia in southern Iraq launched an uprising against his rule following Iraq's defeat in the 1991 Gulf War, so often excluded them from government posts. Sunnis and Shia are both Muslims but separate sects within Islam. Although there are rarely outward indications to distinguish between them, their doctrinal differences date back to the death of the Prophet Mohammad in AD 632 and the conflicting viewpoints as to who should have been his successor as leader of the Muslim community. Mohammad had never stated clearly who should lead the movement after he died and this led to a disagreement that has divided the sects ever since. The Sunnis say that the Prophet's successor was best selected by popular consensus from amongst his closest companions. The Shia maintain that Mohammad wanted his successor to be his cousin and son-in-law, Ali ibn Abi Talib, and that the community's leadership should subsequently have remained within the Prophet's bloodline.

It was one of Mohammad's companions, Abu Bakr, rather than one of his relatives who received the leadership after the Prophet's death. According to the Shia, it was a decision Ali acquiesced to because he did not want to split the faithful. It was only after the assassination of the third person to hold the post, Uthman Ibn Affan, in AD 656 that Ali was finally elected leader of the Islamic community, a position known as the Caliph. This resulted in civil war and Ali's death five years later, while praying at a mosque, from a poison-coated sword. Ali's supporters at first pledged loyalty to his son, Hasan, but those who had organised his assassination bribed many of them to change sides, leaving Hasan's army in disarray. He was forced to sue for peace and step down from the Caliphate. In return for his acquiescence, the new Caliph, Muawiya, promised that his successor would be chosen by council.

Shortly before Muawiya died, however, he made his supporters swear allegiance to his son, Yazid, thereby breaking the key condition of the peace treaty. Another of Ali's sons, Husain, refused to accept Muawiya's deceit. With 72 men, many of them Mohammad's closest relatives, he marched to what is now the city of Karbala, sixty miles south-west of Baghdad, where, on 9 October 680, he was met by Yazid, who had with him several thousand soldiers. Husain and almost all his companions were killed in the subsequent fighting. It was a battle that ensured the Sunnis secured the Caliphate but it was a day that also shaped the future of Shia Islam. It became one of the most significant events in their history, one that was subsequently given an increasingly romantic and spiritual dimension and which made the concepts of suffering and martyrdom central to the sect's sense of identity. The Battle of Karbala is still commemorated each year by Shia in the festival of Ashura when believers mourn the sacrifice of Husain and his followers. The battle came to define the Shia's belief that what had been rightfully theirs was unfairly taken from them and ensured that a history of bloodshed and revenge would forever afterwards colour Islam's doctrinal schism.

Saddam was a Sunni and consequently preferred Sunni Arabs to hold Iraq's most important posts, especially if they were from his own tribe. Consequently Sunnis predominated in both Iraq's military and government and were proportionally worst affected by Bremer's disbandment of the army and his introduction of de-Ba'athification. As a result many Sunnis concluded that they would have no place in the new Iraqi state unless they fought to get one.

On my third day in Baghdad I saw the workings of the CPA first hand when Mike and Danny handed me over to its officials, who were to brief me on the improvements being made to Iraq. I spent a morning in Saddam's Republican Palace as a succession of chino-wearing figures sought to demonstrate that America would not only win in Iraq but that it was already succeeding. Lists of schools and hospitals being built were rattled off. Great store was set on the recent currency change in which Saddam-era notes, resplendent with his image, had been replaced by a new currency featuring Iraq's archaeological monuments. Baghdad's intermittent electricity supply should be viewed as a positive development, I was told, as it was partly due to the vast number of electrical goods the average Iraqi could now buy.

It was explained that the CPA was putting in place the foundations for a modern society, one with legislation that would prevent discrimination in the workplace and a new national curriculum that would ensure Iraq produced the world's next generation of great scientists. A public awareness scheme was planned that would save Iraqi lives by encouraging people to give up smoking. I attended a PowerPoint presentation which detailed how Iraq's new army would be ready for operation by the end of the year. Ambitious plans had been drawn up to reform the tax system. The number of insurgents being killed was cited as an indication of progress. Every official I met that morning seemed to have computer print-outs, complete with coloured graphs and pages of figures, which proved how effectively their area of responsibility was being implemented. It was very corporate and, in its own way, impressive. There was no denying that, whatever their other faults, those working in the CPA had seemingly boundless energy and commitment to its cause.

On my fourth night in Iraq, at the end of my stay with Arawn, Mike and Danny took me back to the Chinese restaurant for a farewell dinner. It was a Saturday night and the place was heaving, every table and chair taken. Mike, who was as Australian as they come, made sure I got stuck into the beers, and made clear that he would have considered it impolite if I hadn't.

Everyone I talked to was confident that the Americans would succeed in Iraq. A number of the security contractors were even buying up Iraqi banknotes in the expectation that the country's exchange rate would soon soar when the war was won. There were some I met who complained about the arrogance of the American troops they dealt with. Those who had served in Northern Ireland were not particularly happy to be lectured on the evils of terrorism by a people whose countrymen had partly funded the Irish terrorists who used to take pot shots at them and their mates. However, they all appeared to believe victory was inevitable. There was an apparent truism they seemed to trust absolutely: the US was simply too powerful for any other outcome to be possible.

It was home, not politics, that dominated conversation that night. I talked to a security contractor from Devon about how his wife would not let him sleep in the main part of the house on his first day back on leave in order to give him time to let the Baghdad stress flow out of him.

'When I came back from exercise or a posting abroad while in the Army I'd be so wound up that if she disturbed me in the night, while I was sleeping, I would grab her. I mean grab her roughly. It was an automatic thing – fight or flight – but it unsettled her. So now she sets up a camp bed in the garage and makes me sleep on that when I arrive home.'

There was a contractor who claimed to have been a bare-knuckle fighter before he joined the military. He said that he had been born a gypsy and had spent his childhood moving around Britain, often living in Wales. His father had been a force to be reckoned with in the gypsy bare-knuckle fighting world and his son had followed in his footsteps. He had the squashed nose and disjointed facial features that indicated there might be truth in what he was saying.

While in the Army he had been accepted by the SAS and had spent considerable time on covert operations in Northern Ireland. After he had been in the regiment for a few years, his father became ill with cancer and asked his son to visit him on leave as he had something to tell him. His father wanted to reveal the story of how his family had ended up gypsies. They had apparently originally come from Northern Ireland, his father born to a family of committed nationalists. He got caught up in the Republican cause and joined the IRA. What exactly he had done for them was not made clear but it was enough for the police to learn who he was and to begin searching for him. He had fled to mainland Britain and adopted the life of a gypsy to avoid discovery.

'It's a funny old world, isn't it,' the contractor said to me. 'There was I hunting down these fellas as part of the British Army when apparently there's a statue of my grandfather in a village in Ireland put up because of his great fighting skills against the British. It hails him as the great nationalist hero!'

At a corner table was an American, marked out as a CPA official by his pink polo shirt and carefully parted hair. He did not have stories about bare-knuckle fighting or having a secret terrorist as a father. He was, in fact, from a preppie family in Idaho. Unlike the others he preferred to talk politics as there was something he wanted to say about what was going to happen next in Iraq.

'The worst is over,' he predicted while enjoying his chicken fried rice and a cold bottle of Carlsberg. His job was to run democracy awareness courses for the Iraqi people, a task he fulfilled by staging workshops at government offices across the country during which the principles of the rule of law, fair elections and the importance of an independent judiciary were outlined. In this role had seen a lot more of the country than most of those in the Green Zone, many of whom had barely even seen Baghdad.

'The people I've met understand they've been given a turning point, an opportunity that won't come again, and they want to grasp it,' he told me. 'The hard work's been done now, the foundations for a new Iraq set up.

'What we need to do is hand power over to the Iraqis as soon as possible so that it doesn't look as if we are occupying the country. That'll take the wind out of the insurgency. I am sure of it. The Iraqis can get on with putting all our plans into action. People will look back and not believe what's been achieved so quickly.'

I said I hoped he was right, that the violence would soon end, and we clinked beer bottles in agreement.

It was perhaps not unexpected that those who ran the occupation were confident of the war's ultimate success. My biggest surprise during that visit to Iraq came at the end of my stay with Arawn when I was dropped off at the building in the Red Zone where the *Telegraph* and a number of other newspapers and TV companies had set up their offices. The news from Iraq that I had read in the UK had been primarily about bombings and military casualties. I was expecting the atmosphere among Westerners in the Red Zone to be that of a wake. Instead, among the journalists, it was as much party time as it had been at my local pub in Hackney or by the pool at Saddam's palace.

Most of the press pack, the *Daily Telegraph* included, had based themselves at the Hamra, a hotel in the quiet residential area of Jadiriyah on the opposite side of the Tigris from the Green Zone. It became the iconic reporter's hotel of the Iraq war, the place to which new arrivals rushed from the airport and where the war's old hands lived. Part of its popularity was based on the fact that the perimeter blast wall that protected it stretched beyond the hotel itself to include the half block of buildings that surrounded it. These included two or three hostels, which provided cheap rooms for freelancers and therefore increased the range of reporters able to stay in the compound, and also a couple of restaurants, one of which occasionally had a guitar player at weekends. It does not sound much but, by Baghdad standards, this was a wealth of entertainment of Las Vegas proportions. Even during the darkest days of the war, in the later parts of 2005 and for all of 2006, it meant I still had a choice as to where to eat dinner, even if I was by then normally too exhausted and strung out to do anything but order room service and slump in front of the television. A handful of the larger media organisations, such as the *Washington Post* and *Time* magazine, had hired villas within the compound, renting the buildings from their owners who gratefully took the thousands of dollars a month offered and relocated to Syria or Jordan. This added even more places to visit for anyone in search of distraction.

At the compound's centre was the Hamra hotel itself. It was a former Ba'athist-run place built in a Frank Lloyd Wright style made up of two towers that were by far the tallest in this neighbourhood of Baghdad. From the balconies on the tenth floor of the main tower there were panoramic views of the city in its grimy glory and many of the largest palaces and government buildings could be clearly made out. The hotel was not, however, particularly comfortable. The decor had not been refurbished since the building was constructed in the 1970s and, in

clothes and only used equipment – whether a watch or a mobile phone – that could be bought in Baghdad. My wardrobe consisted of brown and green-striped shirts and a selection of stonewashed jeans. Two more staff members were hired, joining my driver, Abu Omar, and my translator, Ahmed, as the *Telegraph*'s Iraqi team. They were Marwan, a security guard, and Sajad, who was to drive a second car.

Marwan was a reassuring presence, calm and steady, who belied the sallow dark bags under his eyes with a constant alertness. He had military experience as a former member of the Iraqi army's most elite element, the Republican Guard, and had fought in the Iran–Iraq war. He was also Ahmed's older brother and I trusted that family duty would lead him to do what was necessary in order to protect us. His job was to travel in the back-up car, keep a watchful eye on the road around us and surprise any attackers by rushing to our aid if anything went wrong. It was a task he seemed to take to with remarkable equanimity despite the fact that if anything had happened he would almost certainly have been killed whilst giving us time to flee.

Sajad was a friend of Abu Omar, who vouched for his trustworthiness and bravery. He had been a taxi driver before he started working for me, a particularly dangerous job in occupied Iraq where most people tried to avoid making unnecessary journeys let alone spend all day cruising the streets looking for fares. Escaping that life meant he was delighted with his new, better-paid job despite its potential dangers. He was in his early forties, as was Marwan, and Ahmed quickly nicknamed him the 'giant rooster' as Sajad did somewhat resemble a chicken.

Days spent behind the wheel had given his back a perma-nent arch, his head popped up straight from his hunched body and a shock of greying hair sprouted in an uncon-trollable quiff.

Sajad's task was to drive the second car, which was to trail us discreetly while Ahmed, who was in the front car with me, and Marwan discussed any problems they had spotted via walkie-talkies. The theory behind having a second vehicle was that extra sets of eyes would enable greater forewarning of potential dangers. Moreover, if something happened, Sajad was expected to drive towards the danger and help rescue us. If I was being followed he was meant to put his car between me and my potential attackers and, if things got really bad, suppos-edly force them off the road. I always trusted he would do what was required as, like many Iraqis, he clearly took his pledges of loyalty seriously. He also had Marwan sat beside him to make sure he did not hesitate when needed.

At the start of 2005 the Western media organisations in Iraq banded together to secure advice and training from a group of security contractors. Two of them were to be based at the Hamra, which most commonly proved to be a team consisting of a former member of the SAS and an ex-Royal Marine who had joined the SBS. I got to know both of them well. They were always supportive, never questioning why someone like myself with no combat training was trying to operate in such a place. They did not go out onto the streets with us but instead helped me through the steps that marked my own militarisation.

In a series of training sessions they instructed my team and me on how to move around without drawing undue attention, how to respond if shot at, and what to do in every situation from a breakdown to a car crash (a likely event on Baghdad's chaotic roads and one for which the solution was apparently to thrust cash into the hands of the driver of the other vehicle before a crowd lynched you). Car doors offered no protection from gunfire, we were told. Even a wall would not necessarily stop a bullet if it was fired from a high velocity rifle. Mortars could kill a person standing a hundred yards away. Armoured vests might stop a bullet but they would not prevent ribs getting broken as the Kevlar plate was pushed into your chest.

We went through combat medical training: how to keep a pierced lung inflated by strapping a credit card across the entry wound, what not to do if someone's skin had been burned off, the danger of internal bleeding from bones smashed in a bomb blast, and the best way to tourniquet a shattered arm while using only one hand and your teeth. Then, in the summer, my newspaper decided to follow other media groups and carry a weapon in the back-up car. We bought a semi-automatic pistol, a Browning 9mm, from our security advisers and they took us to the shooting range at the interior ministry. Shell blockages, target selection and the techniques of firing from positions of cover were outlined and practised.

It was a big step deciding that it was time to carry a weapon. Where those of us in the Baghdad press corps had once simply been journalists, we now risked resembling leaders of our own militias. Everyone had their own security procedures, our two-car system being simply the method our budget stretched to, and by 2005 most of us were armed. My team, with Marwan and his pistol, were minor league. The larger American papers had dozens of guards and the TV stations small armies.

While I was the *Telegraph*'s Iraq correspondent I never heard of any media organisation that started shooting, though they would probably have kept it pretty quiet if they had. The closest call appeared to have been when reporters from a US television station were unlucky enough to have been driving past the Palestine at the exact moment when the hotel was hit by a cement mixer filled with explosives and came under sustained machine gun fire. A massive gun battle erupted as its guards shot back at their attackers. The American TV crew was caught in the middle. Their security detail was certainly on the look-out for targets as they sought to get away as quickly as possible. If we had been in the same situation we would have been killed. The correspondent's armoured saloon had bullet marks down one side. I was pretty jealous of their budgets when I saw that. The *Telegraph* was never going to be able to afford a similar level of protection.

This escalation in our security precautions nevertheless left me with mixed feelings. I could not quite accept that a media company might have to kill someone, nor was I sure how carrying guns would help if, like Rory Carroll, we found ourselves surrounded by three vehicles with nowhere to go. As far as I could see it risked only making matters worse if we started going pop-pop-pop with our semi-automatic glorified peashooter. The bottom line, however, was that my newspaper approved of the pistol and my team had made it pretty clear they were unwilling to go out without it. So I hid behind that knowledge and tried not to think too hard about what its presence might turn us into.

The truth, moreover, was that the pistol did make me feel more secure, despite my misgivings. It provided an emotional sense of security if nothing else. I knew that whatever happened I did not want to be the next person shown on the internet being beheaded. That pistol might have brought false hope but it seemed too much to go out with nothing to rely on for protection but the Iraqi-style shirt on my back.

I had been a journalist for a decade by the time I started my job in Iraq. Ten years in which I had learnt my trade, completed my apprenticeship at a local paper in Yorkshire, worked in Hong Kong during the years that straddled the 1997 handover to China, and then fought my way onto the national papers in London. I had secured a job at the *Telegraph*, become one of their foreign correspondents when they posted me to the States and filed for them from countries across the world. I knew how to construct a story, what information was needed, who you had to talk to and how you ordered your quotes to lure the reader in. Journalism is a craft, certainly not an art. You learn the techniques and drill them until they become automatic so that against a deadline events can be put into the required style and set out in a way that is comprehensible to the reader.

Ten years' practice was not enough for Iraq. Twenty years probably would not have been. The situation defied easy packaging and clear conclusions. Facts, facts, facts, editors had drilled into me. Double, triple-check your facts, and then put them in an order that ensures they provide answers. In Iraq there were few facts and far more questions to which no one had answers. Due to the limitations imposed by the dangers we faced, few reporters had a comprehensive understanding of what was going on beyond the concrete palisades that ringed the Hamra.

This lack of understanding did not mean that there was no value in us being there. You only had to hear what was being claimed in Washington and London, let alone by the officials in the Green Zone, to know that it was essential the media publicised even the limited information it could gain. I still believe that now. I am proud that the work done by all the journalists working in Baghdad helped make clear to the world what was really going on in that city. However, it did not stop my efforts seeming depressingly inadequate whenever I let myself think of the hundreds of unreported stories unfolding each day: the myriad of personal tragedies never told, the individual triumphs that would fail to be recognised.

Most of the Iraqis I met were unable to understand much more than I could, which was in its own way reassuring. They would routinely tell me that they did not comprehend how such a thing could have happened to their country and clutched at explanations that might rationalise what had occurred. Maybe it was because the Americans intended to create chaos in order to destroy Iraq for ever, I would be told, or possibly it was God's judgement on the worst moral excesses of Saddam's secular regime. For some the foreign Wahhabi coming into Iraq to impose their brand of ultra-conservative Islam were to blame, for others – and this was a real favourite – it was in some unspecified way all the fault of Iran.

Only America's senior officers and officials seemed unwilling to admit to the possibility that they did not know exactly what was going on. I would come across the odd clued-up officer out in the field who really understood his area of operations and could explain, in detail and with insight, the problems he faced. In the official briefings by the top brass, however, everything was always on course and they still had their flipcharts and PowerPoint presentations to prove it.

One time I did come across a senior American who was willing to acknowledge the extent of his ignorance. I was on a trip to the north-western town of Tal Afar where I stayed with the local US unit stationed there. Their commander was Colonel H. R. McMaster and he was the smartest American officer I had ever met. Shaven haired and bulging with muscles, he looked like the archetypal hard-nosed soldier. In fact, he had been a military history professor at West Point and had a PhD from the University of North Carolina where he wrote a thesis about the mistakes made in the Vietnam War. In the first Gulf War he had headed a tank troop that had taken on units of Republican Guard that vastly outnumbered his own and destroyed them all without losing a single soldier. It was an achievement that earned him not only the Silver Star but a hero's write-up by Tom Clancy in his 1994 book *Armored Cav*. When I met McMaster in his office in the old Iraqi barracks that his unit's camp were built around, he batted away the broad policy question I had flung at him as being impossible to answer.

'Anyone who claims to understand what's happening in Iraq doesn't understand it,' he said.

He was an officer who had successfully done his job, had that year taken Tal Afar and restored it from being a place where freshly severed heads were placed in the centre of road junctions to one that bore some semblance of civilisation. Not that it lasted. After his tour ended it took only three months for his successor to lose control and for the town to once again become a rat run for the suicide bombers making their way towards Mosul.

In our compound, with its blast walls and electricity generators, we were living the good life by Baghdad standards. In the city at large conditions were deteriorating rapidly. This realisation was inescapable, however confused the overall situation might have been. Everyone you talked to, everything you saw, testified to it.

It is hard to conceive the state that Baghdad was being reduced to. Try to imagine that it was where you had grown up and lived. Think what fundamentals you would take for granted and the presumptions on which you had built your life. Then imagine them being stripped away one by one, what you would be left with and what such a situation would do to you.

It was not only the war but the general lawlessness that made Baghdad so dangerous. People could not go outside without fear of becoming the victim of a violent robbery. There was still no effective police force and criminals were taking full advantage of the vacuum. The health ministry was advising doctors to start carrying weapons for their protection because thieves were pretending to be patients to seize drugs and equipment. Gangs preyed on the roads into and out of the capital. The *Telegraph* had been a victim when a colleague on a trip to Basra had found the road in front blocked by a lorry and armed men emerging from a car behind. That time he, his driver and his translator had been lucky. It was only their possessions and the car, not their lives, that were taken.

It was rare to hear of resolutions so bloodless. An Iraqi friend of mine, a receptionist in one of the city's hotels, had his son kidnapped as he emerged from a mobile phone shop in central Baghdad. He paid the ransom and was sitting in the main room of his house when he heard a car stop and someone run to the front door. There was a burst of gunfire. He opened the door to have his son collapse into his arms. The boy died there and then as his family tried, and failed, to stem the bleeding.

The basic necessities for life were eroding. Saddam, as part of his system of state control, had instigated a rationing system to ensure every Iraqi received basic food items on a regular basis. By 2005 the country's new rulers were unable to guarantee supply. The system for sugar and baby formula collapsed, forcing many to go without. By the spring, electricity in the capital was limited to eight hours per day and rarely came on for more than two hours at a time. Output averaged only 850 megawatts, compared with 2,500 megawatts before the war started. Partly it was because of the looting that had followed the collapse of the Ba'athist regime but it was also because the network was a target for those opposing the occupation. They knew that maximising people's discomfort helped turn them against the country's new rulers. Sewage processing plants were another favoured objective. The attacks against them resulted in pipes overflowing and sewage being reported on almost half of Baghdad's streets. Sadr City, the vast Shia slum in east Baghdad, was consequently in the grip of a hepatitis epidemic. In the height of the summer the water plants were hit, cutting off supply to two million homes. The temperature was above 40°C as I watched people queue at emergency water pipes to fill their jerry cans and buckets.

I used to ask Ahmed to translate the city's talk radio

shows. They provided insights into everyday life that the security situation made it so hard to glean. From my office on the third floor of the Hamra I could see Baghdad stretching around me: the stacks of flats with their box-like windows, the roofs covered with their jumble of cables, abandoned furniture and bent television aerials; the streets with their rusting cars pumping out the cheap petrol fumes whose odour imbued the city, and the occasional palm tree bringing a burst of life to the city's otherwise beige exterior. As we listened to the radio I would sit looking at it, hearing the voices coming to me from out there.

I liked Radio Tigris the best as it was usually the liveliest. In the summer of 2005 a programme debated where people could sleep to escape the oppressive heat. I still have the notes I jotted down:

Air-conditioning? None working as the electricity not reliable enough. Children crying because so tired. Very exhausting for the parents.

Woman concerned about danger of sleeping outside on the roof. A popular solution apparently. Has heard of people being hit by falling bullets and shrapnel. That a big worry.

'We heard one night an American plane bombing nearby,' another woman says. Had been on the roof of her home at the time trying to keep cool. 'What should we do when that happens?'

A caller complaining that the five families living in their block of flats could not all fit on the roof and those forced to sleep in the garden were plagued by rats that appeared to be 'bigger than cats'.

An architect, Abu Rhadi, 'This city was once the most beautiful in the Middle East. People would walk by the river at dusk and the restaurants were filled with laughter. Now our life is this.'

That summer I visited a US army unit in Kirkuk, a city in the north of the country which marked the boundary between Iraq's Arab and Kurd populations and was therefore among the country's least stable cities. It was one of Iraq's oldest settlements, a place lived in continuously for 5,000 years. At its heart was an ancient citadel, first built in the 9th century BC, which was ringed by 72 towers. It stood on a 130-foot high mound, dominating the modern buildings that surrounded it.

I arrived at Kirkuk General Hospital just as it started taking in the injured from a suicide bombing. At least thirty had been killed and more than fifty injured, a number of them from bullet wounds inflicted in the aftermath of the blast when local police panicked and started shooting in every direction.

The hospital had been built by the British in 1946 and it had barely been improved since. Brown paint was peeling off the walls and the ceilings were black with dirt. As patients were rolled in on metal trolleys they left trails of blood on the floor of the entrance hall.

In the central ward a dozen beds had already been filled. The skin on the face of one of the wounded had been peeled back and hung in flaps. Blood oozed through bandages on the leg of another, his chest pepper-marked by stones lifted off the street and flung into his body in the blast. A man stood over a bed where a figure lay unconscious. He was holding one end of a tube, the other end of which had been stuck into the patient's nose. He was methodically placing his end next to a ventilation machine to inflate the injured man's lungs, and then moving it away to let them fall. The hospital did not have the valve to enable it to be connected properly.

An Iraqi doctor, a striking man with a strong nose and powerful chin, emerged from surgery and pulled off his plastic gloves. He was one of only three working there. His face crumbled. 'We have no resuscitation devices and no intravenous fluid. We do not have enough equipment and what we do have is twenty years out of date,' he said. 'We cannot save most of these people.'

When they learned of the explosion, the Americans had sent doctors to the hospital to help. Though they had brought their own medicines with them, they were despairing about the level of hygiene. Used needles were being flushed down toilets, blood was left to congeal on floors and there were no antiseptic wipes. It had been one of the US medics, Captain James Schroeder, who had ferried me to the hospital from the base at which I was staying. He was one of those Americans I found throughout the US military, someone who had come out filled with excitement and optimism about how he was going to be doing good by making Iraq better. Now he was faced with this.

'They do their best,' he said of the Iraqi doctors. 'But you can see the reality of this place.' He was called to treat a police officer whom I had seen brought in. His leg had almost doubled in size from the bleeding from a fracture in his hip.

Outside, the ambulances ferrying in the wounded were little more than transit vans equipped with first aid kits and extra bandages. Cars joined them in dropping off the injured. On the ground lay four bodies covered by white sheets. A woman in a black hijab was standing beside them weeping silently.

I sat on a low brick wall and waited for my lift back.

Half an hour later Captain Schroeder sat down beside me. He normally had the demeanour of the High School jock he once was, all white teeth and clean features. Now sweat and dirt marked lines down his face and there were red stains on his uniform. I asked him how his patient was. 'He died,' he said. 'Too much blood loss by the time he got here.'

4. USA

When I visited Iraq in April 2004 American forces had placed Fallujah in a state of siege after four security contractors were ambushed, killed and their burned bodies paraded through the streets. US High Command promised the city would be pacified but plans for an assault were aborted amid concern about the number of Iraqi civilians at risk of being killed. A compromise was reached in which a local Iraqi security force was given the responsibility of stabilising the city. Over the summer of 2004 this unit dissolved and handed over its American-provided weaponry to the extremists. In November, the US military attacked. For nine days its troops battled their way through Fallujah's streets until the city had been wrestled back under American control.

Three months later, in February 2005, the marines who had taken Fallujah were preparing to go home. They had been in Iraq for a year, a year in which they had been involved in the American military's most intense house-to-house fighting since Vietnam, had killed around 1,500 of their enemy and seen a hundred of their own die with a further thousand wounded. These men were the self-styled 'Devil Dogs', troops who proudly had as their motto that there was 'no greater friend; no worse enemy'. Soon they would be back at their base in Southern California, able to enjoy days on the beach, trips to Tijuana and races up Highway 5 to the delights of Los Angeles. First, however, the United States government wanted to influence exactly what would be coming home. Before being allowed on their flight back to the States, the soldiers were being required to undergo therapy. The sessions were given the military-sounding mame of 'Warrior Transition' but what they resembled was a segment from *The Oprah Winfrey Show*. It was time to share.

In February 2005 I was allowed to attend one of these sessions in Camp Fallujah, the marine barracks on the outskirts of the city. It was being held in an auditorium in the Saddam-era military base that the US troops had adopted. Rows of seats upholstered in blue cloth formed a semi-circle facing a raised stage. Normally a TV tuned to ESPN was placed on it, enabling the marines to keep up with the sports news from back home. On this occasion, however, it hosted the unit's senior officers and regimental chaplain, who were warning their charges of the new fights to come, this time ones in their everyday lives.

'Go slow when reconnecting with your children,' the men were told. 'Don't be surprised by the nightmares. Tolerate bad traffic. Don't expect wives or girlfriends to have been transformed into the sexual Houdinis you fantasised about while apart. Feel good about yourselves and what you achieved in battle.'

One of the senior officers stepped forward. 'Iraq is changin' and it all started here in Fallujah,' he said. 'Freedom started in Fallujah. Freedom from fear. Freedom you brought to this place. Everyone is proud of you. Your nation is proud of you. You're the heroes of Fallujah and that will be with you for the rest of your lives.

'When you hear veterans from the D-Day landings they talk about how it was a seminal day in their lives, the formative event of their lives. I submit to you that Fallujah will be a seminal event in your lives, somethin' that is uniquely yours. There can be good things from that, but there can also be bad. The images are seared on your mind. We can't make them go away: the burned bodies, the pieces of humans or the effect of a roadside bomb. Be aware, the battle of Fallujah may go on inside you.'

There were nearly a hundred men present. Their guns lay on the floor in front of those sitting and were slung around the shoulders of those who stood. They all listened intently.

'What good are you goin' to take from here?' asked the chaplain, who despite his job title had the physique and presence of a boxer.

It took a while for an answer. 'To appreciate the smaller things in life,' a voice said.

'Like what?' the chaplain responded.

'Beer!' This got a laugh from everyone, the chaplain included.

'The sense of havin' served my country,' said someone.

'The fact we fought them here so they can't take it to our homes,' proposed another.

The chaplain asked, 'What of the negatives?'

The answers came quicker this time. 'Loss of comrades,' said one Hispanic serviceman. 'Not all of us are here.'

The chaplain nodded. 'They laid down their lives for a cause greater than themselves.'

'Dogs eating corpses,' a voice called out.

'That's right,' said the chaplain. 'I saw a dog comin' from the chest cavity of a man, its face drippin' with blood. That was pretty bad. I've got dogs and I don't think I'm quite goin' to look at them the same way again.'

A marine said, 'The smell of it. When you're barbecuin' on a Saturday morning in your back yard, I'm not looking forward to that.'

'The suffering of the women and children,' another offered.

There was a lot of agreement about that one. 'I know there is not a man here who wouldn't choose to put down their life for a child,' the chaplain said.

'Getting shot at,' came the next response.

'That's goin' to change you fundamentally as a human being,' the chaplain said. 'You need to talk about that stuff but be careful who you talk to. People can't understand what it's like here. They may look at you like you're crazy. This isn't good dinner conversation.'

'What do you do if someone talks shit to you in a bar about the war in Iraq?' he asked.

A marine shouted out, 'I'm goin' to crack them over the head with a bottle of beer.'

That got a lot of laughs too.

The next day their commander took me on a tour of the city. Mike Shupp was like someone out of every war film you have ever seen. He was the trusty tough guy: a strong handshake, straight talking, broad, and emotionally powerful. There was a story about why he should no longer have been in Fallujah which made him seem only more impressive. He had been in Iraq for five months when his wife developed cancer and he was flown home as she underwent chemotherapy. It was terrible to watch, he admitted, but she beat it. He had been given compassionate leave from the rest of his tour so he could help her recuperate. Then a rocket came through the roof of his old HQ in Camp Fallujah and took out his successor, and he was called back to Iraq to lead his men.

Colonel Shupp was one of those people who were rarely quiet. The words flowed from his mouth so fast that even with shorthand I could barely get them down. He was proud. He had fulfilled his assigned task. In fact he had hopefully won the war. Two years into the fight, Fallujah had fallen and Iraq could now start moving towards peace. That was what he believed. He was going home with the conviction that his had been a job well done.

'Look at our accomplishments here,' he said. 'The insurgents wanted Fallujah as a safe haven. We took it from them. My men didn't let me down. They were exhausted and tired but they looked after each other and won. After the battle an old woman came up to me and kissed my hand. She said, "Thank God for you people." It was incredible.'

Although I had read the reports and seen the photographs, I was not ready for the level of destruction I saw as Shupp took me into Fallujah itself. We drove down the main street in a convoy of Humvees and it seemed as if there was not one building that had been left without pitting from shell fragments or machine-gun fire. At the first corner a house had simply disappeared, reduced to a pile of sharp pebbles and dust. Half-way down the next block was a mosque, its dome shattered and the minaret lying in ruins. Doorways still showed the white crosses that had marked buildings as cleared of insurgents. Rubble covered the pavements and street lights lay across intersections. The Humvees had to swerve every few minutes in order to avoid craters in the tarmac.

We turned right at a corner and in front of us was what remained of an apartment block, the windows blown out and three four-foot wide holes running in a diagonal down the side wall where American missiles had struck. Beside it lay the remnants of clothing, a purple blouse and a pair of black cotton trousers the most identifiable, scattered by the force of the blasts. There was another corner and this time we turned left onto a side road. The breeze-block walls of the surrounding buildings had crumbled across the dirt-covered street. Broken wires hung from telephone poles and, ahead of us, a goat was foraging amid the piles of debris and rubbish.

It was February, the end of Iraq's brief but unpleasant rainy season, and craters had become pools. A truck was parked outside a house. Its owner was one of the families drifting back into the city after having originally joined the rush to escape before the showdown between the Americans and Sunni gunmen began. Some of their possessions lay in the back under a black tarpaulin. A figure stood in the doorway to the house, looking dejected as others walked past her to see what else might have survived.

Access to the city was limited by checkpoints, every entrance having been blocked. At the one we passed through on the way back to camp marines were methodically searching every vehicle going into the city, causing a queue to snake back a hundred yards from the barriers. The Americans had taken Fallujah once and were damned if anyone was going to have to do it again. No weapons would get back in if they could avoid it.

A group of marines were taking photographs as final

mementoes. They gathered in front of the checkpoint with the city behind them. 'Smile and say Fallujah,' the serviceman taking their picture shouted.

Colonel Shupp was still talking, now about the reception he expected when he arrived back home. 'I think the people back in the States appreciate what we've done,' he said. 'There may be a difference of opinion about the war in Iraq but there is no difference of opinion about the military. These men will be goin' back as veritable war heroes.

'They deserve it. They were the most heroic people I ever saw. They are the next greatest generation. They're goin' to go back and be the next leaders of our country. They showed a passion here no one can imagine. These are truly amazin' people.'

In the base, marines were lining up outside the camp post office with boxes of kit they wanted sent to the States. These were the physical reminders of the seminal event of their lives. It was a slow queue as everything had to be laboriously approved, checked and weighed. Three marines from San Diego were playing cards and talking about their Warrior Transition while they waited. They had seen *Rambo*, I learned, so they knew what war could do to the psyche.

'It was like being in a movie, it felt unreal,' one, Ivan Getierrez, said of the fighting. He was 21 years old, a skinny little thing with ears far too big for his head. 'Everything was just being played out. There were bombs, explosions, bullets – I was in the zone doing what I had trained for. It was like being in a trance going through it.

'Then I woke up. I'd lost two good friends. I think about why it was them and not me. Most nights I think about that. Go figure.'

His fellow card players really did not want to get into it. Instead they kept studying the hands they had been dealt to ensure there was no way I could attract their attention and ask what it was they might be feeling.

Due to the deteriorating security situation, by 2005 the US military provided almost the only way to get out of Baghdad and into the rest of Iraq. My translator, Ahmed, and the rest of my Iraqi team were always pleased when I did because, in my absence, they did not have to risk coming into the office and could work the phones from their homes, e-mailing me with the information I needed to write my articles. It was a better life for them than having to share a car with a foreigner or waiting to see who might attack the Hamra complex.

Joining up with the American forces was a relatively simple procedure. I would send an e-mail request to the central press office in the Green Zone and they would pass it on to the unit in the area I wished to visit. Nine times out of ten the request was approved. There were far fewer reporters around by then and some of the units would only get a couple, if any, coming to visit them during their entire year in the field. They did not like that. It made them feel that what they were doing was being forgotten – or, worse, was unimportant. Often a visiting journalist, even a Brit like me, would bring a welcome sense of validation.

Getting approval to go somewhere and actually getting there were two separate things, however. I spent days sitting by helicopter landing pads trying to travel from one place to another. It was like an extreme form of hitchhiking. A helicopter would come and I would get as far as I could, then I would wait for the next one that might take me a little bit closer. Occasionally I found myself on a helicopter doing the whole trip in one leg. That was when I knew Sod's Law would leave me grounded halfway by a sand storm, or knocked off the manifest by a sudden influx of soldiers with orders to get somewhere fast.

Sometimes the contortions I went through to get out of or back to Baghdad became ridiculous. Once, while stuck by an airstrip in a base west of Ramadi, I was utterly fed up after having spent four days waiting in a world of transit tents and portaloos, with nowhere to wash and only the semi-tepid contents of self-heating ration packs for food. In the end I boarded the first flight possible, a plane going to Kuwait. Once there, and after considerable effort, I finally got on another flight that was heading to Baghdad via a stop in Qatar. Three countries and seven days for a trip that would have been a six-hour drive in safer days.

When I could get a lift from a helicopter there would be the race to climb in as I pulled my bag onto my back and piled into the side while the gunner urged me to go faster because the pilot had no plans to stop for long. Then the vertical lift-off to weave across the skies of Iraq. One time, going from Kurdistan to Tikrit, we spent the whole journey never more than a hundred feet off the ground – down the sides of valleys, skimming across the desert, rising up to cross electricity lines, scattering goats. Everyone on board had their cameras out for that trip.

The hairiest journeys were always the ones into the Green Zone itself, especially if I found myself on the British shuttle that ferried people to it from Baghdad airport after a stay with the Army down south. On most helicopter trips the pilots had done the route so often they felt it to be almost routine. The British pilots, however, were often out of their normal area of operations and on maximum alert. As a result they knew how to make you feel scared. The automatic defence system would be set to such a high level of receptivity that a sudden reflection of sunlight off water could be enough to trigger the anti-attack flares. They were usually set off at least once every journey. When the flares started firing the pilot would twist and bank so that I would fall against my harness, the passengers who had never done the ride before would look pasty-faced with fear and I would be left desperately wondering if it was just a misfire or if this really was an attack. Only a couple of times did I hear gunfire on these trips, and who knows if we were being fired at or if it was simply the muzak of Baghdad. Nevertheless, on those occasions, the helicopter turned all the way over onto its side as the pilot sought to get out of trouble and I was as pasty-faced as everyone else.

Anbar province was the heart of the Sunni insurgency. It is home to the cities of Fallujah and Ramadi and there was not a settlement in it that did not have its local youths keen to cause as much damage as they could to American forces.

One time in June 2005 I travelled through Anbar along a road north-west of the city of Hit. I was at the back of a six-vehicle US convoy, in a Humvee that made up part of the guard detail for a military investigator who had been dispatched to determine how an Iraqi civilian was killed.

The case was one of those confused stories I often heard in Iraq. The marines had been raiding a house. The oldest son was shot dead. The marines said he had come at them from the main bedroom with a gun. His family said the marines had shot him in cold blood and then produced a gun to put beside him. It became a serious problem for the military when it emerged that the dead Iraqi was related to a senior local politician, hence the investigation. I could not see how, amid the chaos and deceits of Iraq, anyone would be able to get to the bottom of it, let alone the Marine Corps judge advocate the US authorities had sent.

In mid-summer, Humvees were never the most comfortable way to get anywhere. Due to the number of roadside bombs, most vehicles had been fitted with as much armour plate as they could take. This was obviously good in one way but Humvees had not been designed to carry such a weight. The overstretched engine left little power for the air-conditioning system. It was hot in there in your helmet and body armour.

One of the four marines in my vehicle, Private Casey, had just returned from two weeks home leave in California. He was a gangly youth, too tall and at the same time not wide enough for his uniform. His parents lived near the liberal haven of Santa Cruz and he was recounting how the local students had treated him while he had been there.

'They're rich kid hippies,' he said of the Santa Cruz student scene. 'You'll see them sittin' on the sidewalk with their fake dreads. They knew who I was and were giving me shit. I was at this party and this guy was not holdin' back, saying, "What are you doing goin' over there killin' babies and droppin' bombs?" So I told him I was an infantryman so I don't drop bombs and I saw everyone I killed. But he wouldn't get the message.'

One of his colleagues, Corporal Philip Lathrop, wanted to know why he had not beaten him up.

'I did,' Robinson assured him.

Their commander, a bullish staff sergeant called Dan Thompson, was particularly pleased that he had a Brit on board. He was sitting beside the driver and turned round to tell me so. 'It makes me glad that America and Britain are such staunch allies,' he said. 'Not like the French. We heaped a lot of bodies on the beaches in Normandy and they seem to forget that.'

It was a long drive, at least two hours there and two hours back, and there was little to see to break the boredom. Away from the section of the Euphrates river that curls though Anbar, the landscape was a repeating expanse of arid desert broken only by the occasional sand-bank or boulder. In my Humvee, a machine-gunner had been placed looking out of the top hatch to watch for any sign of roadside bombs. For the rest of us the thing to do, it seemed, was talk.

'What I like about President Bush,' Thompson said, 'is he's a man of principle. He says what he believes and does it. I really believe that by being in Iraq we're fighting here so we don't have to fight these people back home. I know some people don't believe that, but I really do.

'The rest of the world doesn't understand what we are up against. What Spain did after that bomb went off on their train, pulling out of Iraq like that, that showed me the rest of the world wasn't willing to step up to it. People like to talk of Clinton's time but he didn't have to face any great threat. 9/11 happened because Clinton took his eye off the ball.'

He took a sip of tepid water. 'I'd actually left the army but rejoined when 9/11 happened. It would've been similar to having trained for the Olympic Games and not being able to race.'

The engine started overheating and the air-con had to be turned down even further. Robinson looked across at me and shook his head. 'It's like a fuckin' sauna in here,' he said. The driver was talking about his father's ranch in Oklahoma and his uncle's ranch in Montana. They were apparently where he would rather be.

An Iraqi car lay on its side by the road. It was a black-ened wreck surrounded by scorch marks. Two corpses lay around it. One had been blown completely in half, its arms stuck out by rigor mortis, so that it looked like an Action Man toy pulled apart at the waist and then discarded. The other had had its head blown off. It lay facing the tarmac, the blackened hole at the top of the neck targeting us as we drove passed. No one else on board seemed to see them, the conversation continuing as if I had imagined the entire scene.

The radio warned of suspicious vehicles parked on the road ahead. There was a lorry and, opposite it, a white car with its bonnet open. As we passed them Thompson rolled down the window and pointed his grenade launcher at the car. An Iraqi, who had been working on the engine, stood up, staring at us with a mixture of terror and bemusement.

We were entering the outer edges of habitation now. There were electricity pylons lying on the desert where they had fallen, others bent at the base so their wires trailed along the ground. Then we reached the Euphrates, the water so blue after the grey of the dust and sand. A thin band of green vegetation was visible around its edges and white horses raced along the water's surface.

The village of the Iraqi whose death was being investigated was like all the others in Anbar: concrete boxes clustered in the middle of nothingness. I was led to a house and sat on a red plastic chair by the front entrance as the marines talked to the family inside. A score of troops had been positioned on the surrounding roads to stop any surprises.

I looked through the window. There was a lot of talking going on. The Americans adopted serious expressions. A woman dressed from head to foot in black robes started crying and shaking her arms at them. A group of Iraqi men appeared from a back-room and also started gesticulating. The American soldiers watched the new arrivals wearily. I was told to stay where I was when I asked a US soldier if I could get closer to hear what was being said. The woman opened the door and placed a grey T-shirt at my feet. It was covered in dried blood, spreading in ever lighter rings from a small burn hole at its centre. Her whole body was shaking. The American troops told their judge advocate it was time to leave.

As we walked back to the Humvees I asked if anyone now had a better understanding about how the Iraqi had been killed in the raid. They didn't, or at least not one they wanted to share. So what would happen? 'Give them money to shut 'em up,' I was told, though by one of the soldiers rather than the military investigator.

My Humvee crew were drinking Red Bulls as I got in. This time, as we made our way along the road, all of them spotted the dead bodies.

'Did you see that!' Lathrop shouted. 'That's half a

person. Can we go back so I can take a picture? That was pretty cool. Go on. Just quickly, one picture, that's all.'

'We really blew that shit up,' Thompson observed. 'They shouldn't have tried to bury a roadside bomb. They got what they deserved.'

Whatever my reason for visiting the Americans, it was nonetheless a good break from Baghdad. Such was the reality of Iraq that operating in the capital was the opposite of normal reporting. Usually journalists sought out the dramatic. In Baghdad that was the last thing anyone wanted to come across. The consequences could be far too severe. A good day was a quiet one. Being with the Americans meant they were in charge of my security. I could simply concentrate on doing my job. There was something therapeutic and relaxing in that.

The US's smaller bases – FOBs, forward operating bases, they were called – were relatively austere. Most had been set up in old Ba'athist buildings or army barracks to which little was added but protective barriers and watchtowers. These were intended as temporary camps, sites to be occupied only until the Iraqi army was ready to take control of them.

The larger US bases may have been covered in the same ubiquitous sand and dust but they had a far greater sense of permanence and, as a result, far more effort had been made to ensure they held as many familiar comforts as possible. The US government liked to ensure its troops did not suffer too much deprivation in the field. I routinely saw American soldiers cooking themselves hot dogs, playing ball or enjoying the latest series of *Lost*; everyday activities which created an impression of unexpectedly normal people that was hard to reconcile with the knowledge of the brutality that was their day job.

In the Hamra, I lived off poor-quality kebabs. In US mess halls there were typically rib-eye steaks, burgers, tortillas, salad bars, fridges boasting twenty different kinds of soft drink, chocolate cookies and even Ben and Jerry's ice cream stands. Camps routinely had recreation centres which offered special dance nights boasting evenings of hip-hop, salsa or country and western music. Some bases had cinemas. Never have I heard an audience laugh as long or as loudly as a group of marines did while watching Brad Pitt beat up Angelina Jolie in *Mr and Mrs Smith*.

Al-Assad, the main airbase in Anbar province, was one of the US's biggest camps and consequently one of its best equipped. It spread over more than five square miles and had two bus routes in it. Red 'Stop' signs, the ubiquitous furniture of American streets, had been placed at its road junctions and US mailboxes installed. Subway, a coffee shop and a pizza parlour were open for business, their counters manned by nervous, if friendly, Indian contract workers from west Bengal. The base had its own football pitch and swimming pool. Its recreation room was kitted out with PlayStations and Xboxes. There were pool tables and a basketball court. On 4 July, pig carcasses were flown in and roasted. Screens were set up so the troops could watch the Super Bowl. The camp even had its own Hertz car rental office providing 4x4s with bullet-proof windows for those wanting to cross camp in something more comfortable than a military Humvee.

It was not only material comforts that the US sought to provide for its servicemen in the midst of a war zone on the other side of the world. A military survey had shown that the soldiers' greatest concern was not being killed or injured but the breakdown of relationships. Divorce, rather than death, was what they meant when they talked about the 'big D'. So America's armed forces had done what they could to help those in the field maintain contact with their families. International calls were subsidised and, most significantly, almost every serviceman had access to a free internet terminal.

Never before had soldiers fighting abroad been so connected to home. This was not an environment where letters were sent with sensitive information blacked out by censors. People were instant-messaging their friends and loved ones directly. They could e-mail, set up internet sites, post pictures, use all the wonders of the multimedia age. The internet was so popular that by the end of 2005 there were 200 blogs being updated regularly by active servicemen in Iraq.

This inevitably created its own problems for the military. A national guardsman was demoted after writing on his blog that his company commander was a 'glory seeker' and his battalion sergeant major an 'inhuman monster'. The Pentagon finally had to ban access to YouTube after there were complaints about the number of gory videos being uploaded onto it from Iraq. However, the internet permitted an unprecedented level of awareness in the States of what the troops were experiencing and the problems they faced. Anyone, for example, wanting to know how their friend Elizabeth Le Bel, a 24-year-old sergeant on her first combat posting, was doing needed only to check the latest missive on her blog. One of them even came from the computer at a military hospital hours after the vehicle she was in had been hit by a roadside bomb. 'I started to scream bloody murder, and one of the other females on the convoy came over, grabbed my hand and started to calm me down,' she wrote. 'She held on to me, allowing me to place my leg on her shoulder as it was hanging free. I learned that the driver [of my vehicle] had not made it through, and that is a very tough thing for me. Thankfully, it was quick, I am told.' It must have been a challenging read for those who had known her in better times.

I often wondered how this level of connectivity affected family and friends back in the States. It certainly must have made the worry that something bad had happened more immediate. When a soldier was killed the first thing his base did was shut down its internet connection until the bereaved family had been notified. Wives were no longer waiting for a figure in dress uniform to come knocking on their front door. They were panicking the moment they discovered there was no one replying to their e-mails.

I visited a camp where a battalion had managed to find a local contractor who could set up WiFi in their barracks. The soldiers barely talked to each other at night as they sat in their cubicles browsing pornography or engaging in cybersex with women back in the States.

On another trip I sat next to a gunnery sergeant in the military internet café at a base in al-Qaim. This was one of the most isolated places in Iraq, a camp located right on the Syrian border, where, during the summer of 2005, the Americans routinely fought al-Qa'eda supporters wanting to cross into Iraq's heartland. It was a battle zone in which one of the American FOBs was so exposed, and so routinely attacked, that those stationed in it had burrowed their barracks underground, covering the tops with reinforced concrete as protection from the mortar fire.

The gunnery sergeant had just come back from a night-time operation. Caked in sand and grime, he was talking to his wife on instant messenger. It was snowing in their home town and she could not find the shovel to clear the yard. He was patiently explaining to her exactly where it was hung in the garage. I asked him if he minded being bothered with such domestic inconveniences. 'Not at all,' he told me. 'Means I don't have to worry there's a problem back home that she's strugglin' to cope with.'

Once, when in Kirkuk, I saw a soldier in his base's internet room bow his head and start praying. Looking at his computer screen I realised that he was communicating with his wife via webcam. She was praying too. He later told me that, as long as operations allowed it, they would pray together at the same time each day for his safe return home.

It was while I was with the US forces invading Iraq in the early days of the war that I first understood what American soldiers are trained to deliver when it is demanded of them. It has coloured my attitude to the military ever since. Not necessarily for better or for worse, it is simply that you cannot look at anyone in uniform the same way after witnessing what they do for a living.

It was on Thursday, 3 April 2003, the day the US army took Baghdad airport and for the first time positioned its forces on the outskirts of the city, that I learnt what this involved. I was travelling with a US tank company, part of the mass of soldiers spreading across Iraq. The previous night our camp had been located on the edge of the Euphrates valley, a place where the roads were bordered by three-foot-high grass and clumps of palm trees flourished beside meandering streams. We had now been told to move towards the capital and into the debris of the fighting that had gone on ahead of us.

I was in the back of an M113, an armoured van that acted as the unit's mobile control centre, and as we made our way forward I looked down into a line of foxholes dug by the Iraqi forces and saw the dead lying in them. There was what must have been a small truck, now just twisted metal sheets. An Iraqi tank had been hit so hard that it had been scattered in a circle fifty yards wide. In an orchard was a dead member of the Iraqi army's most elite unit, the Republican Guard. He was lying on his back amid the rotting fruit, his helmet having rolled down a slope and come to a stop at the roadside.

The shooting started at mid-morning, ten to ten to be precise. It began as a salvo in the distance and then spread until it surrounded us on all sides and there was no escape from the constant sound of combat. Many of the Iraqi soldiers were hidden in foxholes. Others were perched on the roofs of buildings. Cars and pick-up trucks drove up side roads to fire off a round before trying to escape. Banks of missiles were attached to the backs of trucks. Men who had been hit half a dozen times still crawled towards their weapons to have one last shot. Soldiers in the path of American tanks stood their ground to fire their machine guns. The air above was filled with the twisting trails of rocket-propelled grenades and missiles.

I hid at the bottom of the vehicle. I could see nothing; the fighting was merely noise. There was no space in my brain for anything but the necessity of picking up every sound that might explain what was happening on the other side of the metal walls in which I was encased. Above me towered an American soldier who was half in and half out the back hatch. He loaded, aimed, fired, loaded, aimed, fired his grenade launcher. His left leg was twitching. At one point he reached down and cut free a box of extra ammunition. He stared at me with vacant eyes as he filled his pockets with so many shells that they spilled out and rolled around his feet.

The gun casings from the .50-caliber fixed at the front fell through the cockpit in a metal waterfall that bounced off the floor around me. I reached down and picked one up. It was burning hot to the touch.

The machine gunner leaned down to light a cigarette. 'You havin' fun yet?' he asked.

It took four hours to reach the outskirts of Baghdad, but when we did the shooting that had surrounded us stopped as suddenly as it had begun. We parked in a small field beside a street sign pointing towards the international airport a few miles to our west. I pulled open the back hatch and stepped out onto the dark green grass, its blades wide as table knives, and looked at the men around me. Soldiers were climbing from their vehicles, and they too stood staring at each other. Smoke was rising everywhere.

A tall black soldier was walking towards me. His name was Sergeant Scott. I had never seen him before and I never saw him again. 'When do we know when this all ends?' he said. 'When do we know when it's all over? How much longer can this go on? There's been a whole load of killing.'

A group of soldiers had gathered nearby. 'I put five rounds, perfectly placed, in the centre of his chest,' one was saying. 'But he wouldn't go down. I could see him still reaching to try to load another rocket-propelled grenade and I changed my machine gun to three-round bursts and sent two into his throat and one right through his forehead.'

'There was a guy at a big fuckin' machine gun and I was pepperin' his bunker with rounds. First Sergeant saw him too and fired off a grenade. It exploded and I saw this arm fly out and roll through the air. The blast blew up all this dirt. It was so hard it felt like shrapnel and I thought I'd been hit. I reached for my face and found there was no blood so I just got straight back into it.'

The driver of the M113 in which I had made that journey was sitting in the cockpit smoking a cigarette. His face was shiny with sweat. 'Did you see it?' he asked me. 'There were dead people everywhere. When I see that many dead bodies it's time to go home.'

He was not one of those who re-enlisted when his time was up. He is a postman now, driving a van along a route in Atlanta.

During the Vietnam War, GIs who had done well, or who had done something so bad it was felt they should get away from the combat zone for a few days, were sent to China Beach. It was a stretch of sand facing the Bay of Danang where, between the swimming and surfing, soldiers and marines were encouraged to put the war behind them and party. That they did with a passion. The booze flowed, the vice girls laboured and the smell of marijuana drifted on the breeze. At night the bars that had sprung up along the shoreline played Jimi Hendrix and the Rolling Stones.

There was nowhere in Iraq that was considered safe enough for US troops to go for rest and recuperation. In this war the four-day mini-break from fear was an air force base in Qatar. By 2005 everyone who had served four months in Iraq was eligible for one visit per tour. Troops flew in around the clock, C-130s depositing their uniformed cargo, and buses ferried the new arrivals to the self-styled welcome centre. There it was quickly made clear what kind of stay could be expected.

Sex was strictly banned and any trips off base prohibited except as part of an organised tour. Alcohol was limited to three beers a night, a limit that would be monitored via a computer logging system that required military IDs to be swiped with each purchase. The only stimulant available in plentiful supply would be chocolate and cans of Coca-Cola.

There was no Jimi Hendrix here, not even any White Stripes. Instead the song that greeted the new arrivals as they walked into the welcome centre was Mariah Carey's 'Hero'.

The Americans had spent a lot of money on the recreation complex. The events on offer included horseshoe-throwing competitions, the occasional comedian, volleyball games and a chess tournament. There was a giant gym, swimming pool, pizza restaurant and burger bars. DVD screens and a mini-cinema filled the main building and pastel-coloured sofas had been provided for this generation's warriors to rest on.

The centrepiece of the facility was its computer-games room. At work these soldiers were expected to kill and maim. As relaxation they were offered a chance to spend time in the modern American teenager's fantasy living room complete with beanbags, Xboxes and unlimited amounts of snack food. GIs could while away the hours in pretend combat while a male Filipino attendant provided sweets and drinks on demand, bringing them straight to their tables so they did not even have to step away from the consoles.

Anything more daring was strictly off-limits. When a two-week tour of installations in Iraq and Kuwait by a scantily clad female group, the Purrrfect Angels, was staged in 2004, one female officer reported it as sexually offensive and the person who organised it was reprimanded.

The older soldiers primarily spent their time talking to their wives and children on the free telephones. The young ones mostly decided the best distraction was the pool, which was where I found them when I visited the base in the spring of 2005. The few female GIs present had clustered in a group at one end while the boys stared hungrily at them.

'It's like a correctional facility,' I heard one soldier say as a group discussed their officially sanctioned release from danger.

'There is just enough beer that it's a tease.'

'How do we get out of here and find some action?'

'I miss being back on base. At least it's not boring there.'

'This is a severely limited hunting ground. What're you to do for pussy?'

In the gym dozens of soldiers silently pumped weights while staring at the provocative music videos being played on the television screens around them.

At night the military police came out in force and patrolled the paths between the accommodation tents. There were two nightclubs. In them soldiers showed off their hip-hop moves, men mostly having to dance with men, each seeking to prove their skills as they padded out the time they took drinking their lagers. The fundamentalist Christians and the recovering alcoholics were petitioned to spread their three-strong allocation wide.

One of the camp officials showed me around. She told me it was necessary to have strict rules to ensure that soldiers acted in line with the contemporary moral values of the Pentagon and the base's Arab hosts. What did she think was the best thing the camp offered? 'Sleep,' she said. 'These soldiers can have some time away from their operation zones and catch up on sleep. That'll help them the most when they get back.'

I noticed that extra lighting was being put up in the lanes that divided the rows of tents. I asked her what it was for. It was apparently to aid safety at night by ensuring everywhere was suitably well lit. I had heard stories of female soldiers being sexually abused and fights breaking out as rival units squared up to each other. She was not at liberty to talk about that. The rules were there to ensure everyone's safety, she said.

In the beauty centre there was a massage parlour, but it was not the vice den the words would have implied to those American soldiers who fought in the paddy fields of South-east Asia. It was run by the military and a sign on the door stated, 'All male patrons are required to wear briefs during the entirety of their session.'

A sniper based in Samarra was seen getting his nails manicured. Apparently he did not want them to interfere with the smoothness of his trigger finger. He had considered getting his toes done at the same time but decided against it as he had extremely ticklish feet.

The memory of the Vietnam War cast its shadow over Iraq. It was why in briefings US High Command would bristle at the word quagmire. It was why American commanders liked talking about post-war Germany or Japan but never about Saigon. It was why no one would accept any parallels to that earlier conflict even as they followed the same policies of building up a local, hastily trained army and bolstering a corrupt and hated government.

The American soldiers doing the fighting had grown up hearing about that war. It was the one many of their fathers and uncles had fought in. It was why they watched so carefully what was happening in America in case they were not going to receive the homecoming promised. It was why there was not a camp I went to that did not have its messages of support from people in the US on prominent display. American schools, business associations, women's organisations and welfare groups would routinely send banners pledging their gratitude to the troops stationed in Iraq. They were hung in mess halls and by briefing rooms to make sure the soldiers knew their efforts were being appreciated and they had not been forgotten.

As a teenager I had also watched films and read books about Vietnam, drawn to its twisted glamour and exoticism. I had once half expected, maybe even hoped, to find in Iraq an American army of rebels and soul-loving African-Americans. The reality was as far from that as you could possibly imagine for this American army was no Vietnam draft.

In Iraq, the US soldiers I met were usually in impassioned awe of their weaponry and in love with what it could do for them. Air strikes or artillery barrages would be accompanied by whooping and excited discussions about the size of the blast and how they really 'blew that shit up'. They were often unthinkingly patriotic and convinced nowhere in the world could compare with the U S of A, certainly not Iraq where, I would be told, the people did not even care enough about their nation to pick up garbage from the streets. They were as nervous as anyone would be at the prospect of being blown up and gave me the impression that they would kill anyone their officers instructed them to. Though they had their faults it did not mean they were undisciplined, at least in most cases, or doubted the ethos of their country and corps. They were people had signed up to be soldiers and had trained for it. This was a professional army and, nearly every time I saw it in action, it acted as such. It may not have always been right, but it was usually ordered.

The servicemen in the American military normally shared the deep moral certainties that form Middle America. I saw soldiers visibly emotional and angry at witnessing the level of destitution the country had been reduced to by Saddam and the war. Units in Kurdish areas were particularly affected by what the civilians around them had endured. Most soldiers gave every impression of genuinely feeling for the plight of the ordinary Iraqis, or at least of having persuaded themselves that they did. Nor were they hesitant about telling me as much. It was rare to come across an American of any rank who did not volunteer that one of their fundamental motivations was to help the Iraqis and give them that most precious and mythologised of American gifts: freedom.

Few can guilt-trip as well as a US soldier trying to make you feel bad about doubting their ability to achieve what they have set out to – or, worse, their right to interfere. This was often what used to aggravate me the most and was what I had least expected to find. Most soldiers I met, particularly in the first years of the conflict when doubts in ultimate success had yet to set in, held strongly to the belief that the sacrifices and dangers they endured were worth it if they were making people's lives better. The sincerity that came with this belief could at times be overwhelming, its forthrightness making it only harder to take, for this was not how it seemed to me that the war was being playing out beyond the razor wire that marked the edge of their bases.

The Iraqis I talked to nearly all had their story of when they or one of their family members had American soldiers turn over their homes for no good reason. I had seen for myself, when I was with the troops advancing on Baghdad, the difficulty the Americans had in determining innocents from combatants in the heat of battle, particularly as those they fought often wore civilian clothes. The soldiers had admitted as much, worried after the fighting had finished whether they had chosen right or accidentally killed non-combatants. In April 2003 I heard a sergeant describe to one of his friends, a soldier called Trey Black, what happened when his vehicle had come under fire from all sides and he had started firing back. He feared he had hit two people who had merely been trying to hide after finding themselves caught in the crossfire.

'I saw the tops of their heads behind a berm and I shot them,' he said.

'That's why you've got to wait and see them shoot at you,' Black answered. 'You're here to die, boy.'

'But that's the thing,' the sergeant said. 'I'm not.'

My trip to Kufa in 2004 had made me realise that US air strikes were not as clinical as those organising them wanted to believe. Barely a month went by without accusations from Iraqis somewhere in the country that civilians had been killed during a military operation. It was nearly always impossible to know for certain whether these reports were true, but there were so many of them that it was inconceivable that none were. To me there was no question that the operations the American High Command so loved to celebrate resulted in their troops assaulting streets and fields where at least some of those hit had never held a weapon in anger.

Nonetheless I believed the American soldiers when they talked about the intent of their actions, if not their consequences. They were too American in character; too committed to that American conviction that they were the 'good guys' who did the right things. Moreover many were religious, which only added to the urgency of their need to believe that they were acting on the side of righteousness. The soldiers who made up the US military in Iraq were primarily drawn from poor white families from the American south and first-generation Hispanics. Both were instinctively God-fearing. It was what made it so confusing spending time with them, that contradiction again between how the soldiers would behave when

I met them and what they did for their work. When I interviewed them they talked of body counts and the destructive impact of various types of weaponry. When I spoke to them in private, God and Jesus were the figures they were most likely to name-check. Amid the girlie posters stuck to the walls above their sleeping cots would be crucifixes or a prayer to be recited before sleeping.

I once attended a service held by a Southern Baptist, the Reverend Raymond Folsom, for a unit stationed in the midst of the desert. The altar was a cardboard box resting on the back of a Humvee over which a green cloth had been placed along with a cup and a crucifix, their silver plating dulled by exposure to the elements. Another box covered with a camouflage mat stood in front of the chaplain as a lectern. Many of the assembled soldiers clutched their own Bibles, some embossed with gold.

Reverend Folsom cried out praise to Jesus and called on God's protection in times of danger. He told stories of Old Testament prophets who had lived in Mesopotamia. 'Pray, as many times Israel won its battles because they prayed,' he said, 'because it's God who wins battles, whatever your technology. Pray.'

One of the soldiers called for a prayer for his family. Another that he might one day find his own 'special lady'. Reverend Folsom led a rendition of 'Amazing Grace'. An Apache helicopter flew overhead as the congregation was exhorted to raise their voices to offer the final verse as a prayer to God: ''Tis grace hath brought me safe thus far, and grace will lead me home.' The next week he had already planned that the hymn would be 'Onward Christian Soldiers'.

Forty-five per cent of Americans believe that God created the world some time in the last 10,000 years and 59 per cent believe in the message of the Book of Revelation. Seventeen per cent go as far as to say they believe the end of the world will happen within their lifetime. This meant that in the American military there were inevitably some whose passion to be righteous involved more than the satisfaction of religious certainty. Among the soldiers fighting in Iraq there were Christians who viewed what was happening in religious, rather than solely political or military, terms.

I saw an awful lot of soldiers reading the books of Tim LaHaye. Almost totally unknown in Europe, this former Southern Baptist minister is a literary phenomenon in America. His 16-book *Left Behind* series has sold 65 million copies and topped the *New York Times* bestseller list four times. The books are good old-fashioned action adventure stories but their thrust is wholly theological, based on the Book of Revelation and St Paul's Epistle to the Thessalonians. Inspired by pre-millenialism, they teach that conditions are going to get a lot worse before they get better. They say that disasters and wars are good things, signs that the Second Coming is approaching, and that when the day comes Christ will descend from heaven and summon all the true believers, who will instantly disappear in an event known in Christian eschatology as the Rapture. Left behind will be the unbelievers: not only atheists and non-Christians, but Roman Catholics, Lutherans and the rest.

Largely as a result of his literary success, LaHaye was named ahead of Billy Graham as the most influential Christian leader in the US in the past 25 years by the

Institute for the Study of American Evangelicals. The ninth book in the series, which came out in 2001, was the biggest-selling book of the year, ousting John Grisham from the top spot for the first time in more than half a decade. He had met George Bush, and proudly says that the President made clear he was a fan.

In the first of his *Left Behind* books, LaHaye's beliefs were given a particularly dramatic setting. The moment of the Rapture comes just as Rayford Steele, the flawed hero whose journey through the series is one towards salvation, is piloting a commercial craft across the Atlantic to Heathrow. People suddenly disappear from his plane leaving behind their clothes in their seats and an atmosphere of total panic. Steele turns the plane around and when he descends to land in Chicago smoke is rising across the city. Cars, their drivers having suddenly disappeared, crash. A plane, whose pilot was amongst God's chosen, plummets into the ground, killing all on board. People are left terror-stricken as loved ones vanish before their eyes.

In line with LaHaye's religious teachings, what follows in its sequels is seven years of catastrophes before Christ reappears and defeats the Antichrist in a final battle between good and evil, thereby establishing his rule in peace for a thousand years.

I met LaHaye once, shortly after I got back to America from covering the initial invasion of Iraq. I was not expecting the smiling septuagenarian with dyed brown hair who met me at his condo by a golf course in Palm Springs. He was utterly charming and hospitable but it was still one of my more unusual interviews. He had a particularly detailed view of heaven and was keen to reassure me that, although single at the time, I would not be left alone after the Rapture if I embraced God because there would probably be singles groups there.

'If you're alive, your body will be transformed, as it's a corruptible body that needs to be made incorruptible for heaven,' he told me. 'Remember when Jesus rose from the dead? He still looked the same and could eat food, but he could walk through walls. He had an incorruptible body. Scripture says that we will be like Jesus. He was 33 so we assume that everyone will be transformed to their appearance at that age.

'The thousand years of the Millennium Kingdom will be magnificent. We know from the Bible that there'll be trees that each month will grow a different fruit. It will be familiar to this world, but more perfect. Sheep will still be sheep. Grass will be grass. But they will be perfect. What happens after that, none of us can imagine.'

He continued, 'I've had such a fun life serving the Lord so I trust Him completely that I'll be happy doing so for a thousand years. We've been told that we will be able to travel at the speed of thought. Personally, I plan to go planetary exploring.'

He was particularly interested in what was happening at that moment in the Middle East because it was a location at the centre of his literary series. In it the Antichrist is the head of the United Nations, and runs troops called Peacekeepers. His base is orientated around the site of ancient Babylon, which happens to be located only a short distance south-east of Baghdad. There is an awful lot of fighting by God's army across Mesopotamia in LaHaye's books. It must have been an interesting plot twist to have come across for his readers in the American military.

'We're living in very scary times,' LaHaye told me. 'I've studied the signs and I can tell you that our generation has more reason to believe that Christ will return in our life-time than any generation in the history of the Church.'

It was shortly before Easter 2005 that I first realised such beliefs were not unknown among the American troops fighting in Iraq. I was in a US convoy, thirty or forty lorries along with some Humvees and a few Bradley tanks added for protection, on the motorway that heads west out of Baghdad and across the border towards Damascus. For safety reasons convoys like this only travelled at night. That evening the moon was on the wane, so I could not make out much around me, and stars covered the sky.

The road was filled with American vehicles taking men, equipment and supplies to the US bases spread across Iraq's western provinces. We were not, however, going anywhere fast. The radio was reporting that mortars had been raining down somewhere in front and the convoy I was in was waiting for the backlog of cars and trucks to clear. Or maybe we were waiting for the helicopters with their thermo-imaging to come from a nearby strip and check there was no one out there in the darkness still waiting to attack us. The soldiers I was with were not quite sure.

It had already proved to be a particularly difficult journey as the only room available for me was in the back of one of the trucks and it was not a good spot. In a couple of months' time the US would decide journalists could no longer travel this way, the roads having become so dangerous that the military authorities would normally only permit us to be ferried by helicopter. The truck had no roof, and only a two-foot-high wall of armour plating around the sides to provide any form of protection. Two soldiers were in the back with me. One was at the far end, the other right beside me, both of us pressed as close to the shelter of the cab as we could get. We lay on our backs to give the armoured plating the maximum chance of saving us if anything nasty happened.

The soldier next to me, a staff sergeant, was nervous, as was I because it was never good to be stuck in one place for too long if you were in a US military vehicle. He started talking about the war to distract himself from his fears. I could not really see him in the gloom, and anyway I was looking straight up into the edge of the Milky Way, but I could hear him clearly. He had an explanation for what was happening in Iraq and the part he was playing in it that he was keen to share.

'Do you read the Bible?' he asked me.

I would nearly always answer 'yes' to this question because it could make some Americans unsettled if you were not religious.

'Well,' he said, 'in the Bible it says there must be a final battle between good and evil in Mesopotamia. It'll be a time when the Antichrist must be defeated but a time when the fightin' will be so bloody that the rivers will run red with blood. Maybe that is now. Maybe I'm one of those soldiers summoned to fight that battle.'

At the start of 2006 I spent as long as I could jumping from one US base to another. Things were getting very bad in Baghdad and my team's ability to ensure our security felt in doubt, not least because a recent attack on the Hamra hotel where I lived had left us unsettled. I had no desire to be anywhere near the hotel complex and consequently ended up spending almost five weeks away from Baghdad with the American forces. The war was approaching the start of its third year and a number of US troops were already on their second tours, some on their third, most of which had lasted at least a year and some of which had stretched to fourteen months or more. The soldiers knew things were not getting any better because they had seen the situation deteriorate with their own eyes. There was still a general commitment to the mission, to being professional, and a refusal to accept defeat, but it was becoming clear that some of the old certainty was beginning to erode.

It was during that time away from Baghdad that I visited the American camp by Haditha, the town where it was later alleged one of the worst war crimes of the conflict was committed. Only a few weeks before my arrival a unit of marines is said to have methodically gunned down men, women and children, although when I was there this was not yet known. The coming months would bring similar cases from around Iraq: claims that prisoners had been set free so they could be shot while supposedly trying to escape or that drunken US soldiers had raped a 12-year-old girl. It was as if a cancer was growing in the weakest parts of America's exhausted army.

I was only in the camp by Haditha for a few days. The soldiers did not want me to be there and made sure I was on the first convoy out. It was long enough, however, to realise that it was nothing like any base I had visited before.

Haditha is one of Iraq's bad places, a run-down town of ninety thousand people in western Anbar province where the buildings were often merely corrugated shacks and the roads little more than sandy pathways. From the first day the Americans arrived its people had demonstrated their commitment to killing as many of them as possible. Their intransigence, and Haditha's isolation and proximity to the Syrian border, had made the town a perfect point for Iraq's Sunni extremists to congregate. By May 2005 al-Qa'eda ruled it in an alliance with one of the most brutal home-grown insurgent groups, Ansar al-Sunna. Together they decided who lived or died, who got paid, what people wore, what they watched and what they listened to. The right-hand lane on all roads through the town was reserved for their vehicles. All women had to wear headscarves. Pop music and Western films were banned.

Law and order were in their hands. A headmaster who was accused of adultery was whipped with cables 190 times. Two men who robbed a shop were pinned to the ground and had their arms broken with rocks. So many alleged American agents were executed on Haqlania Bridge, the main entrance to the town, that it was renamed by locals the Agents' Bridge and then the Agents' Fridge, in evocation of a mortuary. Severed heads were lined up along the railings that bordered one side.

The American camp was located a half-mile outside Haditha in a hydroelectric dam that spanned the Euphrates. It was the largest such facility in Iraq and one that provided electricity for most of the surrounding region. During the invasion there was concern that the dam might be blown up to disrupt the approaching US troops. A Special Forces unit was dispatched to hold it. For a fortnight there was fearsome fighting until the advancing force finally reached the spot and those attacking the dam abandoned their assaults to adopt guerrilla tactics.

An American deployment had been there ever since.

These troops did not like to go out much, and when they did they usually went in numbers, launching raids backed by armour and aircraft. During these sallies there would be a relative calm and then the Americans would go back to their base, the extremists would move back into Haditha from the surrounding countryside, and things would continue as before. American movements would be disrupted by roadside bombs and snipers, and the occasional mortar or rocket would be fired towards the dam to show who was really in charge.

Even though I knew nothing of the allegations about the marines' recent massacre – that story would not break for another month – it was clear from the moment I arrived that the American troops stationed by Haditha had gone feral. Their main link with the outside world was the convoys that came up from the US camp at al-Assad and they did not arrive very often. The marines, trapped in their slice of territory, had largely been able to determine their own limits and institutional discipline gave every impression of approaching breakdown.

This was not one of those American camps with its coffee shops and polite soldiers who whiled away their rest hours playing computer games or talking about girls back home. This was a place where marines had abandoned their official living quarters to set up their own encampments with signs ordering outsiders to keep out. The daily routine was punctured by the dam's emergency alarm as its antiquated and crumbling machinery risked total collapse.

The dam was made of the same yellow-stained concrete that almost every building in Iraq was etched from. It was at least one hundred and fifty yards long and rose three hundred yards into the air on the downstream side. At its ends were two accommodation blocks, each a series of warren-like floors. Both had at least a dozen different levels and it was in these that the American troops lived, occupying the rooms that had previously acted as offices for the facility's Iraqi engineers. Inside, the grinding noise of the dam's equipment made hearing difficult. The whole place stank of rotten eggs, apparently a by-product of the grease used to keep the turbines running. Lighting provided only a half-gloom. The lifts were smashed.

The washrooms were at the top of the dam and the main lavatories at its base. With around eight hundred steps between them, some did not bother to use the official facilities. Small camps had been built around the dam's entrances. One night I went into one of them looking for a cigarette lighter. A Portakabin had been appropriated and its entrance surrounded by a wooden fence against which were piled empty cans of food, water bottles and tattered magazines. A fire had been lit and a marine, his head covered by a black balaclava against the evening chill, was pulling apart planks of wood with his dirt-encrusted hands in order to feed it. The place stank of urine and smoke. On the door to the cabin was a picture of a skull and crossbones. I knocked on it and pushed the door open. Inside four figures illuminated by the light of a battery-powered lantern were playing cards. Rugs were wrapped around them. Half the room was filled with rubbish. Pictures of half-naked women covered the walls. No one volunteered their lighter.

Unlike in every other stint with American forces, at Haditha I was not allowed to interview a senior officer properly. The only soldiers willing to speak at length were those from a small Azerbaijani contingent whose role was to marshal into and out of the facility the band of Iraqi engineers who kept the dam's machinery going. The US troops liked the Azerbaijanis. 'They have looser rules of engagement,' one said admiringly in a rare conversation.

The camp commandant had a giant poster on the wall behind his desk. It was a cartoon of a terrified-looking Arab in a tribal headdress being stared down by a scowling President Bush. 'You can tell those fuckers with the laundry on their heads that it's washday,' the slogan said.

I busied myself researching who these people were. The battalion had undergone three tours in Iraq in two and a half years. On their last tour more than thirty had died, most when the unit was in the vanguard of the attack on Fallujah. They had been Colonel Shupp's people, among his heroes of Fallujah – his new 'greatest generation' – that he had told me about when I visited Camp Fallujah the previous year while the Warrior Transition sessions were being conducted. These men had left a few weeks before my stay at the camp with the same promises that the worst was now over and that they had done their bit to ensure the war was won. Then they were sent to Haditha after only seven months away.

Six marines had died in three days during August. In nearby Parwana, fourteen died shortly afterwards in the most deadly roadside bomb attack of the war so far. The day before my arrival one soldier had shot himself in the head with his M-16. No one would discuss with me what had happened.

There was only one American civilian at the dam, an engineer sent out five months earlier by the US government to work with the Iraqis to keep the facility

violently they were left paralysed. One prisoner had been blindfolded for three months and electrocuted almost every day.

A Sunni welfare group contacted Ahmed saying it had photographs of Sunnis who were tortured after being arrested by the police. The pictures' provenance was impossible to verify but the mutilation was sickening. One figure had burn marks on the chest, welts on the ribs, scars across one arm and two bullet holes in the head. Another had had both legs broken and his nose smashed. It was reminiscent of the worst Ba'athist excesses. However, this was now happening in a country supervised by American and British forces.

Unsubstantiated rumours circulated among Iraqis of secret Swiss bank accounts into which government funds were being diverted. Corruption was certainly endemic. After one flight into Iraq I was asked at the airport for a bribe by one of the customs men if I wanted to avoid the laborious process of him going through my bags. When Ahmed had to secure the immigration documents that allowed me to work as a journalist in Baghdad, a process he had to go through every time I arrived in the country, he took with him a pile of dollars to smooth over complications. 'Give praise to the new Iraq,' he would say as he disappeared out of our office.

Throughout 2005, ministers routinely made trips to Najaf to seek advice on legislation from Grand Ayatollah Sistani. Politicians would use parliamentary sessions as a stage on which to expound the depth of their religious convictions. Imams were invited to comment on proposed legislation. Religious programming began to dominate parts of the state television network. Asmaa, Abu Omar's sister who I had met while watching the Iraqi football team's match against Saudi Arabia, and for whom not wearing a hijab was a point of principle, said she was now sometimes called a 'whore' if she walked outside unveiled. On Shia festivals crowds of worshippers took to the streets, at times with catastrophic consequences. A thousand people died during one pilgrimage when there was a stampede on a bridge over the Tigris. After that incident bodies were being pulled from the water for days.

Unable to sack anyone or move ministers around due to the delicate state of his ruling coalition, Jaafari was rarely able to assert his authority in the cabinet. Government departments became political fiefdoms that rarely communicated with each other and had their own security forces that operated at their minister's discretion. Despite his office's theoretical powers, Jaafari was often reduced to merely adjudicating on who would live in which former Ba'athist mansion.

The debate during the summer of 2005 on what should be included in the text of Iraq's new constitution confirmed the impression of a political system in crisis. The Americans had gambled that the constitutional process would unite the country. Instead it appeared only to harden divides.

Shia politicians, with the help of their Kurdish political allies, used the overwhelming parliamentary majority they had secured as a result of the Sunni election boycott to force through what they wanted against all objections. The American ambassador pleaded with them for moderation, saying his country had already expended too much 'blood' and 'treasure' for an equitable solution to be abandoned. When the draft constitution was published at the end of August it was clear he had been largely ignored. There was little in it to imply the future would not be just as painful as the present. The US even had to accept its failure to establish Iraq as a secular state. The document's second article sanctioned Islam as a 'basic source of legislation'.

The draft constitution contained a system of federalism that would make Iraq one of the most decentralised states in the world. If approved, any of the country's eighteen provinces could hold a referendum on whether to become a semi-independent region. They would then have the right to ensure their 'internal security'. This clause had been demanded by the Kurds to preserve the autonomy of their peshmerga fighters, the Kurdish warriors who throughout the 1980s had fought a war of independence against Saddam's soldiers. It raised the spectre of regions having their own paramilitaries operating under the label of specialist local police units. With most of the Shia population in the south, Sunnis in the west and Kurds in the north, each region could potentially have its own private armies and be sanctioned by the state to do so.

Shia politicians maintained that federalism was necessary to prevent another Saddam emerging as it neutered the centralised powers he had exploited to subjugate the entire country. To its Sunni opponents, however, it simply looked like a plot conceived in Iran to break up Iraq and gain de facto control over the Shia south and its vast oil reserves.

Three days before polling day I watched a group of election workers, tasked with encouraging Iraqis to vote in the constitution, visit the Baghdad district of Karrada to hand out baseball caps and badges featuring pro-democracy slogans. The authorities had promised it would be a neutral 'go and vote' exercise but the atmosphere changed as 200 people swarmed around the electioneers, becoming one that reflected the real issue of the campaign: sectarian rivalry. This was a largely Shia area and the traditional folk songs being played turned into Shia religious songs. Women in black robes appeared on balconies as the crowd whipped itself into a frenzy. 'Shia, Shia, Shia, vote yes, vote yes, vote yes,' they chanted.

The government had created a lavishly produced pro-constitution advertisement to be broadcast on Iraq's TV stations. It was as glossy as any that might be seen in Britain or the United States during an election campaign. To the sound of nationalist music, a young boy first gathered stones in the desert and placed them to form an outline of Iraq. Dozens of men and women in different ethnic and religious dress then emerged with their own stones, each coloured a lighter or darker shade of brown, which they placed to form a wall. As the music reached a climax, the camera pulled back to reveal a crowd of smiling, embracing people and the coloured bricks spelling the word 'constitution'.

The problem, as the local press reported, was that none of those joyful figures were Iraqi. The advert was as much an illusion as its message of unity. Due to fear of revenge attacks, no local actors had been willing to appear in it and therefore the advertisement had been filmed abroad.

The Sunnis did vote when the referendum was held in October on whether the constitution should be adopted. Their exclusion from the parliamentary debate on the constitution's content had made clear that their previous boycott had been a major mistake. It had left them with no legitimate say in the country's political future. The result of the poll, however, only exposed how deep sectarian divides had become. The Shia and Kurds voted overwhelmingly for the constitution, the Sunnis overwhelmingly against it. The constitution passed. The lesson many Sunnis drew from this was that they were unlikely to gain anything through the ballot box.

In December 2005 another national election was staged so that a parliament could be elected under the new rules approved by the referendum. Once again I saw thousands of people lining up to cast their ballots. This time I was watching Sunnis vote as, despite their disillusionment with the referendum result, most were giving the ballot box one last chance. They did not have much of an alternative. The Sunnis' electoral boycott at the start of the year had led to a parliament dominated by their enemies. At the very least they wanted to ensure that this time they had some say in its composition.

I was in Tal Afar, a town in northern Iraq which only six months earlier had been one of the most dangerous places in the country. Located 30 miles west of Mosul, it had been controlled by Sunni extremists who used it as a staging point for suicide bombers coming in from Syria. According to the Americans, horrific atrocities had been committed. There were beheadings and executions. People were grabbed from their homes and tortured if suspected of being Western sympathisers. A mass grave was later found containing twenty-one bodies, nineteen of which had been shot through the back of the head.

In May, the American 3rd Armoured Cavalry Regiment was dispatched to restore order. When US soldiers first approached the town scores of gunmen stood in their path firing rocket-propelled grenades. Taxis had brought up reinforcements. The American commander, Colonel H. R. McMaster, responded by building an embankment around the city. He stationed guards to stop anyone hostile going in and out. His troops then moved into the town itself, using barbed wire to close off each district and clearing them house by house.

The impressive thing about the job McMaster had done was that he had expended as much thought on how to get the town up and running again as he had on the killing of the enemy. In Fallujah, which the US had stormed more than a year earlier, many people were still living in the ruins of their former homes. In Tal Afar the streets were filled with building sites. Shop windows that had been destroyed during the US assault were replaced and new sewers laid. Two thousand goats were distributed to farmers. These were little things but such steps were not normal and that tells its own story of the American failure in Iraq.

The evening before election day, I arrived in the US base on the outskirts of Tal Afar in a military helicopter. As in Amarah the previous January, the soldiers stationed there were nervous that night, uncertain if anyone would come out the next morning to vote and what violence might accompany the ballot. They need not have worried. The following day was mostly peaceful in Tal Afar, bringing only a few mortar rounds and a sole rocket-propelled grenade attack, and the Sunnis came out in their tens of thousands as soon as the polling booths were open.

The polling station I was taken to visit was in a secondary school in the district of Zahawi. It was one of the largest structures in the city, a four-storey concrete block with horizontal windows framing the main entrance and brightly coloured murals of palm trees and oxen lining the corridors. As in most of Tal Afar, work had already started to repair the marks of combat. Bullet holes had been cemented over and walls decorated. A new lick of paint, however, could not hide the gaping holes left by two American Hellfire missiles. They had struck four months earlier, an American soldier told me, when Sunni gunmen turned the school into their command centre. In the aftermath of the fighting to capture the building, mangled bodies had lain in the school's corridors, bloodstains marked the tiled floors and the playground was left pockmarked with craters. Now the school was filled with hundreds of people waiting to vote. It was the smell of drying sweat, not burned flesh, that pervaded its crowded rooms. Similar scenes, I was told, were occurring across the city and in Sunni areas throughout the country. In Fallujah demand for ballot papers was so high it risked outnumbering supply.

Due to concern about suicide bombers, those seeking to vote at the school in Tal Afar had to be frisked three times before they could reach the ballot box, which slowed down the process and left many voters waiting for hours before they had their chance to join the democratic process. The queue stretched from the classrooms where the polling booths were located, through the school's entrance, around the building and down the street. I walked the length of it, trying to gauge the number of people. There were six hundred, maybe a thousand, though it was difficult to judge as families clustered together and individual Iraqis moved from one part of the line to another as they sought out friends with whom to chat. The atmosphere was one of patience and content-ment, despite the gaps in the queue that the US had instructed be left every thirty yards to try to limit the carnage that would follow if anyone did fire a mortar shell at it. Seeing me, many of those waiting smiled and waved.

A week before election day, I had interviewed Iyad Allawi, an Iraqi politician who headed one of the country's largest secular parties, the Iraqi National Accord. He was a committed opponent of the religious political parties and was a confidant of both the American and British ambassadors. His analysis of what would happen if the coalition of Shia religious parties that had won January's vote was again victorious was little less than apocalyptic. Iraq would descend into civil war, he said, unleashing a wave of 'evil forces' around the world.

'The stakes are very high,' he warned. 'Imagine that the same group comes to power for a further four years and maintains the current situation. Everyone will get hit. You can't have the streets of Iraq split between terrorists and insurgents on the one hand and militias on the other.

'If Iraq continues down this route it may dismember and fragment. If it fragments, God forbid, it'll be quite bloody. Not only for Iraq. It will trigger a chain in the whole region, and perhaps beyond, which could not be controlled and this will unleash evil forces throughout the world.'

What would he do, I asked, if the same parties won? 'I'll relocate abroad,' he said, throwing up his hands to indicate he would have little choice.

On election day, similar warnings were repeated by the voters I talked to in Tal Afar. Even in a place that had experienced first hand the worst insurgent excesses, they were still more terrified of the Shia religious extremists than their own fanatics. They were voting, but they were doing so in desperation.

'We want to change the government because this government is attacking Sunnis,' said one man, a 29-year-old Sunni Turkoman who worked as a construction worker in a nearby street. I asked him what would happen if the current government remained in charge. He stroked his moustache. 'I do not know,' he said. 'Only God knows but I fear it will be very bad.'

When the election result was announced the following month it revealed that the same Shia political parties had won. Iraqis had again chosen to vote along ethnic and sectarian lines in overwhelming numbers. The secularists were nearly annihilated. Allawi saw his party's parliamentary seats reduced to half the number won in the election at the start of the year. The coalition created by Ahmed Chalabi, a former Pentagon favourite who had put together a list of secular and nationalist candidates, failed to win a single seat.

This time it was not only Shia but also Sunnis who ignored the moderate political parties. The Shia gave the religious parties backed by their clerics another overwhelming victory. Four-fifths of Sunnis voted for the Islamic Party, the Sunni political party with the most fundamentalist agenda, ensuring it became the largest opposition body in parliament.

The Americans had launched the political process with the objective of giving all factions in Iraqi society a stake in Iraq's future so that they would unite in working together to ensure its stability. The result was a parliament filled with zealots who hated each other. Perhaps it was inevitable. The chaos that had engulfed Iraq was now feeding popular fundamentalism because it made people angry and desperate. This was no environment for promoting moderation.

Throughout 2005, when senior officers in the US military talked to each other about the possibility of civil war they referred to it as the 'subject of which we do not speak'. With the announcement of the December election results came the expectation that they would not be able to avoid speaking about it for much longer.

6. Insurgency

Ahmed did not need an alarm clock. First light would come through the windows of his flat and wake up his daughter, Labibah, who slept in the same bed as her mother and father. Although she was four-years-old, and had her own room, after the war started she became frightened of sleeping by herself, often having nightmares built around the snippets of news about killings and bomb blasts that she had overheard. So it had become the family routine for her to sleep with her parents. Ahmed said he had come to prefer it because if anything bad happened at night – a raid by soldiers or an explosion nearby – he knew immediately where all his family were located so would not lose precious time establishing if they were safe.

When his daughter woke she made sure everyone else was awake too. It was not an unpleasant rising. Labibah, Ahmed told me, would start hugging her mother and father until they gave up their slumbers. They would then take turns to cuddle her. He would hold Labibah to him, place her between his arms and kiss her on the forehead. Their day started with a moment of comfort and love.

By September 2005, the first hour was usually spent trying to preserve the family's propane gas to ensure there was enough to make breakfast, and transferring water from the tanks on the apartment's balcony into the bathroom so the family could wash. The price of gas was rising fast. It had doubled during the previous two months to 20,000 Iraqi dinar a cylinder, which was about $17, a lot in Iraq where the average wage was $300 per month, especially as each canister rarely lasted more than three or four days. In order to limit wastage, as much food as possible would be cooked in the same pan at the same time. This inevitably challenged the skills of the cook, who in Iraq is always one of the women of the household, and therefore in Ahmed's family his wife, Raha. Water was a different problem. As supply could be intermittent, many Iraqi families, Ahmed's included, directed it into tanks so it could be stored in preparation for when nothing came out of the taps. Shortages usually occurred at the time of most demand: the early mornings and late evenings. Ahmed had to carry water in plastic buckets from the storage containers to the bathroom, where those who wanted to wash could scoop it over their bodies.

My day started later. I did not want Ahmed or the rest of my Iraqi staff to arrive at the office too early. The early part of the day often brought some of the worst explosions as roadside bombs buried overnight were detonated by passing US patrols. I asked them to arrive at work at ten. My alarm went off at nine. In my suite at the Hamra I always had electricity, provided by the hotel's generators, and the vast tanks on the roofs of the hotel's twin towers ensured there was a steady supply of water. My morning consequently began with a long shower. I would then usually make myself a cup of coffee and eat a bowl of cereal while watching the news bulletin on BBC World. I was not able to buy either of these food items for myself. Visiting shops was dangerous as I might be identified as a foreigner. Buying a packet of Shredded Wheat did not seem a good enough reason to risk being kidnapped or killed. Instead I drew up a shopping list for my driver, Abu Omar, and every few days he would go and buy me food and also the office supplies I needed.

Even though Ahmed did not have to be at work until ten o'clock, he still left his house at nine. In safer times Dora, the district of Baghdad where Ahmed lived, was only a fifteen-minute drive from the Hamra but, with roads closed off by the war and checkpoints routinely set up by the military to try to catch suicide bombers and those carrying illegal weapons, it now normally took four times as long to complete the journey. Ahmed was always insistent that he did not like to make a big deal of the goodbyes as he headed out of the front door. If he did it would make him and Raha more emotional, which did neither of them much good because he had to work and she knew it. Raha and their daughter would nevertheless come out onto the balcony to watch and wave as he climbed into his car and started his drive across Baghdad.

It normally took him an hour to get to work but it could take longer. On one day in September 2005, Thursday the 8th, it took him almost two hours. The roads on the route he normally took were chaos because four checkpoints had been set up. When he finally arrived at the Hamra he was stressed out and cursing. I was at the computer in my office, trawling the internet to see what had been written about Iraq that day and what developments were being reported on the news wires, when he came in to apologise for being late.

'This wounded country of mine is becoming unbear-able,' he said. 'Four checkpoints today. Four! I would not mind if they were not so useless. At the bridge [crossing the Tigris river] the Iraqi police had closed all the lines on the highway except one. It was a terrible crush as everyone tried to get through. And when we arrived at the checkpoint what do you think was happening? They were not even checking any cars. The policeman liked to sit under the shade of their awning and wave everyone through. I became so mad. They are so useless!'

The rest of the team, Abu Omar, my security guard Marwan, and the second driver Sajad, had come from different parts of Baghdad and had already been at the Hamra for almost an hour. They were sitting watching al-Jazeera on the television, drinking strong coffee from espresso cups. Ahmed began organising them. Abu Omar was asked to go to the offices of Iraqna, the local mobile phone operator, to pay our bill. Marwan and Sajad were instructed to read through a pile of documentation we had received from a Sunni religious welfare group detailing a rise in child malnutrition. Ahmed wanted them to highlight the most pertinent and shocking bits so he could later translate them for me.

I rang the *Telegraph* office in London on the satellite phone. The foreign desk had just arrived at work, the time difference between Britain and Iraq being three hours, and they wanted to discuss what stories I was going to put forward that day. Things were quiet, merely a few routine reports of a US patrol attacked near Ramadi, rumours of a gunfight in Kirkuk, nothing partic-ularly major or out of the ordinary, so the conversation was short. It was arranged I would ring back in two hours to give an update on how the day was developing.

I rang back far quicker than that. Almost as soon as I put down the phone there was the sound of an imploding blast and we knew that somewhere in the city a bomb had gone off. The news reported that the explosion had been in Kadhimiya, a district in north Baghdad that was one of the few Shia enclaves to the west of the Tigris. A car filled with 500lb of explosives had apparently driven into a crowd of unemployed labourers, killing 114 of them and wounding a further 156.

Baghdad's unemployed often gathered in the city's main squares in the hope of picking up some work for the day from a building contractor or factory boss. They knew that if these companies found themselves temporarily short of staff they would drive to where labourers congregated and single out those who looked the most fit and strong. The economic collapse caused by the continuing violence had resulted in thousands of labourers gathering across Baghdad each morning. It appeared that they had now become too tempting a target for the bombers.

This was a big explosion even by Baghdad standards. We prepared ourselves to go to the bomb site. The procedure was that Marwan and Sajad left the office first. They drove around the block outside the Hamra's entrance in our second car to see if anyone appeared to be waiting for us and if anything looked suspicious or out of the ordinary. If it was safe they contacted us on their walkie-talkie and Ahmed, Abu Omar and I would leave the office and climb into Abu Omar's car. Once we had driven around 50 yards from the hotel, Marwan and Sajad would emerge from a side street and slot onto the road behind us. The intention was that the two cars would not be seen leaving the Hamra together, and then stay far enough apart so that anyone watching would not realise they were associated.

The traffic was still terrible and it took us forty-five minutes to get close to Kadhimiya. We were on one of the main highways headed north through the city, an over-pass that enabled us to look down on the streets around us and which had only a handful of entry and exit junctions, thereby limiting the likelihood of someone taking us by surprise. Ahmed was in the front passenger seat, I was in the back. He held the walkie-talkie between his legs. To avoid looking suspicious, he would not look down at it as he spoke to Marwan about the vehicles around us and their likely intent.

We could see the smoke from the fires started by the explosion, the black plume drifting up into the still air, dissipating and curling into mutating clusters. Lines of US and Iraqi army vehicles were visible ahead as they approached the bomb site. Marwan reported that some of them seemed to be slowing down and he was concerned that they might be about to close off the road to secure the area. That would leave us stuck in a traffic jam for hours as the damage caused by the explosion was examined and cleared. Ahmed pointed out that even if we did reach the attack site there would already be so many soldiers at the scene that we would never be able to get close to it. We decided to turn off the highway and head to a nearby hospital to see if there were any wounded there who could talk about what had happened.

The Yarmouk hospital is one of the city's main casualty centres. From the outside it looks like almost every other building in Baghdad, the bricks of its walls covered by an expanse of concrete into which are inlaid rows of domed windows. There was no mistaking the building's function that day as the road in front of it was filled with ambulances and cars dropping off the injured. We had pulled over and parked when a police patrol truck appeared. Half a dozen officers were standing in its back and they started firing their Kalashnikovs into the air to tell the vehicles in front to clear out of their way. When the truck stopped at the hospital entrance, three of the policemen picked up a figure who had been lying in the back, the blood seeping through his blue police uniform visible from where we sat, and carried him into the building. Another officer followed them, turning just before he disappeared inside to fire another burst of gunfire into the sky.

Ahmed turned around from the front seat to look at me. 'Wait in the car,' he said. 'Do not get out. This is not a good situation. I will go inside and find out what it is possible to discover.'

I did as I was told. Abu Omar and I watched him disappear, notebook in hand, into the building. It was twenty minutes before he returned, twenty minutes during which a parade of vehicles dropped off their dying cargos. Ahmed reappeared, notebook still in hand, climbed into the front seat and said, 'It is time to go. I have a good interview. I will tell you about it when we reach the Hamra.'

Back at the office we learnt that there had been other bombs going off, none of which we had heard about or been aware of. It appeared as if they were co-ordinated attacks, intended to feed Baghdad's fear and chaos. A suicide bomber had killed eleven people waiting to fill their gas canisters in the north of the city. An Iraqi police convoy had been hit near the Baghdad offices of Moqtada al-Sadr, killing five and wounding twenty-four. Soldiers training to join the new Iraqi army had been targeted near the northern district of Shu'lah, killing at least two people. In Adhamiya, a Sunni district to the east of the Tigris, gunmen opened fire on a car, killing four. As passers-by rushed to help, a suicide bomber detonated, killing seven more. This was proving to be a particularly bloody day.

Ahmed described the situation in the hospital, reading back his notes. 'It was very bad,' he said. 'Many police were around and they were very angry. I found one of the injured unemployed labourers. His name is Hassam Jabar. He is 32 years old and has five children. He said he considers himself lucky if he gets two days' work a week. He was wearing black baggy trousers that had been cut just below the groin. His left leg was broken and his right leg almost severed at the knee. He was the only one I could find conscious on the ward to talk to. The man beside him had terrible facial injuries.' He grimaced and then gave a little laugh. 'It really was terrible in there!'

He looked back through his notebook. 'Jabar said to me that he had seen the car come in from the east side of the square. It looked normal. "Cars might mean work," Jabar told me. "Everyone moved towards it. There must have been a thousand people. The crowd pushed closer as news spread that the driver was saying he had jobs. People started shouting 'I am a carpenter' or 'I am a painter'. Some were so close to the car they were touching it." At that moment its driver detonated his explosives.'

Ahmed continued, 'Jabar said to me, "I found myself on the ground. There was blood on me. Then I saw there were bodies – many, many bodies – and severed limbs lying around me. Then I heard shooting and I was frightened but my legs could not move. People were running away screaming and shouting. I realised the police were shooting into the air to get people away but I still could not get up. Then people started to grab me and pull me away. I found myself in a minibus. The first hospital was chaos. They could not take any more people so they took me here."

'That was all I got,' Ahmed said. 'A doctor came and told Jabar they had to take him to surgery to have his right leg amputated. The police were starting to look at me in a strange manner so I left.'

For the next few hours, Ahmed and I tried to gain additional information and kept the office in London updated on developments. Abu Omar provided us with cups of tea, while Marwan and Sajad monitored the TV. There was another attack: a US patrol rammed by a suicide bomber. No one at the US military press centre would tell me about the extent of casualties but the Iraqi news channels were showing the burnt-out shell of a Humvee.

At five o'clock, I told everyone to go home. It would get dark soon and the most important thing was that none of them were still out on the streets after dusk. When night came the situation in Baghdad was always particularly dangerous as those seeking to cause harm used its anonymity to conduct their business.

Ahmed arrived home at six, he later told me, just as the sun was beginning to set. His wife had spent the day cleaning their flat. Her work had used up all the water so he could not wash. He did not mind, however, as he knew his wife liked to clean on days when she heard that the situation was particularly bad in Baghdad: it distracted her from worrying about her husband's safety. Ahmed's daughter, Labibah, had not been allowed outside because of the day's events and was consequently restless. She demanded her father play with her and for the next hour he sat on the floor pretending to have tea with her and her dolls.

I spent the evening at my computer. Due to the time difference between London and Baghdad, my final deadline was 9 p.m. On days like that I would work right up to it because casualty counts had to be updated and new facts incorporated into my article. In total 152 people died and 542 were wounded in Baghdad on 8 September 2005. It was one of the worst days in the city since the defeat of Saddam. Al-Qa'eda in Iraq claimed responsibility. At around 8 p.m. its leader, Abu Musab al-Zarqawi, released an audio tape in which he promised 'all-out war'.

Once my work was finished I was too tired and stressed to want to meet up with anyone else staying at the Hamra for a drink or a meal. Instead I ordered a kebab through room service and put on a DVD while eating my dinner. I usually watched boxed sets of American TV series, something that would absorb me and transport me as far away as possible from where I was. When I first arrived in Baghdad I had started with slightly more cerebral programmes like *The West Wing*. However, I quickly found myself becoming addicted to *Buffy the Vampire Slayer*. On nights like that one in September 2005, it was all that my brain had space left to take on board. I saw a lot of undead get staked during my time in Iraq.

Ahmed and his family turned on their diesel-powered electricity generator that evening to watch an Egyptian comedy film, sitting in the light of the TV screen because all the other lamps were turned off to limit the amount of electricity used. They went to bed at around ten. Every evening he liked to hold his daughter to him before she went to sleep, placing her between his arms and kissing her on the forehead, so that the day ended as it started: with a moment of comfort and love.

In April 2005 there had been a real fear that civil war, Iraq's greatest nightmare, was about to break out. Reports emerged that Sunni extremists had seized control of Madain, a city just south of Baghdad, and were giving the Shia who lived there two days to leave or be killed. Jalal Talabani, Iraq's newly appointed president, warned that the stretch of the Tigris that passed through the city was awash with bodies. At least 58, some of them women and children, had been pulled from the water in recent weeks. The cabinet's national security advisor announced that Sunni insurgents wanted to massacre peaceful Shia families in order to turn the city into a fundamentalist Islamic bastion.

As three battalions of the Iraqi army, supported by US troops, were dispatched to restore order, I began to explore what had gone wrong in Madain. It took a long time, weeks of work, as anything like that always did in Iraq. At one point I ignored Ahmed's protestations and risked the journey south to knock on doors to see if people's stories confirmed the reports of what had happened. Often in Iraq, the deeper I dug, the more confused I became but this time my efforts paid off. A picture emerged and it bore little resemblance to the Iraqi government's neat description.

During 2005 the situation in Iraq deteriorated with every passing month. While US High Command outlined their programmes for success, and soldiers on the ground sought to control their areas of operation, a void had emerged where the mechanisms of government once stood. Security, food, electricity, water, medicines: these basic necessities could no longer be relied on. The state was failing to look after its people. What I learned in Madain gave me my first indication as to what was filling the gap it had left. It is worth explaining in detail what I discovered because it was in Madain that I realised events were developing a dynamic of their own and that the situation was moving beyond anyone's ability to control. Madain was not merely a story about ideology or nationalist conviction. It was about power, money and people's overwhelming instinct for survival.

Although aspects of what happened in Madain remain unclear, its problems appeared to have originated in the aftermath of Saddam's defeat. Before then it had been a relatively tranquil place, somewhere to which families from Baghdad would travel on a day out in order to picnic in the lush fields that surrounded it. Then, in the second half of 2003, tens of thousands of Shia moved to the city from Iraq's impoverished south. The Shia had missed out on the best economic opportunities during Saddam's time, the real prizes being kept for Sunnis, particularly those who came from Saddam's hometown of Tikrit, and they had grown up hearing how much richer people were in Baghdad and in its Sunni hinterland. With the Ba'athist regime now deposed, they were moving north to see if they could secure some of that bounty for themselves.

At first, conditions in Madain had been relatively peaceful, despite the large number of Shia moving to the city. In Iraq, Shia and Sunni had lived alongside each other for generations and were used to focusing on their common identity as Iraqis and Muslims rather than the difference of their sects. Madain's local Sunnis even paid to have a new Shia mosque built to accommodate the Shia's growing numbers. The situation started to deteriorate in late 2004. A new, predominately Shia, police unit was sent from Baghdad and there was an influx into the city of Sunni fanatics fleeing the US military's November assault on Fallujah. These newly arrived Sunni extremists believed the Shia to be apostates who had turned away from the Prophet Mohammad's true message and therefore deserved to be killed. Frustrated by their defeat in Fallujah, they attacked Madain's Shia and its local symbols of government, such as its municipal offices. The police, a unit of Shia that had come from the Shia district of Sadr City in Baghdad, apparently took out their anger at these attacks on the city's entire Sunni population.

On a Shia feast day, local Sunnis told me, the police drove through Madain firing guns into the air and playing Shia religious songs. An officer grabbed a 14-year-old girl from the street, sat her on the back seat of his car and threatened to rape her. A Sunni wedding was being held that day. The police gathered outside and one of the officers started shouting at the wedding party, saying no one could leave because he wanted to molest the women. Many of his colleagues joined in, flinging insults of their own. There was a riot, gunfire and numerous police cars were burned. The police responded by taking refuge in the police station and, in the following weeks, limited patrols to a minimum.

The Sunnis from Fallujah continued their fundamentalist vendetta. With the police essentially having handed over control of the city, the Shia had little choice but to look to their own for security. Shia armed groups began to emerge across Madain and its surrounding region. The most powerful came from a nearby village, Hurriah, and was led by a 16-year-old Shia, Fadil. The techniques he adopted will be familiar to anyone who has ever seen a Hollywood gangster film. Local people claimed that anyone who wanted his gang's protection had to provide them with money or sustenance in order to secure it. Those who refused risked a knock on the door and a warning of what would happen if they did not co-operate in future.

It was perhaps inevitable that the Fallujahists began to exploit this money-making enterprise just as enthusiastically as the Shia gangsters. The local Sunnis, now terrified of both the Shia armed groups and the police, had concluded that they alone could provide any form of defence. The Sunni extremists had experience of fighting and the weapons with which to do so. As a result they were able to start their own protection rackets.

By March 2005, the situation had deteriorated to a level where assassinations were routine, tit-for-tat kidnappings commonplace and businesses regularly burned out as the Shia and Sunni gangs struggled for supremacy. In the midst of all this, an arms race had begun as each side tried to outdo the other. They amassed rocket-propelled grenades, AK-47s, and mortars. One Shia group was even reported to have got its hands on an old Iraqi army artillery piece.

The crisis reached its conclusion when a Shia group ransacked a Sunni mosque, an affront that brought all sides onto the streets, prompting the Iraqi government's claims that Sunni extremists had taken over the city, the Shia were being butchered and the Tigris filled with bodies. It had been the final showdown, the moment when it was concluded that one sect had to leave for good or there could never be peace. This was what had been interrupted by the sudden influx of Iraqi and US soldiers, who were now desperately trying to work out how they could possibly pacify such hatreds.

This was not the Iraq I heard about from officials in Baghdad, or in the reports being issued by governments back in the West. In these reports armed Iraqis were known as 'former regime elements' or 'Islamo-fascists', hostile forces labelled 'insurgents' or 'terrorists', and their motivation primarily said to be nationalism or a desire to defend a radical view of Islam. The situation in Madain did not fit any of these labels. It fact using them could only hide the reality of what was happening and give an unwarranted credibility to what was essentially mere banditry or a struggle for survival that bordered on anarchy.

In the coming months, the more I learned about what was going on in Iraq, the less the situation in Madain seemed exceptional. It soon did not surprise me that I would often arrive at a US base to find the senior officers working their way through boxed sets of *The Sopranos*. It was, they would tell me, one of the best guides to understanding the mentality of those in their area of operations.

At times I would read analysis by commentators based in America or Europe that described the strategy of the 'insurgency' in detail. 'Baghdad is now under siege', they would say, or 'the insurgency is preparing for its own Tet offensive'. As far as I could see the insurgency did not exist as they understood it. There was no phantom Ho Chi Minh figure pulling the strings. There were extremists out there motivated by loyalty to Saddam or religious conviction who were stoking the chaos. However, much of the violence was the work of the unscrupulous exploiting the weak for their own benefit, or countless individuals taking up weapons for their own protection, protection that was sometimes against the Americans barging around their villages kicking in doors. The American-led invasion, and the subsequent misjudgements of the CPA and heavy-handed approach of the US military, had created the circumstances that enabled such a situation to flourish. But what was now happening appeared increasingly separate from any action being taken by the Americans or those who had originally taken up arms against them. This was a breakdown of society being fuelled by fear and the necessity for self-preservation.

Moreover, the Sunni armed groups who did claim to be pursuing political objectives, and who propagated them through web sites and leaflets, defied easy categorisation. According to the US authorities there were three main players and a dozen smaller ones in the Sunni insurgency. The largest ones were Al-Jaysh al-Islami fil-Iraq (the Islamic Army in Iraq), Al-Jabha al-Islamiya lil-Muqawama al-Iraqiya (the Islamic Front of the Iraqi Resistance), and Jaysh Ansar al-Sunna (Army of the Partisans of the Sunna). The smaller ones included Jaysh al-Rashidin (the First Four Caliphs' Army), Jaysh al-Ta'ifa al-Mansoura (the Victorious Group's Army), Harakat al-Muqawama al-Islamiya fil-Iraq (the Islamic Resistance Movement in Iraq), Saraya al-Ghadhab al-Islami (the Islamic Anger Brigades), Saraya Suyuf al-Haqq (the Swords of Justice Brigades) and Jaysh Mohammad (Mohammad's Army).

The fighters in one group would have separate objectives to those in another and often strikingly different interpretations of their responsibilities as Muslims. Most also had their own protection schemes and smuggling rings that they ran alongside their more obvious insurgent activities. It was often hard to determine which they considered more important, or even if either aspect could be separated from the other. In some cities there could be half a dozen of these insurgent groups. At one point the US announced it had identified 24 different militias in Baghdad alone.

In addition to all these warring and shifting paramilitary organisations, there was al-Qa'eda in Iraq, the official al-Qa'eda franchise in the country, under its terrifying leader Abu Musab al-Zarqawi, the man who all Westerners in Baghdad knew wanted to put them in an orange jumpsuit and behead them, just as he had Ken Bigley. This was the organisation that was widely accused of being responsible for the worst atrocities and the most horrific suicide bombings, and was the ideal that most of the young men flooding into Iraq from across the Arab world had come to join.

As with so much in that conflict there was far more confusion than fact surrounding al-Qa'eda in Iraq. This was partly due to the very nature of al-Qa'eda itself, which is as much a state of mind as a terrorist organisation. All anyone has to do is accept its beliefs, adopt its particularly violent solution to destroying materialism, and they become a member. This made it difficult to judge how closely involved al-Qa'eda was in guiding those who fought under its name in Iraq, particularly as Zarqawi's loyalty to Osama bin Laden was tenuous. It was known that the two of them had argued in the past, Zarqawi refuting bin Laden's right to be the symbolic head of militant Islam. Occasionally the Americans would release messages that they had intercepted in which bin Laden or his closest lieutenants would plead with Zarqawi to alter or moderate his tactics. These instructions were clearly being ignored as his organisation's attacks on soft targets, such as markets and mosques, continued unabated. It was possible the organisation's adoption of the name al-Qa'eda was merely a marketing technique rather than a symbol of close affiliation.

So scarce was information about al-Qa'eda in Iraq that the Americans were not even sure if Zarqawi had one leg or two. It was debated whether he had lost one while fighting in Afghanistan. Al-Qa'eda in Iraq was clearly operational. It was clearly nasty. It was probably responsible for many of the worst attacks. Yet it was unclear how many people were operating under its name. It could have been five hundred or five thousand. Nobody seemed to know for certain.

When al-Qa'eda in Iraq claimed culpability for a bombing or an attack it did not necessarily mean it was responsible. Other insurgent groups would also often claim responsibility, sometimes with far more credibility. Determining who was to blame was only made harder by the Americans' apparent penchant for publicly blaming al-Qa'eda in Iraq if it was at all possible. This played well back in the States and avoided them having to admit that the people primarily shooting at them were Iraqis rather than foreign jihadists.

Some Iraqis were so cynical about the whole situation that they would argue al-Qa'eda in Iraq did not even exist and that Zarqawi was merely a CIA creation to justify America's continued presence in their country. It was, in its own way, as justifiable a conclusion as any other.

Amid this chaos and confusion the Americans announced plans to create a new Iraqi army and police force to remove responsibility for security from the US and its allies. In 2005, the US hoped it would be the establishment of this force, combined with the rallying effect of the political and constitutional process, that would pacify Iraq. An ambitious timetable was announced in which these new security forces would be up and running within two years, by which time it was intended that Iraqis would be leading the fight against the insurgency and securing the nation's borders. There is a military truism, however, that I repeatedly heard from officers in Iraq, both American and British, which states that it normally takes ten years to win an insurgency, and fourteen years to lose one. This new plan intended to stabilise Iraq far quicker and this brought its own dangers.

The pressure for prompt action was particularly acute in the case of the new army. The US desperately needed Iraqi soldiers if it was to have any hope of stabilising the country or of reducing its own casualties. Iraq's Saddam-era army had been abolished on 23 May 2003 by a stroke of Paul Bremer's pen. During 2004, the Americans first attempt at creating a new Iraqi army failed when a battalion turned tail when ordered to go into Fallujah and 40 per cent of its recruits deserted. The remainder of the force had largely been disbanded and a new training programme drawn up to ensure the soldiers it produced would be willing to fight. In 2005 this was now being implemented. Thousands of Iraqis were recruited and millions of dollars spent on salaries and equipment. American and British soldiers were taken off combat operations to whip the new military into shape. A staff college opened south of Baghdad.

The need for fast results meant many Iraqi recruits were placed with active units after only six weeks of training, so keen was the coalition to get Iraqi boots on the ground as quickly as possible. Doubts were raised in some quarters as to whether they could possibly have the discipline and skills needed. The American response was that there was a war going on and therefore no alternative to a significant degree of on-the-job training.

It was not easy to gain permission to spend time with the troops in the Iraqi army, even though by mid-2005 there were meant to be 57,000 of them. The Americans knew they were a work in progress, and that what was being reported back by those who had managed to see them in action was not always favourable. Nevertheless, in late May I managed to secure approval to visit a brigade based near Muqdadiya and accompany it on an operation. It was to be the first time Iraqi soldiers had been allowed to operate independently of American troops and US High Command wanted to show off this achievement to the media. I was told I would be joining an Iraqi army unit commander called Captain Haider in one of the white pick-up trucks that at that point were the Iraqi army's only mode of transport. A US army Iraqi translator would be assigned to accompany me.

On the day of the operation, five of us squeezed onto the front seats of the pick-up truck – myself, my translator and three Iraqi soldiers – while six more Iraqi servicemen sat on the metal benches fitted to the back. Despite the supposedly multi-sectarian composition of the army, all the soldiers were Shia. They were dressed in second-hand uniforms donated by the US military. These were of the same design as the ones the marines had worn while fighting the Iraqi army during the 1991 Gulf War. The Marine Corps had been told to pass them on now that their own uniforms had been upgraded to a new computer-generated camouflage design. Few fitted their new owners properly, the average Iraqi soldier being far smaller than his American counterpart. Leather belts held up trousers and sleeves hung to the tips of fingers. None of the Iraqis had any body armour and weaponry was largely limited to second-hand Kalashnikovs.

The operation was to be a sweep of local villages that for months had been considered home to the prime suspects for the roadside bombs which kept hitting American patrols in the area. As we waited for it to start I asked my companions what had drawn them to the military life. The answer seemed to depend on their rank.

For the officers it was apparently patriotism. 'I am aware I could be killed but there can be no room for fear in my heart,' a Lieutenant Mohammad told me. He had the stare of a true believer. 'I must protect my family and country. When I went on my first raid I let my soldiers enter the house first and I could see they were scared. The second time I led the way so they knew my strength and now they fight like lions.'

Captain Haider, his commander, nodded in approval.

A private sat on my left, a man hairy even by Iraqi standards with black curls covering the backs of his hands and pushing out of the top of his camouflage jacket. He had a far more pragmatic reason for enlisting. 'There are no jobs so I become a soldier,' he said without a hint of embarrassment. 'I dream of owning a little shop but it is impossible with the present conditions in Iraq. In two or three years, when I have saved money, I will leave. This job is very dangerous and my family begs me to finish it, but for now I need to work.'

181

Captain Haider nodded again, though this time not with approval but rather with an air of resignation to the fact that it was true and a common story.

Haider was a rotund man, his stomach falling over the front of his trousers, who was hardly ever without a cigarette. He was a committed patriot and keen to assure me that the new Iraqi military was the right organisation to bring stability to his country. Its soldiers, he insisted, were among the bravest in the world and had some of the best training methods.

'I am special forces,' he said. 'To finish our training we must catch a wild rabbit or cat with our hands, kill it with our hands and then eat it raw. I have eaten five cats. That is how strong the Iraqi soldier is.'

Haider's role in the operation was to gather information for his commanding office and, once it started, the first few hours involved him listening to the radio so that he could report what was going on. The situation was mostly quiet. There were a few mortar rounds, a rocket-propelled attack and some gunfire, but the impression was that most of the local armed groups had been forewarned that the operation was coming and had disappeared before it began.

This, I was told, was not an unusual occurrence in operations that involved the Iraqi army. The links that existed between the soldiers and the local communities in which they lived resulted in confused loyalties that made secrecy difficult. Due to the speed with which the new army was being put together there had been little time for adequate screening of people's true motivations for joining the force. Sometimes this problem went to the highest levels. The previous month a battalion commander had been arrested for feeding information to local extremists.

It was mid-morning when we were finally ordered to visit the villages being searched. A number of Haider's troops donned balaclavas even though the temperature was around 35°C. This, I learned, was so that no one could recognise them and later take reprisals against the soldiers or their families. My translator, a local university student who could not have been more than 19 years old, had kept his balaclava on from the moment we had joined the Iraqi soldiers, such was his view of their integrity.

The countryside was lush and well irrigated by a series of slow-moving streams and ditches. Reeds lined the road-side and the fields were dotted with groves of date palms and poplar trees. Haider drove fast, the speedometer rarely dropping below 70 mph. The roads were not good, mostly dusty tracks beside irrigation canals, but there was no regard for tyres or shock absorbers as he pushed the accelerator to the floor.

'We go fast so they do not hit us,' he reassured me. 'There is no need to be worried. Iraqi soldiers are very brave.'

We began to meet other units. At road junctions groups of Iraqis sat or squatted on the ground, most of them smoking. At one turning the private on my left waved and shouted a hello. 'He is my cousin,' he said, indicating a figure waving back. Everyone seemed remarkably relaxed.

In the first village we reached, more than a hundred soldiers were milling around the streets, many sitting on benches or walking into and out of houses. It was a typical Iraqi village. These, like almost all Iraq's built-up areas, were rarely attractive places: featureless in their repetitive-ness – lines of houses, one or two shops selling bottles of water and vegetables, a few trees, a couple of sad-looking shrubs – and drab in their colouring of brown and grey. The buildings were mostly concrete blocks, most less than thirty years old, with the roofs flat in case someday the money miraculously appeared to enable another storey to be built on top. However, those who lived in them had rarely travelled far and as a result they had the atmosphere of entrenched communities, places where the villagers knew with unthinking familiarity every corner and pot-hole. Families had usually lived there for generations and so understood, for better or worse, all that was good and bad about each other.

A half-dozen local Iraqis stood to one side, silently watching. There was the sound of a shot and for a moment every soldier was alert. It became apparent that it had come from one of their own and the target had been a dog. A soldier was gesticulating and pointing at it. The animal had blood coming from its haunch and was lying on the ground, trying to pull itself up on its front legs. The soldiers started laughing and a few ran forward. They trained their Kalash-nikovs and started shooting. Not one hit. Then a soldier produced a pistol and shot the dog in the head.

'It tried to bite them,' my translator explained.

In the next village two prisoners were waiting outside a house, their hands bound behind their back. They looked like farmers. We stopped beside them and an Iraqi soldier came over and said something to Captain Haider. He got out of the truck and slapped both the prisoners hard across the face. He thrust them against the side of the truck and started shouting at them.

'These insurgents pushed some of the soldiers when they entered the house,' my translator said.

An old woman, presumably the men's mother, ran over. She was pulling at her clothes and wailing. The soldiers started laughing again.

I looked around. Soldiers were coming out of a building carrying a locked chest which they then smashed to see if it held any weapons. Another group were taking a loaf of bread from a shop. Some villagers were having their hands secured behind their backs by plastic binders. Trucks were roaring up and down the road. Captain Haider was still shouting at his prisoners and pushing them in the chest. Two hoods were placed over their heads but he did not stop pushing them.

A US patrol drew up. A colonel, a man at least six foot three inches tall, tanned and oozing confidence, stepped out of the middle Humvee and started congratulating the Iraqis on a job well done. The American soldiers guarding him had black bands for sunglasses and webbing weighed down with weaponry. The colonel went on a walkabout accompanied by two female GIs, both of them blonde and so beautiful they could have stepped out of a TV show. The women had bags of sweets which they offered to the villagers. The children took them but the men stared back with such hatred it was numbing to behold.

'These are brave men,' the colonel told me as Iraqi soldiers gathered to have their photograph taken with him. 'Iraq has a golden future.' They liked that, when it was translated for them. Soldiers started hitting each other on the back and flexing their muscles before raising a cheer for the colonel's benefit. It felt like quite a carnival for a moment there.

7. Home

Abu Omar, the *Telegraph*'s driver, was a Sunni from the Dulaimi tribe, one of the largest tribes in Iraq and the one from which many senior military and intelligence officers in Saddam's regime had been drawn. He held no affection for the Americans and saw their occupation as a national humiliation, but he cared even less for those Iraqis who were killing Iraqis.

'Kill an American and you're a hero, kill an Iraqi and you're a criminal,' he would say.

He was the oldest son and, with his father dead, took his filial responsibilities seriously. His family was originally from the city of Baqubah, an agricultural centre on the Diyala river 30 miles north east of Baghdad. It was the scene of some of the heaviest guerrilla fighting but he still insisted on seeing his relatives regularly, despite the journey's hazards, as it was of fundamental importance to him that the family remained emotionally close to each other. He would bring back figs from a tree in his uncle's garden that were the most delicious I have eaten anywhere in the world.

He prayed regularly and kept a prayer mat in the office to ensure that he fulfilled his duties as a good Muslim. He once gave me a collection of writings explaining the teachings of the Prophet Mohammad that emphasised the peaceful nature of Islam and the spirit of shared humanity that underlined much of their message. On the front, written in English, were the Prophet's words, 'A Muslim is the brother of a Muslim. He neither oppresses him nor disgraces him, he neither lies to him nor does he hold him in contempt.'

When I first met Abu Omar in the summer of 2004, he ridiculed the idea that there could be a civil war in Iraq. Indeed he laughed at the possibility. Sunni and Shia had lived beside each other for generations, he said. They worked together, inter-married and lived as neighbours in many districts of Baghdad. Their most important sense of identity was that they were Iraqi above all else. That was what foreigners needed to understand. Sunni and Shia were both Iraqi and Iraqi Arabs might fight foreign invaders but not each other.

By the middle of 2005, when Iraq's newly elected Shia politicians were beginning to misuse their power to settle old scores and exert their authority, Abu Omar began to talk darkly about the influence of Iran. One of his cousins had been a pilot in the Iraqi air force and scores of pilots from the Iraq–Iran war era were now being assassinated. These people were particularly hated by the Iranians as they were the ones who had dropped the chemical weapons that Saddam had used against Iran. His cousin fled to Syria after the most famous Iraqi pilot of his generation, Ismael Saeed Fares, whose repeated raids in the Iran-Iraq war had earned him the nickname 'The Hawk of Baghdad', was shot dead. He was hit by 24 bullets as he sat in the garden of his north Baghdad home.

Abu Omar was convinced, as many Sunnis were, that the pilots' personal details were being taken from old records in Iraq's defence ministry. He blamed the Badr Brigade, the paramilitary wing of the Shia political party SCIRI, for the killings and viewed it as an instrument of the Iranian military. To him, the influence of Tehran was everywhere. He was not alone in that. As a result of the close links that existed between Iraq and Iran's political leaders even some US State Department officials liked to say, only partly in jest, that 'the war's over – and Iran has won.' However, for Abu Omar this belief began to cloud every facet of his thinking. The Iranians and their acolytes, he said, had assumed senior positions in Iraq's police force in order to arrest, torture and kill innocent Sunnis. It was they who were murdering Sunni clerics and were responsible for the worst excesses occurring in his country.

By late 2006, a time when the sectarian civil war was being fought in earnest, Abu Omar did not view many Shia as fellow Iraqis any more. They had betrayed their right to such an honour by siding with the Iranians to help them destroy the Iraqi state. He lived in an area of the capital called New Baghdad. It was a mixed sectarian neighbourhood and by then Shia militias were breaking into Sunni houses at night to threaten and kill their owners.

Abu Omar's wife suggested they leave the city, maybe even get out of Iraq itself. If he wished to continue working, she said, then he could stay behind while his family sought sanctuary and visit them whenever he could. He would not tolerate this idea. For a start he would not allow the social impropriety of his wife and daughters living apart from him. More importantly, he would not accept that the enemies of Iraq could force him from his own home. The family, he said, would live together and if necessary die together. What they would not do was betray their principles by escaping the land that was their birthright.

Marwan, Ahmed's brother who was my security guard, and Sajad, the second driver, became good friends after they started working for me. It was an unlikely pairing. Marwan was a Sunni who was proud of his military background and was extremely patriotic. He had served in the Iraqi army and still sported a closely clipped military moustache. He had been in two of the nastiest fights of the Iran-Iraq war: the one in which the Iranians first gained Iraqi territory when they seized the al-Faw peninsula south-east of Basra, and the one two years later when the Iraqis drenched that same peninsula in chemical weapons while taking it back. After that he had lost faith in Saddam, refused to join the Ba'ath Party and had his army career curtailed.

Sajad was a Shia, and like most Shia had never had much time for Saddam or the Iraqi military. What linked the two of them, other than a basic good humour, was the knowledge that they did not take their religion too seriously. They considered themselves Muslims, fasted at Ramadan and noted their sects' holy days, but neither seemed to spend much time praying.

Marwan had a Shia wife, a not uncommon situation in Iraq where – as Abu Omar had so rightly told me – before things got out of hand Shia and Sunnis had lived alongside each other for generations. His wife was the daughter of the family that lived next door to his. While in his early twenties and still in the army he had returned on leave and spotted her walking along the street. He had gone to his parents that very day and told them he had seen the woman he wished to marry. They organised for her family to visit. It was the first time the future husband and wife had met properly. They were not permitted to talk to each other in private while their families discussed the suitability of the pairing.

Marwan's future wife was asked by her father if she was willing to go ahead with the match. She said she was. Marwan and his bride-to-be had barely spoken a hundred words to each other by the day of the marriage ceremony but both had been the ones who had permitted the wedding to go ahead once their families had agreed it was acceptable. It was the traditional way of doing things for the educated Iraqi middle class. They now have five children.

Neither of their families had considered religious differences a stumbling block. What primarily mattered to both was that their child was marrying into a respectable family, and as they lived beside each other they already knew that to be the case.

When, during 2006, conditions got really bad in Baghdad and Shia and Sunni armed bands were killing each other with real enthusiasm, I asked Ahmed if the situation had made any difference to Marwan and Sajad's friendship.

He looked at me as if I was an idiot.

It was during that period that I came into the main room in our office and found Marwan repeating phrases as Sajad looked on, nodding encouragingly.

Sajad was checking Marwan's knowledge of Shia religious history and customs. Marwan's wife had been teaching them to her husband so that if need be he could bluff his way through the illegal checkpoints that the Shia death squads were setting up across Baghdad. When an Iraqi was stopped at one, and if those manning it identified him as Sunni, the likely result was torture and death. So Marwan was practising his newly gained knowledge of the twelve imams revered by Shia Muslims, the sect's key historical dates and the significance of its festivals. Sajad corrected any mistakes.

I asked Sajad how Marwan was doing. He was doing okay, I was told, 'for a soldier'. Marwan stared at him. Then he stood up and started to pretend to whip himself. It was a parody of the Shia faithful who would commemorate the anniversary of the death of Husain in the Battle of Karbala by publicly beating themselves with ropes and metal strips until the ground was covered in blood.

He hopped around saying, 'I have become a good Shia now.'

Everyone, Sajad included, loved it.

It was a strange life, the one I led at that time. To give me opportunities to relax the *Telegraph* let me take regular three-week holidays from Iraq. I would finish a stint, board a flight out of Baghdad airport, arrive in Amman, and the next morning be en route to Heathrow for the start of a break back in Britain. After landing I would find myself on the tube, sitting alongside the commuters as we passed under central London, they on their way to work, me on my way home. It seemed incredible that life in these two cities could be going on at the same time in their own very different ways separated only by two short bursts of reading a book on a plane.

London has been the one constant location in my life. I was born there, and though I have lived away from it I have always come back. My friends and family live there. I know many of its streets so well that I do not even need to look to see where I am going. It is predictable and consequently reassuring.

In the Middle East a country was dying. In London people were preoccupied with the usual talk of house prices, dating and jobs. I would spend weeks living in Iraq, then fly back and find the conversations were still exactly the same. People knew that the war was going on, most knew it was not going well, and a number had demonstrated to try to stop it from even taking place, but it was not – thankfully – the most important thing in their lives. It was, in fact, rarely mentioned. There would be moments when what was happening in Iraq would come to the fore when another squaddie died or something catastrophic happened. Even then people's reaction seemed to focus back on themselves, dealing with how they hated the hypocrisy of Tony Blair or wondering how a Labour government had gone so wrong.

During my first week in London I would largely stay at home, watching TV late into the night, so that I could shake off the residual stress before I started meeting up with people. During the second week I would go out and enjoy myself, delighting in the simple pleasure of being able to go to shops and bars. Often during the day I would walk for miles, revelling in the sense of movement and the sight of people going about their everyday lives. Nothing I saw seemed predictable. It was as if I had hyper-vision, every person fascinating me as they went about their normal routine. In the third and last week I would feel the tension coming back into me and I would start waking up earlier, becoming more frantic about trying to fit what I could into every day. Then I would find myself on the tube with my bags. A day later, there I would be, back in Baghdad.

There were moments in Britain when I could not escape

the effect of Iraq, however hard I tried. Normally it would come when I was sitting around people who started complaining a little bit too much about stresses such as a pushy mother-in-law, a delay at an airport while going on holiday or a washing machine that kept on leaking. I did not have much sympathy at the time for such problems. It seemed to me that people in London had life pretty good and that they should enjoy it as much as possible, though to give them credit, most of the people I knew did. I kept my mouth shut when those moments came. It was normal for people to be dwelling on such details; lucky even.

Then I met a girl. Previously London had been a place in which to relax and forget. Now I had a reason to be there. On my breaks back in Britain we would swim in the pools on Hampstead Heath, sit in pubs during cold nights, go and see films together, do all the good stuff normal people do. We had a lot of fun. In fact, it was fantastic. The more I got to know her the more I realised that she somehow already knew the most important lesson that living in Baghdad had taught me. She understood that all the inconsequential strains of life were not things to get caught up in and distracted by, that only the really big stuff mattered and the rest was too often merely an impediment to actually living.

Until then I had enjoyed a pretty self-centred life. Being a foreign correspondent often does that to you because when things get tough you can simply weigh anchor and move on. I had made homes on three continents and travelled around the world at least twice. There had been a period in my youth when I had happily partied too hard, and another in my twenties when I probably drank too much. I had never given much thought to where it would all lead. The priority had been what might be the next exciting place to visit or story to cover.

Being in Iraq changed people. Some it made angry and too quick to snap. Others it left feeling invincible because they believed they had seen the worst and survived. I saw a lot of that, especially among the troops. They would get through their tour of duty, arrive home, and then be killed in a road crash. They could not conceive how they could be hurt in such familiar surroundings and as a result drove far too fast. A private in the unit I had been placed with during the invasion had died that way. He arrived back to Georgia in July 2003 after having spent a year training in the Kuwait desert, fighting his way to Baghdad and then coping with the first stirrings of the insurgency. A month later he was dead after he refused to ease off on the accelerator and his motorcycle hit a tree.

A significant minority were left feeling that they needed to find ways of escape; that they wanted to forget everything and let alcohol and drugs make them live only in the moment. To me, however, it did the opposite. For the first time in my life I did not want to find fresh distractions. Doing so seemed a way to waste time and no one has much of that. That was another lesson I learnt in Iraq.

It was an amazing feeling to get on a plane, circle up above Baghdad airport and then head west, knowing it was taking me to someone who wanted to see me, and whom I wanted to see just as badly. In Iraq I witnessed people's emotion as they lost everything and everyone that they had cared about. That was a powerful thing to behold. While on breaks in Britain I started looking carefully at the lives of my friends with families, people who had settled in one spot and made the best of it. I realised they had made a choice and, for the most part, they were content. More than that, it had made them who they were and what they would be. My time in Iraq had a surprising effect on me. It was terrifying and terrible but it did finally make me grow up.

I was on one of those breaks in London when, shortly before the December national elections at the end of 2005, the Hamra hotel was attacked and my office destroyed. I was watching Fern Britton on *This Morning* discuss a comb that was supposed to cure baldness when my boss rang to tell me the news. When I first heard it, I could not believe it. That building had been my safe space, a refuge where I could pretend I was somewhere sane. Two cars, piled high with explosives, had driven into the perimeter blast walls. There was nowhere sane in Baghdad any more.

While I digested the news, I wondered for a moment if it was worth going back. That dilemma did not last long. In fact it was gone almost as soon as the question had been raised. I had got too involved in what was happening in Iraq to be able to step away now. I needed to know what happened next, whether the catastrophe that I feared was approaching would unfold or if the Iraqis and Americans could somehow pull the country back from the brink of total collapse. What was happening in Iraq was important and even what had happened to the Hamra was not enough to make me want to stop reporting on it. I rang Ahmed and he said the team were already organising themselves to drive to the hotel to see what remained and that they needed me back soon as they did not know what to do next. I booked a ticket and, a couple of days later, was waiting at Heathrow for my flight.

The Hamra escaped being totally destroyed because the bombers got their calculations wrong. The first explosion not only took down our defences but blew such a colossal hole in the tarmac that the second vehicle could not drive over it. The bombs still caused considerable damage, however. My office was on the side of the building that bore the brunt and afterwards it resembled the collapsed shacks one sees in photographs taken after a major earthquake. The ceiling had come down, windows were blown in, cupboards reduced to tinder and the metal front door was buckled and left hanging by one hinge.

The Iraqi houses around us suffered the worst. They did not have any blast walls to protect them. I used to watch the people living in them from my window: the women stepping onto their balconies to hang up their washing, or the children gathering to kick a football around on an adjacent stretch of wasteland. They had found themselves targets solely because the international press corps had decided to move into the hotel next door. No one asked them if they minded. Afterwards those of us at the Hamra, myself included, did not like to talk about that too much. Everyone sought to put this knowledge to one side, the knowledge that they were hit due to our presence.

Two apartment blocks disappeared in the bombing to be replaced by a pile of rubble and a couple of stubbornly standing supportive struts. At least eight people died, among them the little boy who had ferried hot pastries to the hotel bakery. He had been making a delivery just as the bombs went off. They never found his body. Indeed the strange thing was that the only bodies people could locate in the immediate aftermath were those of the bombers themselves. Bits of them had gone everywhere. One of the Westerners hired to supervise security at the hotel claimed to have found a penis in a shrub. Half a

with the US claiming that the political process had been a success and the soldiers were going to be able to start coming home soon. The events of that day, however, pitched Iraq into an orgy of bloodletting that would defy anyone's attempts to downplay.

Beyond the general lawlessness, the violence until then had been primarily caused by the efforts of the Sunnis to resist the American occupation that had marginalised them in a country they had once ruled. The Shia government was settling scores against their former Ba'athist political enemies and intimidating Sunnis to try to stop them aiding insurgents, the Kurds were doing what they could to force Arabs out of Kirkuk so they could one day incorporate it into their new Kurdistan, and the religious extremists were busy trying to bomb and brutalise the Shia, whom they had labelled apostates and therefore worthy of being killed. Before that day in February the Shia had not properly fought back, however, certainly not en masse. The majority had ignored the provocations and heeded the instructions of Grand Ayatollah Sistani, their most senior cleric, for restraint rather than retaliation. It had been a heroic act of fortitude for which they never really received enough credit.

On 22 February, shortly after midnight, half a dozen men overwhelmed the guards at the Shia's Golden Mosque in Samarra, forced their way inside and set explosives on the building's five supporting pillars. It was a lengthy job and one that took considerable skill. To ensure the structure's collapse holes had to be drilled into the stone supports and the explosives packed inside. Then the firing mechanisms were set to detonate simultaneously.

The work took five hours and it was dawn by the time it was finished. The mosque had stood for more than a thousand years, though the golden dome from which it now took its name was a relatively recent addition, having been constructed shortly before the First World War. It was one of Shia Islam's holiest sites, a centre of pilgrimage and prayer, exceeded only in veneration by the shrines at Najaf and Karbala. The explosions sent up a cloud of dust that hung in the air for almost ten minutes. When it cleared, the crowd that had gathered could see that the dome and most of the mosque's side walls had been destroyed. Wails of lamentation went up. In the following months such cries of anguish were repeated across Iraq as the consequences of that act became apparent.

Outraged, the Shia came out in force. It was unthinking and unplanned. No one controlled it at that point as throughout Iraq vengeance was enacted. Convoys of Shia roamed the streets of Baghdad. Sunni mosques were targeted and a number set on fire. In the coming weeks, Sunnis with no sympathy for the more extreme elements of their sect concluded they had no choice but to fight back in order to defend themselves. Neighbours who had lived side by side for generations turned on each other as fear of proximity to a member of the rival sect overtook their previous bonds of fellowship. Thousands piled their most treasured possessions into cars and fled their homes. The city's morgue brought in freezer trucks to cope with the number of corpses.

No one knows the full death toll from those first few days after the bombing of the Golden Mosque. Mixed Sunni-Shia areas surrounding Baghdad were off limits to any Western reporter. Even Iraqi journalists found themselves under attack if they ventured too far from the capital. Atwar Bahjat, a correspondent for the al-Arabiya

TV station, was lynched in Samarra, her body and that of her cameraman later found mutilated. What was certain, however, was that the whole dynamic had altered. The civil war in Iraq had begun.

It was the bodies that denoted how much had changed. Suddenly they were everywhere, each day bringing reports of the latest discoveries. Iraqis were being killed before, of course, but now the danger was constant and in every quarter. The militias were not only guarding their own districts but rampaging through surrounding streets. Homes were broken into and the men in them rounded up and marched away. In the months after the Golden Mosque was destroyed vehicles were stopped in broad daylight, identity cards checked and those from the wrong sect rewarded with a bullet. A bus carrying Shia and Kurd students was raided, everyone on board told to leave their seats and line up outside where they were summarily shot. Gunmen slowed down as they passed a Sunni market, stuck out their guns and killed 23 people. Rockets fell into a Shia neighbourhood, killing 62 people and wounding more than 100. In the Sunni area of al-Jihad the gunmen did not even bother to make an event of it. One afternoon Shia militiamen simply took to the streets, firing into shops and killing whoever they wanted. By the time Iraqi security forces arrived the streets were littered with the dead, the bodies of men, women and children left lying in the dirt.

Night-time was worse; the time of mystery when the real work was done. The police were supposed to be the only ones out, the whole of Baghdad under curfew, but it was still between dusk and dawn that most killing occurred. The corpses would be found dotted across the city the following morning. You had to draw your own conclusions as to what the police had actually been doing and who their friends really were.

Pathetically, there was not even a functioning Iraqi government that could act to try to stop what was happening. The politicians chosen in the previous December's election still could not put aside their bitterness and rivalries. They continued to wrangle that spring over who should get which post in the cabinet.

I went to the city's morgue. No one knew exactly how many bodies it was dealing with. Previously I had relied on the director of the facility, Faik Bakir, to provide me with the number of victims of violent death that it processed. That was no longer possible because, following the bombing of the Golden Mosque, he had been forced to flee the country, reportedly for revealing to the media the unprecedented number of dead being delivered to the morgue.

The stench of corpses rotting in the heat reached me before the sight of the pale-yellow brick medical centre where they were stacked. The refrigerators were full and bodies were now being piled in rows on the floor. A group of armed men were checking the identity papers of all those going inside. They were Sadrists, representatives of the Moqtada al-Sadr supporter now in charge of the country's medical services. They scared me.

Ahmed went to find out what he could. The narrow, crumbling lane that led to the morgue was filled with people. They had all come, as we had, for answers. In their case though they sought answers to what had happened to those they had lost: the husbands, the sons, the cousins or the friends who had disappeared amid the slaughter. An old woman was standing by the metal gate that marked the entrance, her sorrow so total that she had to be held upright by two male relatives. A young man was shouting at the sky in anger. Those passing him barely acknowledged his pain, so preoccupied were they by their own fears.

Pictures of the dead could be seen on computers placed in the morgue's lobby. Families were clustered around them, scrolling through the photographs in the hope, and the dread, that they might recognise someone. It was acutely unpleasant viewing. People in Baghdad were not simply being killed; they were being beheaded, garrotted, and tortured. Victims were having electric drills used on them and cigarettes stubbed out on their flesh. Eyeballs were being gouged out. Bones were broken and body parts hacked off.

It was said to be the Shia who preferred the drilling and gouging. The drill bits pressed into the temples of Sunni heads would apparently 'destroy their stupid minds'. The Sunnis preferred beheading because it was believed to be the Prophet Mohammad's method of dealing with apostates. As a result of the level of mutilation being inflicted, tattoo parlours began offering customers 'death tags' featuring names and next of kin as a possible safeguard should they end up among the facially unidentifiable.

Those who had recognised someone in the photographs told their stories. Four brothers living in Mansour had been taken from the home they shared with their wives. Their bullet-ridden bodies were found in a drainage ditch, their toes and fingers cut off.

Jabar al-Azawi's face was covered in purple welts, he had drill holes in his legs and both shoulders broken. He had been working in his shop in southern Baghdad when he was grabbed by a carload of armed men.

Ahmed did not say much as we drove back to the office. In fact he did not say much at all during that time, focusing instead on his work, busy pushing his contacts and travelling the city to interview those he trusted to gather the information we needed. It was as if by putting in the hours covering what was happening he could avoid worrying about what it meant for him and his family.

When, weeks later, the Iraqi government finally released a figure for the number of people killed in Baghdad in March 2006, the month after the bombing at the Golden Mosque, it was 1,294. By mid-summer the official monthly death toll in the city had reached 1,500. More Iraqis were being killed in Baghdad every couple of months than the number of American soldiers who had died in the entire conflict. Plans were announced to build two new morgues so that Baghdad could cope with the influx of bodies.

What was really haunting, however, was the knowledge that even these numbers did not tell the whole story. There was no way of knowing how many more bodies were simply being thrown into the Tigris or the city's sewer system. The 4th Infantry Division, the American unit unfortunate enough to have the Iraq rotation at that time, announced that its men were going to plug the holes where the sewers could be accessed from ground level. This would not do anything to limit the slaughter but it would at least mean that families were more likely to have a body to bury.

Families of the wrong sect in the wrong place woke in the morning to find letters pushed under their front doors telling them to get out by nightfall. The message would sometimes be delivered by someone simply shooting at the building. No one with any sense needed to be told twice. It was not a time for stubbornness. Around thirty thousand people became refugees in those first few months. By July there were 180,000 of them. Eighteen months later it was approaching three million. Whole streets in the bloodiest districts had been abandoned.

The Western security contractors in the Hamra, the ex-Special Forces men hired to provide guidance to the press corps, began providing regular updates on where the latest militia checkpoints had been spotted. Roads that I had previously driven along dozens of times were now firmly out of bounds. A reporter from the *Washington Post*, and he must have been half mad to try it, attempted to get into the Shia bastion of Sadr City. He came back with stories of children as young as twelve standing at road junctions, dwarfed by their AK-47s, checking everyone who went past.

Abu Omar, my driver, lost his eldest sister. She was five months pregnant, a teacher who had been at the front of her class when a bomb went off outside the building. The brother of Sajad, the driver of our second car, disappeared while driving on a highway near Ramadi that he had to use for his job as a truck driver ferrying goods to the Syrian border. As he was Shia it was presumed he had been taken by Sunnis and was being tortured or had already been killed. The elders of Sajad's tribe sent a delegation to the Sunni tribes around Ramadi seeking information about what had happened to him. They pleaded ignorance. I worked my contacts in the American military to see if there was any chance that he had been accidentally arrested. They knew nothing.

His eight children and wife moved in with Sajad's family. Sajad already had six children of his own. He now had sixteen mouths to feed and sixteen lives to protect from the madness.

Ahmed was at home when the gunmen came to his street. They stopped outside his house and he heard them break into the building next door. He sat with his family in their living room praying that they would be spared. There was gunfire. He heard the gunmen leave and then a tap on his door. He opened it and there was his neighbour, his hands clutched over his chest to try to stop the bleeding. He could not even speak to ask for help but instead collapsed on the floor. Ahmed tried to put into effect the medical training our team had received, while his five-year-old daughter watched a man die in front of her. Ahmed moved his family to his parents' house that night. They did not even bother to pack, so desperate were they to get away.

I went to one of Baghdad's psychiatric hospitals with the hope of finding what effect this might be having on the mental state of the city's population. It was a small building beside a roundabout in the centre of the city accessed through a metal gate covered in flaking green paint. Inside the walls were covered in white tiles. There were only four doctors working in the facility with half a dozen nurses to help them, the rest having fled abroad.

They had almost no medication with which to treat their patients. Instead they relied on more antiquated solutions. In a small room on the second floor was an electroshock machine. It had leather straps to hold the patient down and a metal headset was attached by two wires to a wooden box. Patients were given two to three sessions of electroconvulsive therapy a week, a plastic mouth guard placed between their teeth before each treatment.

When we arrived, the patients, watched by their supervisors, were wandering around a whitewashed courtyard. The doctors, in their white jackets, chain-smoked. They were notably introspective about their task.

'In Iraq 90 per cent of people have some form of mental problem due to the lives they face,' the duty consultant, Dr Nour Bassim, said. 'We, the doctors here, have diagnosed each other and know that we ourselves are suffering. But is that necessarily madness or is it a rational reaction at a time like this?'

He pointed at a man standing by a small statue of the hospital's founder. 'He is delusional. He is convinced that if he leaves this hospital he is destined to die. It is acute paranoia, so much so that he cannot even step outside.'

'That man,' he said, indicating a middle-aged Iraqi with a bald head and bushy moustache. 'He has concluded he must be divine as he was in a bombing but survived.

'How can I say with certainty that neither is right? Is it correct to say they are clinically unwell? That they are wrong to believe they will be killed outside these walls or did not only live due to a miracle of divine favour? How do I know the answer when nothing seems certain? I could be the person who is delusional, they the ones who are sane.'

Despite the suicide bombing of the Hamra most of the press corps stayed in the hotel, moving into the main tower that had escaped the worst of the damage. I checked out, partly because the staff had been seen looting the worst-damaged rooms but primarily because, in the aftermath of the bombing, the locals living beside the Hamra had made clear that they had had enough of our presence. When reporters drove in and out of the main entrance they started having stones thrown at them. There was a whip-round of all the media bureaus to raise money for those affected by the blasts, which for a while did pacify the more aggressive instincts of our Iraqi neighbours. Nevertheless I could still only feel embarrassment and apprehension when I saw them.

I moved the office to another hotel in the compound. It used an alternative entrance to the Hamra and was in a spot where the surrounding buildings had been unaffected by the bombing. The hotel had been the Australian embassy until the general security situation deteriorated to such a level that it had been thought sensible to join the other diplomats in the Green Zone. During their time at the hotel, however, the Australians had renovated it to ensure the building had proper escape routes and this made it feel secure.

The only other alternatives within the complex surrounding the Hamra had been a hostel, which had exotic, if frayed, decor that betrayed its former use as a brothel, and the faux-Classical Greek glamour of a hotel opposite the Hamra itself, which seemed to me the most exposed of them all because it was closest to the main road. Not staying there proved to be the right choice. A few months later its staff became convinced that it was only a matter of time before the whole compound was overrun. One night they stole everything they could get their hands on and disappeared.

I liked our new residence. It was clean and the owners friendly. The family who ran it lived in rooms on the ground floor and I often spent time with their children and relations who would tell me the latest gossip from their day. The Australians had built a pool table that sat in the basement. The Iraqis were extremely good at pool but played in a style of their own. There were no tactical soft shots or snookers in their game. Every ball had to be hit as hard as possible into the pocket otherwise it did not really count.

The building in front of it had been taken over by a security firm run by an Iraqi-American who had come to Baghdad from New York. There was an uncertainty about what his company did, although whenever you asked people working for it they answered that they were in the 'packaged food transportation' business. This was clearly more of a money-spinner than might have been expected. While staying overnight in Jordan waiting to go into or out of Baghdad, members of the Hamra press corps routinely said they had spotted the Iraqi-American outside the Four Seasons hotel in Amman in a white Rolls-Royce.

I was concerned that this firm was a likely target for attack. There had already been a failed bombing attempt on it the previous year and, a month after we moved into our new office, a half-dozen or so of his people were shot while they were out in the city. In response the Iraqi-American brought dogs in to patrol the perimeter walls at night. In the autumn of 2006 the Iraqi police raided the company and seized an arsenal of weapons said to include heavy machine guns and a storage room filled with AK-47s. The Iraqi-American fled the country while leaving instructions for his remaining men to mount extra guards to overlook every exit.

I heard recently that the company left Baghdad in 2007, finally forced out of Iraq, only to be replaced at their old base by a new set of security contractors. They are Russian and they can apparently be heard singing at night as they work their way through cases of vodka.

Iraq's old institutions of state had been stripped away when the American administrator Paul Bremer disbanded the Ba'athist instruments of rule. The new organs of government that the US established in their place had largely failed, a result of the security situation, the unrealistic expectations introduced at their inception by the American ideologists who governed Iraq in the year following the US invasion, and the incessant political wrangling caused by the country's year of elections.

As Iraqis now flailed in the knowledge that their lives were under acute and imminent threat, the traditional Arab bonds of charity, tolerance and communal responsibility finally started to fray. These had done much to maintain social cohesion despite the strains caused by the war, but the enemy was now their own countrymen not a foreign invader. After the bombing of the Golden Mosque individual people in individual districts concluded that the only logical response to what was unfolding was to seek their own defence. If that meant taking out the family in the neighbouring street before they got to you, so be it.

The militarisation of Baghdad was taken to the next inexorable step. While the number of tit-for-tat killings continued to spiral and the death squads prowled the streets with ever more menace, Iraqis sought to protect themselves. The price of an AK-47 trebled to $350. People talked of burying rocket-propelled grenades in the garden. Women began carrying pistols in their handbags.

In the worst-affected areas individual streets started organising their own paramilitary groups for security. This was neighbourhood watch, Iraqi-style. When the sun set, zigzags of obstacles – palm trees, old air-conditioning units, unused cars – were pulled across roads to slow approaching vehicles. The men of the street would take turns to stand guard, some at ground level and others on the roofs of surrounding buildings to give them a better angle of fire.

I talked to members of a group in a Sunni neighbour-hood in the south-west of the city who were adamant that, with so many people having suddenly developed a taste for killing, they could not trust anyone but those who lived in the same row of houses as themselves. Their mistrust was particularly directed at the police whom they considered nothing more than a legalised extension of the Shia mili-tias. They were deeply concerned about the extent of their present weaponry. They only had Kalashnikovs and they wanted much more firepower, particularly heavy machine guns and rocket-propelled grenades. Feelers had been put out to a street a dozen blocks away whose defenders were rumoured to have got their hands on a collection of mines. Laying them across the entrance at night was considered an attractive precaution.

In the Adhamiya district, Sunni guards fought a two-day pitched battle when police tried to enter the neighbourhood. A rumour had spread that the officers were members of the Badr Brigade, the paramilitary wing of the Shia political party SCIRI, a name synonymous for Sunnis with murder and kidnapping. Omar bin Abdulaziz Street, Adhamiya's main thoroughfare, was racked by assault rifles, machine guns and the occasional grenade as the police were caught in crossfire from the surrounding buildings. Loudspeakers in the Sunni mosques shouted slogans praising 'the heroes of Adhamiya' and calling on them to 'defeat the aggressors'.

The US army, accepting the inevitable, began to issue weapons licences to those guarding their homes. Some groups did not survive long enough to be accredited. One north-western Sunni district had to disband its neighbourhood watch after eight of its members were killed in the first two days.

Across the capital, battle lines were drawn up as the two sects faced each other. Zones of control were guarded and raids launched into bordering districts. Members of a minority sect living on the wrong side of these new demarcation lines were expunged for the perceived safety of the majority. Tens of thousands of people were threatened, killed or forced from their homes. By August the scale of this sectarian cleansing meant that 95 per cent of Shia were believed to have fled the southern Sunni stronghold of Dora. Sunnis had left the Shia parts of Zafraniya. A similar cleansing of Sunni occurred in Mashtel, while in nearby New Baghdad, where the sects were more matched in size, they fought nightly battles in a desperate attempt to gain control.

One man, a Sunni, told of what had happened when rival gunmen succeeded in infiltrating his area. 'They started firing at our houses,' he said. 'They didn't expect a very quick response, but we gave them one. We surrounded them. They were in a trap and gunfire on them was from everywhere.

'We killed a lot of them. After defeating them, it was our turn to attack. We followed the ones fleeing and we saw them entering a mosque, which we shot with two rocket-propelled grenades. And then we returned home.'

Very occasionally there were people who tried to preserve the old ties that had once appeared so enduring. A Shia community leader in the central commercial district of Karrada publicly issued a warning against anyone intending to hurt the Sunnis who lived there. 'If anyone touches them, they touch us,' he said.

In a city where fear now ruled that was the exception, and anyway I heard later that he had been tracked down and killed.

Working in Baghdad was relentless and exhausting. To have a break from its terrors, Ahmed and I flew on Iraqi Airlines to Irbil, the capital of the Kurdish region in the north of Iraq. It was the first time Ahmed had been on an aeroplane and the corkscrew ascent did little for his confidence. Every few minutes he asked if it was normal for the plane to be wobbling so much. I did not have the heart to say no.

Kurdistan was different to the rest of Iraq. The presence of the peshmerga, the guerrilla force who for decades had fought Saddam from strongholds in the mountains, was felt across its four provinces as they guarded checkpoints and scrutinised strangers. It was why, along with the relatively homogeneous nature of the local population, the area was relatively peaceful.

The result had been a building boom. Where Baghdad was a place of blast walls and debris, Irbil was one of new shops and emerging high-rises. There was even a five-star hotel in its centre where you could sit by a pool and drink cocktails. It was a hotel where a concierge opened the front door in welcome, bell boys carried your luggage and waitresses in fitted suits drifted around taking orders. It truly was a different world.

I caught sight of myself in the line of mirrors that covered the wall opposite the hotel's check-in desk. There was a short, dirty figure in Iraqi-style lime green stonewash jeans, the hems too long so that they came down over his shoes. The shirt was from a shop in Baghdad, short-sleeved and long-collared, brown with thin orange stripes in a zigzag motif. I did not like to shave, the Iraqis being so naturally hirsute that I thought it helped me blend in, but I had never been able to grow a good beard so there was merely an embryonic moustache in the making. I had cut my own hair, barbers being in short supply in Baghdad by then and ones who would risk touching a foreigner even more so. I had trimmed the top and back but had clearly not done a good job as parts were sticking out in chunks. Sweat stuck dirt to my face. My skin was burnt by the sun, my nose red, and my eyes tired so that they squinted slit-like against the electric lighting.

Previously starved of investment, Kurdistan was being pulled out of poverty and into the modern world. Seventy-eight international companies had invested hundreds of millions of dollars in the previous two years. The area's previous poverty made it a blank slate while its oil reserves promised rich rewards. Roads were being blasted through mountains, bridges built, underpasses created and the edge of the city ringed by new housing projects. It was an indication of how events might have unfolded across the rest of Iraq if things had worked out differently.

My aim was to spend time at Lake Dukan, a reservoir

in Suleimaniya province where the altitude provided relief from the summer heat. A cousin of Ahmed's, who was half Kurd and half Arab, had agreed to be our driver. On the evening before we set off, we drove to a pizza restaurant for a meal. Some children dropped firecrackers on the road beside us. Ahmed and I hunched automatically. Our driver was in hysterics. 'This is not Baghdad,' he said. 'This is Kurdistan.'

When we arrived at the lake we found families picnicking along the water's edge, while on the surrounding roads cars deposited their cargo of delighted children. It was a beautiful spot with the aquamarine water ringed by mountains whose cliffs had been eroded into sharp peaks and whose lower reaches had been softened by centuries of alluvial deposits. Heather tipped with rose-coloured flowers grew by the lake's edge. Men and young boys had stripped to their underwear and were splashing in the water.

Most of the visitors were Arabs who had also come north for a break from the violence. One group was preparing food on a small camping stove, a blue rug laid out beside them. 'Have some, please,' said the women in charge of the cooker, a simple gesture to two strangers. It was chicken and okra piled on fresh rice. Tea was poured for us into thin glasses and three teaspoons of sugar stirred in.

The family had not had a pleasant drive up. 'It was terrible,' the cook, Bekal, told us. 'All the way I was berating my husband for taking us on this trip. When we went through Baqubah there was a bomb in a car on the road in front. I was sure the whole way we were going to be killed. But it was worth it. I cannot put into words what I feel to be here. It is wonderful – quiet and full of water. At home I feel myself to be in a prison. Here I feel a different person. I feel happy.'

There was only one clear winner from the chaos that gripped Iraq that year and it was Moqtada al-Sadr. His position was one that had always relied to an extent on violence. It dated back to the moment he emerged as a key player in Iraq, when his supporters killed the traditional hereditary holder of the keys to the Imam Ali mosque in Najaf, Haidar al-Raifee, and America's favourite Iraqi cleric, Imam Abdul Majid al-Khoei, days after the US troops entered Baghdad in April 2003. Sadr's followers viewed Raifee as a Ba'athist collaborator and Khoei as an American stooge. When the two men approached the mosque to try to broker a peace agreement with the Sadrists who now controlled the site, they were attacked by a mob. Raifee was killed, stabbed with bayonets and knives, and Khoei was bound and taken to Sadr's head-quarters. Witnesses later told the investigating judge who examined the case that Sadr had appeared at the entrance and told them: 'Take this person away and kill him.'

Sadr's supporters were fundamental in propagating the sectarian violence now spreading across the country. His personal responsibility for these attacks was ambiguous. In public he would often call for restraint, saying that civil war would only play into American hands by giving the US an excuse to prolong its occupation. No one knew what he was saying in private, however, and the men in his Mahdi Army militia were the ones seen attacking Sunni mosques and forming the illegal checkpoints that now ringed Shia districts. They were the people who the Sunni said were telling them to abandon their homes and were rumoured to be carrying out much of the night-time killing. Whatever Sadr's rhetoric, his followers' actions increasingly had the appearance of an orchestrated assault.

In the absence of a functioning state it was to Sadr that the Shia turned for security. He had already started building up his mechanisms for a state-within-a-state the previous year with his religious schools and programmes of welfare relief. His followers now took on the responsibility of protecting swathes of the country from Sunni attacks. Visitors to Najaf reported that Sadr's followers were manning roadblocks accompanied by the police officers whose task it was officially supposed to be. In Sadr City, the Baghdad Shia neighbourhood named after Moqtada's father, it was his supporters who acted when a bomb went off, killing dozens of people. Members of his Mahdi Army militia seized two suspects, judges he had appointed tried them, and his followers hanged them from a lamp-post. The Iraqi government, let alone US forces, had little influence in these places. It was Sadr's face that stared from posters on street signs, in shop windows and from the walls of people's homes. He was their protector and the one to whom they were willing to publicly pay allegiance in exchange for the security he brought.

There were times when Sadr's organisation appeared to be fragmenting and the authority he held over his supporters seemed less than absolute. In late 2006, the Americans said they had identified at least twenty former Sadr militia leaders who were now acting independently of him as they sought to carve out their own little fiefdoms. The most feared of these was Abu Deraa, or Father of the Shield, a man known as 'the Shia Zarqawi' because of his bureau would shut, fled to Syria as refugees. Their relation was almost certainly dead by then anyway, his corpse presumably having joined the bodies plugging the city's sewage system or rotting in the Tigris.

Abu Omar, my driver, hid himself in a district of Baghdad where almost everyone was Sunni like he was. He began to work part time as a driver for the oil company that employed his sister, Asmaa, and this ensured he could still pay the bills. As for Sajad, the driver of our second car, he did not have many choices because he had so many dependants. He went back to being a taxi driver and from dawn to dusk drove the streets of Baghdad looking for customers. He had two IDs, one identifying him as Shia and the other as Sunni, and trusted he would get it right when stopped at a checkpoint. The last I heard he had judged it correctly so far.

On my final day in Baghdad my team drove me to the airport early in the morning. I had spent the previous evening saying my last goodbyes. It had not taken long, so few reporters were left. Most of what I had I threw away or passed on to my Iraqi team. In the end everything I took with me fitted into two bags, my own physical reminders of a seminal event in my life.

The sun was only just up when we left the Hamra complex for the last time. It was one of those soft Iraqi days when enough sand was being blown up into the air to give the sunlight a dirty glow. There were few people on the road. By then Iraqis had to queue for five hours for a tank of petrol and so everyone was conserving fuel for important journeys. Pedestrians mostly avoided going out until later when, it was calculated, there would be enough people around to avoid becoming too distinctive a target.

Unusually, we sped through the streets. Few shops were open and the throng on the pavements was notable by its absence. One old man was out, setting up a vegetable stall at a road junction. He had a box of cabbages and another of tomatoes already on display and he was staring at them with pride. I saw a couple of stray dogs, a cart being pulled down a side road, a truck or two, a dozen cars, but otherwise nothing. There was little noise and less movement, a city without a pulse.

As we drove over the Tigris, two American Apache helicopters swung low over the water, beautiful in the elegance of their technology, like science fiction apparitions from an unimaginable world. They flew up above us, the noise momentarily deafening, and then disappeared into the yellow gloom.

At the airport it was bedlam. A tumultuous mass of people were seeking salvation. Baghdad airport was never an easy place to get out of with its security checks and archaic technology but on this occasion it was worse than I had ever seen it before. There was not even time to properly say my goodbyes because the throng pushed around me and the cars lining up at the checkpoint pressed for those ahead to move on. All there could be was a shake of hands as I grabbed my bags, a quick promise to never forget what we had done together, an inadequate expression of thanks to the people who had kept me alive, and then I was jostled forward by the crowd, on through the checkpoint, while they, my Iraqi friends and colleagues, began their drive along those empty streets back into their city.

There must have been at least five hundred people already at the airport, maybe twice that by lunchtime and another thousand by mid-afternoon when I finally flew out. All had only one thought: escape. They were lined up outside the terminal building trying to get onto one of the few commercial airliners still willing to fly into Baghdad. There were whole families with their most precious belongings packed into multi-coloured bags. Children ran through the crowd as the adults argued with the guards at the terminal's security gates to let them in. Black 4x4s pulled up with their tinted windows to release contingents of Western, shaven-headed military security guards who were intent on getting home. They pushed their way through the masses, ignoring the cries of outrage as they forced their way to the front, airport security stepping aside to let them pass with a half-smile and a nod.

I had suspected what it was going to be like and had with me fistfuls of dollars, at least seven hundred dollars-worth, to ease my progress. It still took me almost six hours, forcing notes into the hands of any who could help me, and being as ruthless and selfish as everyone else in holding my position in the queue. In the end I latched onto a youth who said he knew of a spare ticket to Istanbul, which coincidentally was a good place for me to be heading at that point. He led me through a side entrance and we passed security guards who waved me on. At the check-in desk I pushed over my pile of remaining dollars, everything I had, took the ticket and ran to the coach that ferried passengers to the plane.

There was not one spare seat on the flight. An Iraqi woman seated beside me was praying. When we took off she cried with relief. I was sitting by the window and looked down. The runway fell away and slowly the American military vehicles that surrounded it disappeared. The barracks merged into each other and the city began to spread out around them. There was the expanse of ordered streets with their rows of houses. There were the imperial buildings of the Green Zone with their Ba'athist desire for dominance. There were the mosques, office blocks and highways, all of them the landmarks for a host of interrupted lives. The curve of the Tigris opened up before me, the river snaking its way across that land as it had done for centuries before the Americans came and would for centuries after they left. There was a fishing boat, the wake falling behind it as it pushed itself out beyond the edges of the city. It was going with the tide and even from that distance I could see it was making good progress, heading south to cast the nets that it was hoped would come up filled with fish to take home to sell. That would be a successful day. One worth living. Then we banked again, up into the cloud cover, and it all disappeared from sight.

Epilogue

It was a year before I returned to the Middle East. The intervening period had been spent getting my life back on track. I bought a house in east London. Boxes that had spent years in storage were retrieved and unpacked. My girlfriend moved in and we started decorating. Walls were painted, cupboards built and floors laid. The house became a home. Roots were being put down at last.

I stayed in regular contact with Ahmed. He was having a difficult time coming to terms with life as a refugee in Damascus. His wife was still in a bad way, unable to accept what had happened to her brother and the demise of the life she had grown up with in Iraq. Their daughter became ill and had to have an operation, a treatment that used up a significant chunk of their savings.

The Syrian government, mindful that it already had a significant unemployment problem and therefore keen to dissuade Iraqis from seeking sanctuary within its borders, made it hard for refugees to find work. Companies were encouraged to hire a Syrian over an Iraqi with the same skills. As a result Ahmed was only earning £150 a month as a functionary at a translation agency. It was not enough even to pay the rent on the apartment he had found. After Christmas I became really worried about him. His normal good nature seemed engulfed by pessimism and he began to talk as if it would have been better to have died in Baghdad than to live like a beggar outside his homeland.

In the spring of 2007, however, he came up with a plan that he put into effect with his old gusto. He had originally dreamed of moving to London but discovered that Britain was doing little to help Iraq's refugees, even those with links to British companies. Then he contacted PEN International, a charity established to defend freedom of expression which was one of the few organisations working at the time to provide assistance to Iraq's journalists and translators, and it informed him of a US programme which allowed endangered media workers to settle in America. As PEN guided him through the application process, Ahmed put his networking skills into effect, queuing for hours outside the US embassy in Damascus, knocking on doors and bombarding those responsible for the programme with e-mails. American reporters whom he had met in the Middle East but who were now back in the States were browbeaten into applying pressure at their end. I organised a sponsored event in London to raise money for his family so that they could afford to stay in Syria while their application was processed. Everyone I approached, pleased to be able to help at least one family caught up in the mess of Iraq, was notably generous.

Summer 2007 turned into autumn and Ahmed still did not know if his application was going to be approved. There were interviews, background checks, medical examinations, and then a long period during which he heard nothing.

'The Americans are very useless as we know from Iraq,' he wrote to me, 'so I am not very worried by how long it is taking for them to give me an answer. I am glad, in fact, about the delay. Until we know their decision there is a chance for happiness, a chance for my children to have lives that will not have the sorrow of my own. If we know that they say "no" then that chance has gone. Then what will we have to live for?'

In December 2007 I flew to Damascus for a visit. He met me at the airport and I was surprised by how emotional I was to see him. I had been able to forget those years in Iraq but during the intervening months my life had moved on. I was focusing on the future and embracing normality. Seeing Ahmed was a reminder of my time in Baghdad.

On my second day in Damascus we drove to his apartment in the city's Harasta district. It was a run-down area where a constant trickle of water flowed down the street outside his front door. There were no lights on his building's communal landings, and once inside his flat there was a strong smell of damp. On the walls of the main room Ahmed had put up colourful posters of Thailand. He liked them, he said, as the landscapes were very green and therefore pleasant to a person from a desert country like himself. The main reason they were there, however, was to cover the mould growing through the paintwork.

Ahmed was the first to admit that he was not doing as badly as many of the Iraqis in Damascus. On my first night in Syria we had gone to Jaramana, the district where Iraq's Sunni and Christian refugees had primarily congregated. The Shia had mostly gone to a different area, Sayyida Zaynab, the sectarian division having remained even among those in exile.

Jaramana was eerily reminiscent of Baghdad with the people wearing the same clothes, the roads lined by the same style of apartment blocks and the shops selling the same food, their owners knowing what would appeal to their new Iraqi clientele. It lacked Baghdad's war damage but it was nevertheless still clearly poor. Many of the thousands of Iraqis living there were dependent on money sent from relatives who had succeeded in escaping to the West and that left little to spend on fripperies. Rubbish had accumulated by the kerbside and the overhead electrical wires were frayed. When there was a surge in the power supply they crackled and emitted a stream of sparks. I met some of Ahmed's friends, fellow members of the new Iraqi diaspora, and as we sat drinking coffee the conversation focused on how it might be possible for them to start afresh. They spoke of people-smugglers who could get them to Australia in the back of containers, or an aid programme that allowed Iraqi Christians to settle in France if they could prove they were Roman Catholics rather than Coptic Christians. Each scheme was outlined and its chance of success carefully weighed.

Some of those I met that evening were considering going back to Baghdad as the latest news implied that the situation there had improved, that the nadir might have been reached. Economic growth was reported and the value of the Iraqi dinar was rising on the back of the high price of oil. The Americans were saying that areas of Baghdad and central Iraq previously classed as 'lost' had been wrested back from the extremists. The daily death rate was falling and the worst of the sectarian cleansing appeared over. As a result morale had also apparently improved among US troops.

It was a turnaround primarily achieved by the American 'surge', though it was not the only reason. Moqtada al-Sadr announced a ceasefire in August, which had stopped his Mahdi Army's sectarian killings, and a new phenomenon had emerged called the 'Sunni Awakening'. Sunni tribes had formed an alliance to stop al-Qa'eda and the other extremist Sunni groups from enforcing Islamic fundamentalism on their homeland. It had begun in Anbar, the former insurgent stronghold province in Sunni western Iraq, and then spread to Baghdad. Al-Qa'eda and its supporters were now primarily limited to Diyala province, where most of the fighting in Iraq was now focused. On witnessing the Sunni fighters' achievements, the American military offered them help. It was accepted and the US armed them, providing the weaponry needed if they were to continue taking on and beating the religious fanatics. Consequently, Iraq's Sunnis had been able to not only fight their own extremists but also resist the Shia militias. Parity had been reached and with it came a form of stability.

The fighters of the Sunni Awakening were mostly the very same Sunni militants who had fought so determinedly against the foreign invaders during the first years of the war. Many were tacit supporters of Saddam. Mutual self-interest now allied them to America. Once again in Iraq your enemy's enemy had proved to be your unlikely friend.

Ahmed introduced me to a former army captain from Baghdad who had fled Iraq after his son was killed. He had recently revisited his native city. He said there was still little electricity or other basic services and described how the city remained shut at night because most people continued to be too scared to go outside after dark. During the day, he said, the worst of the random slaughter seemed to have abated. People were not being dragged from their cars and killed in such numbers although it was still wise not to travel too far from areas dominated by your sectarian brothers.

'How safe is Baghdad now?' I asked him. 'Maybe 30 per cent,' he answered. Would he go back? 'Not if I do not have to. It is a tense calm. We do not know what it is that will happen. In Iraq there is still so much mistrust. To regain confidence will take a long time.'

The latest official figures showed that more than six hundred people were killed in Baghdad during November and, in Diyala province, families were still being forced from their homes. America's arming of the Awakening may have meant that the Sunnis could hold their own with the Shia militias and al-Qa'eda extremists but it also ensured that the Sunni fighters were now as strong as other groups in the country, there being no pretence that the US-supplied weapons were ever going to be handed back. Around 69,000 Sunnis had been trained and armed by America and no one knew what this force would do next. Iraq's prime minister, Nouri al-Maliki, was refusing to allow it to be amalgamated into the army, seemingly worried about what this might do to his Shia-dominated force. Moreover the Mahdi Army, though quiet, remained at large and SCIRI's Badr Brigade continued to dominate the upper ranks of the police force. The Shia were still pre-eminent in the south, as the Sunni were in the west and the Kurds in the north. All three groups had the weaponry and experience to fight each other if conditions deteriorated again. The future of Iraq remained uncertain.

During my time in Baghdad I had never been able to spend time with Ahmed's family at his home. Dora, the neighbourhood in which he had lived, was always among the most dangerous in the city. Neither he nor I wanted to endanger his family by organising a visit in case I was spotted and his association with foreigners consequently known. However, I had heard many things about his family and felt part of the drama that had surrounded his wife's pregnancy, their struggle for survival, and the grief that had come when those they loved had become Iraq's victims. Now we could finally meet, talk, share a joke and enjoy a meal. Such things are so easily taken for granted but, as I realised that day, they are very precious.

Ahmed's six-year-old daughter, Labibah, and son, Mohammad, were dressed in their smartest clothes, her hair held in bunches by two clips in the shape of orange ladybirds and he in a brown corduroy waistcoat. They were standing by the door when I walked in and had been told to hold out their hands so I could shake them. Ahmed's wife, Raha, stood behind her children. She was not what I had expected. In the photographs I had seen she was always dressed in a headscarf, but now she was bare-headed, her brown hair with blonde highlights held back in a bun, and dressed in a bright pink tracksuit. She wore pale lipstick and her eyes were heavily made up with eye-liner. Gold-plated earrings decorated her face. Attractive, vivacious and smiling, she was the antithesis of the stern black-clad Islamic figures that too often dominate the West's popular image of the Arab Muslim woman.

She had worked hard to prepare the meal. The dishes were so numerous that they covered the fold-up table erected in the main room. There were starters of marinated apricots and dips. Chicken and rice was the main course, supplemented by salads and a selection of breads and sauces. There were a considerable number of us present for lunch: not only Ahmed and his wife, their daughter and toddler son, but also the wife of his brother Marwan, my former security guard, and their four children, as well as the new wife of their oldest son, Othman. Marwan himself was not present, having gone on a fact-finding trip to Baghdad to see for himself what conditions were like.

While we ate the conversation first dwelt on news of what had happened to those we had known in Iraq: those who had died, those who had survived, and those who had fled abroad. Iyad Allawi, the Iraqi politician who had told me before the second national elections back in December 2005 that he would have to relocate abroad if the Shia religious parties again won at the ballot box, had proved true to his word. He apparently now lived mostly in London and Dubai, returning to Iraq when urgent business required his presence. Haider, the translator who had worked for me in Basra, had been seen in Damascus. He was apparently well, if impoverished, and his wife was pregnant with their first child.

I heard for the first time what happened in the days after I left Baghdad and how Ahmed and Marwan's families had all managed to escape alive. It had been a closer-run thing than I had previously realised. The day before they were to leave, Marwan's oldest son, Othman, had been kidnapped by Shia militiamen. He was seen being pushed into a car and driven away. Ahmed had known the Mahdi Army commander in the area where Othman had been abducted. By coincidence, he had been in the same class as him at school, a time when they were friends. Ahmed went to his former schoolmate's house and pleaded for mercy. It had been granted. Othman was released, his face battered and his body bruised, but alive.

Othman sat across the table from me while we ate our meal in Damascus. There was no outward sign of what he had experienced. He looked like most other young Arab men of his age: his hair cut fashionably short and dressed in a blue fitted T-shirt and loose jeans. I asked if he dwelled on what had happened. He still thought about it every day, he said, and at night woke from nightmares in which he was still being held captive.

The day after Othman's release both families had driven to the border. 'For three hours I could not utter any word,' Ahmed said. 'I felt completely isolated from the world. Everything I had known I was leaving behind. I had no idea what to do when we arrived, just that I had to get out of my country quick.'

There was a pause in the conversation as they all remembered that time, Ahmed thumbing the prayer beads he held in his right hand. Then those memories were put aside and happier moments brought to mind. This was not a day for regrets, it was a day of celebration.

Two days earlier the American embassy had been in touch with the news that Ahmed and his family's lives were going to be taking a new direction once again. The application for resettlement in the US had been approved. In a week they would be on a plane flying across the world to their new home in Atlanta. It was a phenomenal thing: a decision that would change their lives forever, and its impact – the hope it brought – had already begun to cast its spell.

Ahmed and his wife had a seemingly endless list of questions about what life would be like in the States. As I answered I tried to imagine how they would find America. Lives previously lived in Iraq, and then for the last year as refugees in Damascus, an Arab city not that dissimilar to Baghdad, were now to be transported to the US with its shopping malls, commercialism and secular schools. Ultimately it would be a life of commuting along the freeway for Ahmed, navigating the aisles of Wal-Mart for Raha, and high school and prom nights for their children. I tried to imagine it and failed. I could not possibly conceive what it would be like for them or how they would react to it.

Nor, as they made clear, could they. They did not care, however, because for the first time since civil war had come to Baghdad they had something that they had previously feared might be lost forever. They had a future.

They were nevertheless well aware of the irony of their situation. The country that had destroyed their previous lives was the one now offering them sanctuary. Ahmed joked that he would now become as 'useless' as the US administrators who had tried to reinvent Iraq. Raha was nervous that there might be anti-Iraqi feeling in Atlanta due to the fact that her countrymen were killing American soldiers. I assured her that it was far more likely that most people they came across would feel guilt at what had happened to them and their country. I hoped that my prediction would prove to be true.

It was a wonderful afternoon. Ahmed's daughter, Labibah, insisted on proudly demonstrating how she could already count to ten in English. His son, Mohammad, took control of the camera and consequently we ended up with lots of pictures of our feet. Photographs were produced showing the day of Othman's wedding, which had been held shortly after they arrived in Damascus. I was shocked to see how tired and beaten Ahmed and his wife looked. At the time, Ahmed pointed out, they had not known how they could afford to survive in Damascus and were terrified of the consequences of what moving back to Baghdad would entail. 'That period is over now,' he said.

When it was time to leave, his family formed a line to say their farewells. Each wished me good fortune in the future. Then Ahmed drove me back to my hotel. I felt emotional again as I said goodbye to that figure in his brown stripy shirt and oversized blue jeans who was off to start his new adventure, not knowing what he faced, only what he had already endured.

'We had interesting times, eh,' he said, holding both my hands in his, 'but we are alive and our families live. It is a stupid crazy world but what can you do about it? Go in peace, my friend. Stay safe.'

He climbed back in the car, a battered yellow Ford Fiesta, and then wound down the window and leaned out.

'I always say that at least some good things came out of all that badness and one was that we became friends. We showed that you do not have to be so bad, stupid crazy fucking world, that there is some goodness in it. Come and see me in America. Come and see what it is that I become. Let us hope we live for a long time and be happy.'

The next morning I arrived back at Heathrow and took the Piccadilly line across London. It was Sunday and the journey was a quiet one, the people in my carriage hidden behind their newspapers, many of whose front pages were dominated by news of the celebrity romance of a couple who had met on a reality TV programme staged in the Australian jungle.

I walked across the park to get from the tube stop to my house. It was a beautiful December day, the sky a pale wintry blue. Leaves had fallen from the trees and gathered in clumps by the side of paths. I stopped for a while and sat on a bench watching families enjoying the crisp air. Two young men were practising their golf swing by the edge of a municipal football pitch, trying to see who could chip the ball against a tree thirty yards away. A squirrel tentatively made its way forward and looked at me quizzically, hoping for food.

My house was near the park's northern entrance. I put the key in the door, opened it and shouted a 'hello', searching for my girlfriend, Kate. She was in our spare room. I knew that while I was in Syria she had been planning to cut pictures from children's books to make a multi-coloured frieze on one of its walls. I walked upstairs to see how she had got on. She was sitting on a white leather sofa that I had once picked up in a yard sale for $10 when living in Los Angeles. I knew she hated the ugliness of that sofa. She was using it now though, scissors and paper in her hands as she tried to make the room as cosy and as special as possible, the baby bump showing underneath her black wraparound dress.

Kate looked up as I walked in. 'Can you help me put the cot together? The instructions are in the box. And your mum rang. We're going to go there for dinner a week on Saturday. We should probably take our presents over so we'd better hurry up doing our Christmas shopping.'

Then she laughed. 'Welcome home,' she said.

Postscript

At present there are two sources most commonly cited for estimates of the number of Iraqis who have died in the war. The most often used is the Iraq Body Count, an international non-governmental body which notes every mention of Iraqi civilian deaths in the English-language press, including any Arab media that has been translated into English. Iraqi soldiers, suicide bombers, those termed insurgents, or anyone else killed while engaged in what is commonly regarded as war-related activity, are excluded from the count. A running total is then displayed on its website.

Its organisers, mostly academics in Britain and the US, are the first to acknowledge the weakness of this methodology. 'It is likely,' they admit, 'that many, if not most, civilian casualties will go unreported by the media. That is the sad nature of war.'

This is unquestionably true. Areas that are least under US or Iraqi government control, such as Anbar province, are often the places where most people are being killed and where the world is least likely to hear about it. Baghdad morgue is the only one in Iraq that has released figures for the number of victims of violent death that it receives.

Despite this fundamental flaw the Iraq Body Count's strength as a source is that every one of the deaths it records is a documented one. It is not an extrapolation or conclusion from a statistical model. Compared to other studies, the number of civilian dead it cites is therefore the least likely to have been inflated even if, as a result, it probably provides a minimum figure.

The count's findings are nevertheless depressing. It reported 12,000 civilians were killed in 2003, two-thirds of them in the invasion of Iraq itself. In 2004, 10,500 died, a number which rose to 14,000 in 2005 and 26,000 in 2006. According to Iraq Body Count by the end of 2007 the total number of Iraqi civilians killed since the war began was between 80,129 and 87,279.

The second, and far more controversial, source popularly used is the survey published in the medical journal, *The Lancet*, in October 2006. Unlike the methodology of the Iraq Body Count, which is a passive study dependent on the reporting of casualties, its authors sought to estimate the number of total deaths caused by the war. This included not only those killed due to the fighting but also due to the lawlessness, declining healthcare and lack of basic services that came with it.

The survey was sponsored by a number of reputable bodies, including the Centre for International Emergency Disaster and Refugee Studies, and used a team, led by Les Roberts, experienced in estimating death tolls in war zones. Its previous findings on the Democratic Republic of the Congo, where it concluded 1.7 million people had died, have been used as evidence by the United Nations Security Council and the US State Department.

The survey adopted the same methodology as it had in the Congo. It drew its conclusions from a study conducted between May and July 2006 in which 1,849 households were visited in 47 selected areas across the country. Every household approached was asked to present death certificates or documentation as evidence for any family members said to have died since the end of 2001. In the vast majority of cases such proof was provided. From this the pre- and post-invasion mortality rates were calculated and this figure then extrapolated across the Iraqi population as a whole.

The Lancet survey concluded that it could say with 95 per cent confidence that between 392,979 and 942,636 Iraqis had died because of the war, giving a mean of 654,965, or 2.5 per cent of the entire population. Of those killed violently, 56 per cent died from gunshot wounds and 14 per cent due to car bombs and other explosions. Coalition forces were found responsible for 31 per cent of those who had died violently since the invasion.

These findings have been extensively criticised, not least because they were considerably higher than any other study, including those by the United Nations and the Iraqi Ministry of Health. Critics have questioned if the survey areas chosen were representative enough and the numbers questioned large enough. It was also queried how the study's conclusion that Iraq's pre-invasion mortality rate was less than Australia's could be credible, although its authors did subsequently argue that this was due to the relative youth of Iraq's overall population which meant proportionally there were fewer elderly people.

Les Roberts, the survey's head, defended the methodology saying it was 'tried and tested' and the 'best estimate of mortality we have'. It had, he said, been used by the US government in both Kosovo and Afghanistan. A number of epidemiologists and demographers did come out in his support, although just as many have challenged his findings.

When President Bush learned of the study he dismissed it, as did the Iraqi and UK governments. In late 2005 Bush estimated the number of Iraqis that had died at around thirty thousand. He argued that the 'six hundred thousand or whatever they guessed at' was 'just not credible'. When asked what he believed the correct number was, he did not respond with an exact figure but instead said that 'a lot of innocent people have lost their lives'.

In that, at least, he is correct. Although nobody knows for certain how many people have died because of the Iraq war, we do know unquestionably that there have been 'a lot' of them.

DONATION

Part of the profits from the sales of Red Zone will go to International PEN, the world writers' organization, which has been working to support and resettle Iraqi writers, translators and interpreters who have been threatened as a result of their work. A significant number of Iraqi writers and their families have been given asylum by the US government as a direct result of PEN'S support, among them Ahmed Ali.

With 145 centres in 104 countries, as well as consultative status at UNESCO and the United Nations, International PEN seeks to promote literature, defend freedom of expression and enable people worldwide to develop a love of reading and writing.

International PEN is a registered UK charity and welcomes support of its important work worldwide. Please send donations to:

International PEN, Brownlow House, 50 – 51 High Holborn, London WC1V 6ER; Tel (+44) 020 74050338.

ABOUT THE AUTHOR

OLIVER POOLE first went to Iraq in March 2003 when he crossed the Kuwait border in the back of an American armoured vehicle as the only British daily newspaper reporter 'embedded' with the US Army. Eighteen months later he returned as the *Daily Telegraph*'s newly appointed Iraq correspondent. For two years his home became a hotel room in the middle of Baghdad's 'Red Zone'. He witnessed the bloody impact of car bombs, saw first hand the consequences of the growing sectarian conflict, travelled across Iraq with British and US troops and had his own offices destroyed by a suicide bomber. Finally in November 2006, with the *Telegraph* closing down his office and his Iraqi assistants fleeing the country, he joined the masses escaping Iraq through Baghdad airport.

Born and brought up in London, he was educated at Oxford University. After working for two years at the *South China Morning Post* in Hong Kong, he joined the *Telegraph* Group in 1999 and was appointed West Coast of America correspondent in September 2001. He now lives in Hackney, east London.

His account of the 2003 invasion *Black Knights: On the Bloody Road to Baghdad* was published in November 2003.

Praise for *Black Knights*

'The best reporter's book of the war so far – and it deserves to be one of THE books of the whole Iraqi crisis. The eyewitness accounts of the fighting, the terrible guilt of the soldiers and bystanders at the killing of civilians, the overwhelming confusion, the continuous question of why they are there are exhilarating and chilling' – Robert Fox, *Evening Standard*

"He [Poole] understands the risk of being infected by gung-ho militarism when reporting brutality and stupidity, at the same time tempering this with fellow-feeling for the men on whom his life depends... This is an exhilarating, honest, often scary account of modern war as close-up spectator" – Peter Millar, *Sunday Times*

'A very honest account, devoid of false heroics, and an admirable lesson in how a reporter can share the solidarity of enduring fear and discomfort with troops to whom he owes his survival, but not lose his critical detachment' – Jonathan Steele, *Guardian*

'Poole is a great reporter...possessed of a cool eye, natural sympathy and curiosity, and brisk honesty. He has immortalised them [the Black Knights] in such a true, funny and poignant book' – Patrick Bishop, *Daily Telegraph*

'[Poole's] account of the baptism of fire endured by a US tank company is starkly horrific in places. It is also witty, often laugh-out-loud funny, and spiced with some wonderfully colourful pen-portraits' – *Soldier* magazine